CLOTHING DECISIONS

CLOTHING DECISIONS

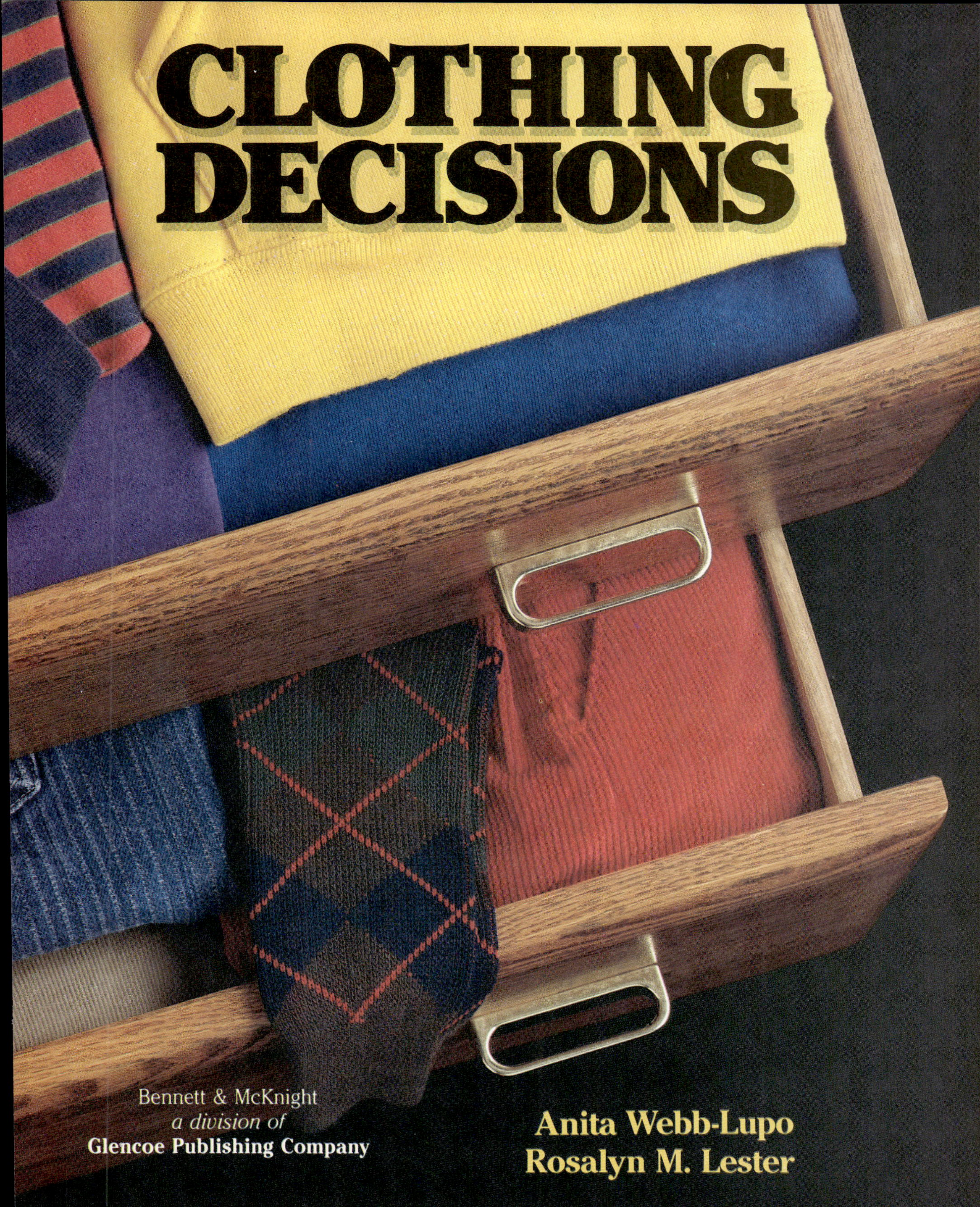

Bennett & McKnight
a division of
Glencoe Publishing Company

Anita Webb-Lupo
Rosalyn M. Lester

Send all inquiries to:
Glencoe Publishing Company
15319 Chatsworth Street
Mission Hills, California 91345

Printed in the United States of America

ISBN 0-02-668010-6

3 4 5 6 91 90 89 88

TABLE OF CONTENTS

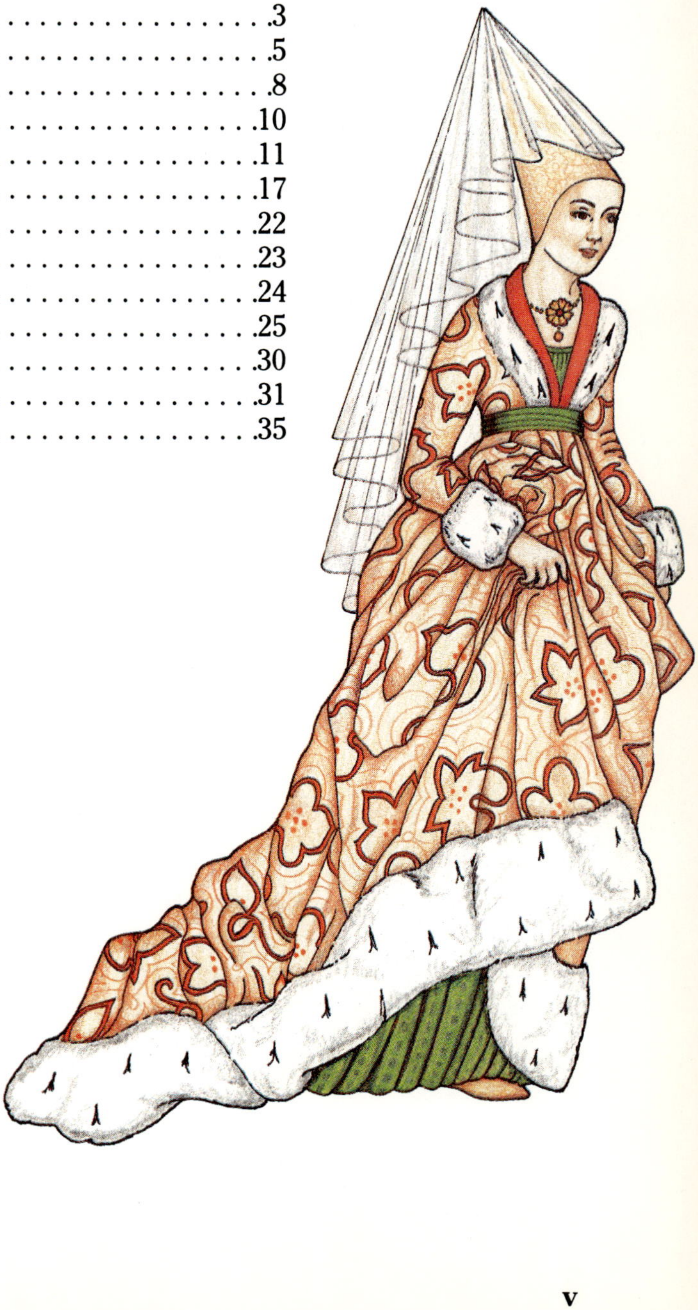

Unit 2—Choosing Clothes . . . 42

Unit 3—Fabrics for Clothes . . . 100

Unit 6—Taking Care of Clothes 220

Unit 7—Clothes and Careers 250

Special Interest Articles

The Way It Was

Getting Your Money's Worth

Perspective

THE MEANING OF CLOTHES

How do you decide what to wear? Do you think about the weather? The places you're going to? What others will be wearing? What looks good on you? You probably think about all these things, but have you ever wondered why? Why are clothing decisions important? Why do we care about how we dress?

Clothes are much more than just a covering for the body. Clothes protect us from the weather. In certain jobs, special clothes are needed for safety. Clothes also help us express ourselves. They let others know who and what we are.

In this unit you'll learn the reasons why people wear the clothes they do. You'll see how people's clothing choices are influenced by their society, their personalities, their culture, and the fashions of the time.

Unit 1

CHAPTER 1

CLOTHES AND SOCIETY

What would you think if you went to a wedding and one of the other guests showed up in a running suit? How would you react if you were at a baseball game and you saw someone in the next row wearing a tuxedo? Those clothes would not seem right, would they?

There's no law against wearing a running suit to a wedding or a tuxedo to a baseball game. Still, very few people would do it. Why not? Other people would think it was strange. Even though we would not want to look exactly like everyone else, most of us do want to fit in. We dress the way our friends do. We choose clothes that are considered right for the occasion.

As you read this chapter, think about the following:

- How do other people affect your clothing choices?
- How do clothes help us belong?
- What do our clothes say about who we are?

Look for These Terms

group
peer
leader
role
status

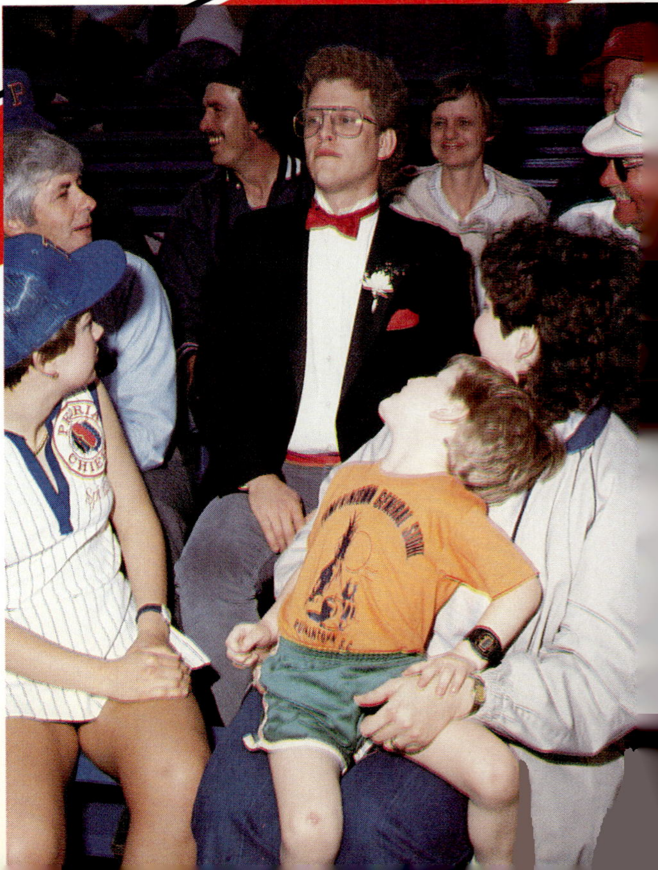

Many teens prefer to dress the way their friends do. How do your friends influence your clothing choices?

CLOTHING HELPS US BELONG

Most teens want the approval of their classmates or friends. They dress to be like others. To be accepted by others is very important to them. Dressing a certain way is an outward signal to others that they "belong."

GROUPS

A **group** consists of people joined together because they share a belief or interest. For example, members of a religious group share common beliefs. Members of a musical group share an interest in a certain type of music. To what groups do you belong?

There are groups of many sizes. Family groups may be quite small. Community groups may consist of several hundred people. Can you think of small and large groups in your school?

How Groups Influence Clothing Choices

The groups to which you belong influence (affect) the clothing you wear. If your mother tended to dress you up as a child, you probably feel comfortable dressed up now and may choose clothing which is "dressy."

Authorities also influence our clothing choices. There is certain clothing we would not wear while in the company of a pastor, priest, or rabbi. Some places, such as stores or restaurants, may have rules about the type of clothing that customers must wear. Some schools require students to wear uniforms.

Many stores post signs such as this. Why do you think they would have rules about how customers dress?

The group which probably has the most influence on our clothing choices is our peer group. A **peer** is someone who has the same standing as another. Your classmates are your peers. They are the same age as you. Like you, they are students.

People of the same age often share the same interests. They also tend to spend a great deal of time together. People want to be noticed and liked by their peers. For these reasons, a peer group has a big influence on clothing choices.

Sometimes we want to signal others that we are *not* a part of a particular group. A group's values or ideas may not be acceptable to us and so we reject that group's style of clothing. By wearing a different style of clothing, we are letting others know that we reject one group and belong to another group.

How Clothing Influences Groups

Not only do groups influence clothing choices, but clothing choices also influence groups. "How can this be?" you may say. Recall that a group is formed because of common beliefs or interests. We cannot see beliefs or interests. But we can see clothing. Clothing becomes a way to show common beliefs and interests.

Clothing gives the group members a sense of unity. The uniforms a sports team wears give the members a feeling of togetherness. The clothes help create a team spirit. Perhaps you have been a member of a sports team, a school band, or a scout group. Did you feel or act differently when you were wearing your uniform?

BEING PART OF A GROUP

Groups require leaders. Someone must take charge of the group. Someone must set the group's purpose or determine how the group is going to operate. These actions are leadership behaviors.

A **leader** guides, directs, or influences the thoughts, feelings, or behavior of oth-

Uniforms give members of a team a sense of unity and power.

Which of These Descriptions Apply to You?

Leader	Nonleader
Appeals to the best in each person	Distrustful; believes all people are lazy and dishonest
Advice giver and "cheerleader"	Expects orders to be followed without comment or question
Comfortable with people	Hard to get to know
Thinks of ways to motivate and help others	Thinks only of his or her status, how he or she looks to others
Simplifies—makes the work look easy	Complicates—makes the work seem more difficult
Gives credit to others	Takes credit; complains about lack of good people
Straightforward	Tricky; manipulates people
Admits own mistakes; comforts others when they admit theirs	Never admits mistakes; blames others

ers. All of us are leaders at one time or another. You may have been a team captain or the head of a committee. A person does not even have to be in a position of authority to be a leader. When you are with two or three friends, one of you will be a leader, influencing the way the group behaves.

To be a good leader takes skill. You need to be willing to listen to others, but you must also be able to make your own decisions. You need to understand people's strengths and weaknesses so that you can help them do their best.

People look up to a leader. They want to be like that person. Therefore they will act like the person and even dress or wear their hair like he or she does. Can you think of clothing styles that became popular because a leader wore them?

Of course, where there is a leader, there must be followers. Every group needs followers. If everyone tried to be the leader, the group would become divided and might even stop being a group. Followers are the "doers." They carry out the purpose and goals of the group. It is important that followers think about the directions their leaders give. Good followers do not follow blindly. They ask themselves, "Am I doing what is right? Will this make me a better person, or will it bring harm to me or to others?"

You can be a leader in one situation and a follower in another. You may be a leader with your best friend, a follower in a school club, and a follower in most of your family situations.

CLOTHING DEFINES ROLES

Within every group, members have roles. A **role** is a purpose or function. The role of a club president is to preside over the meetings. The role of a band member

The clothing and hairstyle of Diana, Princess of Wales, have influenced fashion in many countries.

differently from freshmen? Do school leaders dress differently from students who have a high absence rate?

TYPES OF ROLES

Roles may be either given or learned. Given roles are those that occur without your control. They "happen" to you. Your sex, your age, and your position in your family are all given roles. You didn't choose them. You were born male or female. You age according to laws of nature. You had no choice about whether you would be the oldest or youngest child in your family, or somewhere in between.

Learned roles are those that you choose or take on for yourself. If you get a job in a department store or a record shop, you take on the role of a salesclerk. You choose to be a swimmer, a club president, a "slob," a friend, a babysitter, or the class jokester. You learn different roles as you become a member of different groups.

is to play at school functions. A role may be to follow the group's leaders or to be the "clown" of the group.

Clothing identifies roles within the group. The military is a good example. Uniforms identify the Army, Navy, and Air Force. Roles within the groups are identified by certain hats or special badges. A family is another example of a group whose members have different roles. A young child is dressed differently from the mother. The mother dresses differently from the grandmother. The short skirt that is so cute on a two-year-old girl is not accepted by society as appropriate for a sixty-year-old woman.

Think about the roles people have in school. Do seniors in your school dress

Members of a family dress differently, according to their roles. Can you imagine the grandmother dressed as the little girl?

Can you guess these people's roles by their clothes?

ROLE CONFLICT

Sometimes roles conflict. The role you have in one group may not agree with the role you have in another group. You are growing up and want to be more independent. Your parents may still think of you as a child. Thus your role as a teen may be in conflict with your role as a son or daughter. Role conflicts such as this sometimes focus on clothing. Parents and teens may have different ideas about the correct way to dress. If you have such a conflict, ask yourself, "Do I really like these clothes, or am I just trying to show independence? Am I acting like a responsible person or like a small child?" Talk with your parents. Find out why they object to your clothing choices. Explain to them why you want to dress a certain way. Instead of letting clothing choices become a battleground, try to find a solution you can all agree to.

CLOTHING REFLECTS STATUS

Status refers to the rank of a person within a group. In your school group you may rank as a good, average, or poor student. In your community you may be considered rich, poor, or middle class.

People's clothing may indicate status. Team members wear letters on their jackets to show their status as good athletes. Cheerleaders often wear a symbol on their uniforms to indicate how many years they've been a member of the group.

Fashionable clothing gives some people a sense of status. A fur coat or a "designer original" outfit shows others that the wearer can afford expensive clothes. The clothes are a status symbol. They indicate success and wealth. Can you name other status symbols? How important do you think such status symbols are?

—The Way It Was

CLOTHES AND STATUS

Throughout the ages, clothes have helped to indicate status.

- Prehistoric hunters wore the skins of animals they had killed. The skins not only protected them from the cold but also showed their skill and power as hunters.
- Egyptian kings wore a special apron. It was a triangular piece of cloth or metal which hung from the waist. The apron was decorated with colored feathers, beads, and jewels.
- Handkerchiefs were once symbols of wealth and power. They were made of fine cotton or silk and decorated with lace or embroidery. Only wealthy people owned them, and they carried their handkerchiefs in their hands or wore them on their clothes.
- Items of clothing may indicate marital status. In ancient China, married women wore silk hair nets.
- Sometimes laws were passed in an attempt to regulate the use of status symbols. Laws that control what people are allowed to wear are called sumptuary (SUMP-chu-wer-ee) laws. During the 1400s men wore shoes with long, pointed toes. A law was passed that noblemen could wear shoes which extended beyond the toes by two feet or more. Commoners, however, were limited to shoes that reached no more than six inches beyond the toes. Today we have sumptuary laws of a different sort. They set standards of quality for clothing, state what information must be included on labels, or regulate foreign imports.

SUMMARY

Our clothing choices are influenced by the groups to which we belong, especially our peer group. Dressing like others in a group helps us feel a part of that group. Every group needs both leaders and followers. We may be leaders in some situations and followers in others. The members of a group have roles. Roles may be given or learned. Clothing can identify a person's role. Sometimes there is conflict among the various roles a person has. Clothing also indicates status, or rank. For example, the clothing people wear can tell about their accomplishments or their financial standing.

CHECK YOUR KNOWLEDGE

1. *True or False:* One reason people may choose to dress a certain way is to win the approval of others.
2. What is a group?
3. Our ______ group includes people of the same age and social standing as we.
4. How can clothing influence a group's behavior?
5. *True or False:* Good leaders make their decisions without listening to anyone else's opinions.
6. *True or False:* A good follower never questions what the leader says.
7. Roles that you choose for yourself are called ______ roles.
8. Roles that happen to you without your control are called ______ roles.
9. *True or False:* When one of a person's roles does not agree with another, the situation is called a role reversal.
10. What is the difference between role and status?

EXTEND YOUR KNOWLEDGE

1. This chapter explained why people dress like others in their group. Some people deliberately dress *differently* from anyone else. What are some reasons why they might want to do this? Name some people (from the past or present) who dressed in unique ways.
2. Name a favorite school outfit and describe why you like to wear it.
3. Name five groups to which you belong. What are the common beliefs or interests of each group? In what ways do the groups influence your clothing choices?
4. Many items of modern clothing are worn by both males and females; for example, jeans, sweatshirts, and jogging suits. Do you think the time will come when males and females dress exactly alike? Give reasons for your answer.
5. Many years ago, children were dressed as miniature adults. Compare the children's and adults' clothing of today. How are they different? How are they alike?

CHAPTER 2

CLOTHES AND CULTURE

When you see old movies on TV, do you notice the clothes? Clothing in the 1930s and 1940s was very different from what we wear today. By looking at their clothing, you can learn something about the way people of that time thought and felt. It's the same with old photos. You can see the changes in American life reflected in the styles people wore, from the carefree flapper style of the 1920s (see drawing) to the more functional clothes of World War II.

Clothing also differs from country to country. The styles reveal much about the people's customs and beliefs. We refer to the customs, beliefs, values, and skills of a group of people as their **culture.**

This chapter tells about clothes and culture. Do you know the answers to these questions?

- What did early humans wear?
- How have methods of making clothing changed?
- How does culture influence clothing?

Read on to find out.

Look for These Terms

culture	custom
spinning	values
weaving	economics
mass production	technology
division of labor	

Early humans wore animal skins. What might be some advantages and drawbacks of such clothing?

Egyptian royalty, about 1350 B.C. The basic garments were simple, but they were richly decorated with gold and precious stones.

THE HISTORY OF CLOTHES

Why did people begin wearing clothes? One reason is protection from the weather. People in cold climates needed clothes to keep them warm. People in hot climates wore clothing to shield themselves from the sun. Another reason is modesty. People felt it was shameful for certain areas of the body to remain uncovered. A third reason is adornment (decoration). Since earliest times people have decorated their bodies, not only with clothes but also with jewelry, tatoos, and body painting. They did this to make themselves attractive or powerful, to show that they belonged to a particular group, or to indicate their status. Throughout history, the styles of clothing and the methods of making them have changed greatly. Yet the reasons for wearing clothes have remained basically the same.

THE FIRST CLOTHES

Early humans were hunters and gatherers. They killed wild animals for food and also ate various kinds of plants which grew wild. These people usually did not stay in one place very long. When food became scarce, they moved on.

These early humans left no written records. Writing had not been invented yet. But they did paint pictures in caves, and they used tools of stone and bone. Some of these cave paintings and tools still exist. They tell us something about how the early humans lived, including how they dressed.

A Greek couple, about 400 B.C. The loose, flowing garments could be draped in a variety of ways. Note the border designs on the garments.

A Roman couple, about A.D. 50. What similarities and differences can you see between their clothes and those of the Greek couple?

The first clothes were made from animal skins. At first people simply draped or tied the skins around themselves. Later they sewed them together, using animal sinews (tendons) and bone needles.

Eventually people learned to tame certain animals, such as cattle, goats, and sheep. Instead of having to hunt animals for food, they could raise them. They also learned how to grow crops. People no longer had to wander in search of food. By growing their own food, they could stay in one place, and they had more to eat. This more stable, settled way of life led to rapid progress in many areas.

THE DEVELOPMENT OF FABRICS

By the time of the first villages (about 10,000 B.C.), people already had discovered how to spin yarn and weave cloth. **Spinning** is a process in which fibers are twisted around each other to form long strands. **Weaving** is done by interlacing yarns to form cloth.

Once people settled in villages, they learned better ways to make cloth. They could build larger looms, and they had a better supply of materials. The sheep they raised for food also provided wool, and they began to grow flax, the plant from which linen is made.

Flax and wool, along with cotton and silk, became the most widely used fibers for fabrics. These four natural fibers remained the most important for thousands of years. Then, in the late 1800s, people discovered how to make fibers in a laboratory. Today many of our fabrics are made

Medieval costume, around A.D. 1100. Note the wide sleeves on the woman's garment.

By the 1400s, clothing had become much more elaborate. Tall, cone-shaped caps called hennins were popular among women. Men showed off their legs in parti-colored hose.

from manufactured fibers. The natural fibers, however, are still widely used. Often, a natural fiber and a manufactured one are combined to make use of the best properties of each. You'll learn more about fibers and fabrics in Unit 3.

THE DEVELOPMENT OF MANUFACTURING

For thousands of years, spinning and weaving were done by hand. The spinning wheel and the loom were important items of furniture in most homes. Garments were made one at a time, without a pattern, and all sewing was done by hand. Rich people had their clothes made by tailors and dressmakers. Poor people made their own.

The Industrial Revolution changed all that. During the latter half of the 1700s,

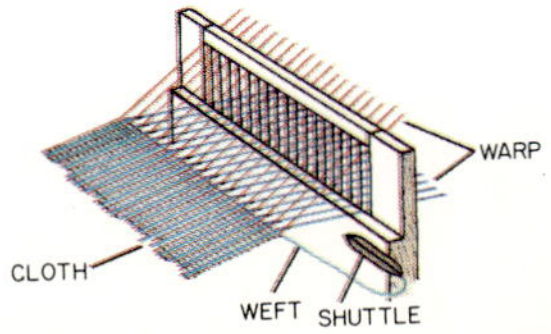

Looms such as this one were run entirely by human muscle power.

In the late 1500s, women's skirts were often open at the front to reveal a beautiful underskirt. Men wore short, padded trunks, long stockings, and a close-fitting jacket called a doublet.

A well-dressed couple in the 1600s. Note the accessories, such as the hat, garter, and fan.

many new machines were invented. Instead of relying on human or animal muscle for power, these machines were run by water or steam. The new machines made it possible to produce goods faster and in greater amounts than ever before. However, most of these machines were large and expensive. It was not practical to have them in a home or a small shop. Instead, large factories, employing hundreds of workers, were built. This new way of producing goods brought about great changes in the way people worked and lived. That's why this era is called the Industrial Revolution.

Here are some of the important changes that took place in the manufacture of fabrics and clothing.

- 1733, England: John Kay invents the flying shuttle. A shuttle is a tool used to move crosswise threads back and forth through a loom. (See the drawing of the loom.) The shuttle used to be thrown by hand. For wide fabrics, two weavers had to work the shuttle. One moved it from right to center. The other moved it from center to left and then back to center. Kay's device sends the shuttle flying across the loom by itself. The flying shuttle makes it easier to weave wide fabrics.
- 1764, England: James Hargreaves' spinning jenny enables a spinner to make eight or more yarns at the same time.
- 1767, England: Richard Arkwright invents the water frame. Powered by

Fashionable ladies and gentlemen of the 1700s wore lace, ruffles, and powdered wigs.

By the mid 1800s, men were wearing long trousers. Women's skirts were still very wide, propped out by stiff petticoats.

water instead of human muscle, this machine is faster than hand spinning and produces stronger yarns.

- 1779, England: Samuel Crompton combines features of the spinning jenny and the water frame to produce the spinning mule. It can do the work of 200 spinners.
- 1785, England: Edmund Cartwright patents the first power loom. It is driven by steam.
- 1789: England will not allow the plans for machinery to be taken out of the country. Samuel Slater memorizes the plans for building Arkwright's water frame and other machines. He travels to America and sets up a mill in Rhode Island. This is the beginning of the textile industry in the United States.
- 1793, United States: Eli Whitney invents the cotton gin. This machine separates cotton fibers from seeds, a job which took a lot of time when done by hand.
- 1805, France: Joseph-Marie Jacquard invents an attachment for the loom which makes it possible to weave complex patterns automatically.
- 1846, United States: Elias Howe patents a sewing machine. Although not the first of its kind, it is better than earlier machines. It makes machine sewing popular.
- 1859, United States: Isaac Singer invents a sewing machine operated by a foot treadle.

By the late 1700s, fabrics were being produced in factories. By the late 1800s, mass production of clothing was in full swing. **Mass production** is the manufacture of goods in large amounts. Garments were no longer made one at a time but by

Clothing of the early 1900s. Note the man's derby hat and spats and the woman's narrow skirt and wide-brimmed hat.

In the early 1960s, women's fashion was influenced by First Lady Jacqueline Kennedy. Note the pillbox hat and short jacket. Note also the man's conservative business suit.

Elias Howe's sewing machine. It was run by turning the handwheel.

the hundreds. Instead of one person sewing an entire garment, the work was divided among several people. Each person sewed only one part of the garment. This **division of labor** made it possible to produce garments faster because each worker became very skilled and quick at his or her particular task.

Mass production made available more clothes at lower prices. Before, only the wealthy were able to own a lot of clothes. Now, most people could afford to buy several outfits. They became more interested in fashion, and that resulted in a greater demand for new clothes. Greater demand led to increased production. Clothing became big business.

The Industrial Revolution changed not only the way clothes were produced but also the types of clothes that were made. Before 1800, men's clothes were as decorative as women's. Like women, men wore lace, satin, and embroidered garments. With the Industrial Revolution came a new middle class—people who had made their fortunes in the business world. They wanted to appear dependable and serious-minded. They rejected the frills of upper-class clothing and chose what became the standard business suit: long trousers, jacket, vest, shirt, and tie. This is one example of how culture affects fashion. The following section describes others.

CULTURE INFLUENCES CLOTHING STYLES

Every culture has had its unique clothing styles. The natives of Hawaii used grass for skirts. Their climate was very warm. The grass was loose and allowed air to circulate around the body. The grass skirt was a practical, simple garment. It suited the Hawaiian way of life. In contrast, the clothing of French nobles in the 1700s was very complex. They wore rich fabrics, yards of ribbon and lace, and elaborate wigs. (See the drawings on page 15.) Their clothes reflected the strict, complicated values and beliefs of that time and place.

As features of a culture change, so do the clothing styles. By studying the clothing of different periods in history, you can understand the customs, beliefs, values, economics, and technology of that time.

CUSTOMS

Custom refers to a long-accepted practice or tradition. The customs of a nation influence people's clothing choices. For example, the long, white wedding dress is a custom of western countries. In the East, other colors are worn. In China, for instance, red is traditional.

Many customs in clothing are disappearing from our society. Once it was the custom for only males to wear pants. Now it is acceptable for both males and females to wear pants. It used to be the custom for people to wear hats whenever they went out. Today hats are seldom worn. Can you think of other clothing customs of the past which no longer exist in our present society?

The clothing of the Amish reflects their belief in plain living and their rejection of modern technology. They wear dark colors and simple styles. Instead of zippers, they use buttons or hooks and eyes to fasten their clothes.

BELIEFS

Clothing can reflect beliefs of individuals and groups. Religious groups often adopt a certain style of clothing. The Amish, for example, believe that wearing fancy clothing is proud and vain. Their clothing is very simple, and they do not wear bright colors.

Beliefs about magic and luck have been held by people of many cultures. Their clothing reflected these beliefs. Masks and elaborate headdresses were worn by American Indians when they wanted to chase away evil spirits. Do you know anyone who wears a "lucky hat" to go fishing? That person believes wearing the hat will improve the chances of catching fish.

VALUES

Clothing can reflect the values of individuals and groups. **Values** are the things which people believe are right and good. They are the things which are considered important. The basic beliefs which you rate highly are your values.

Modesty is a value of many people. During the late 1800s, English women would wear low-cut dresses but would not expose their ankles. It was thought immodest for a woman to show her legs.

The American colonists valued hard work and practicality. They wore clothing that was plain and sturdy. There are people today who value practicality. They seek clothing that is comfortable, easy to care for, and long-lasting.

Others value appearance. They wear clothing that is of the latest fashion. They may sacrifice comfort and practicality in order to be in style.

ECONOMICS

The term **economics** relates to the way people produce, distribute, and use goods and services. People were once limited to the clothes the family or individual could produce. If there was a good weaver in the family, the family had good clothes. Then people began to barter (trade) goods and skills for someone else's goods and skills. Someone who was good at farming might trade some wheat for cloth made by a skilled weaver. Thus, a change in economics led to a change in clothing choices.

The economy of a culture also affects clothing styles. World War II took many

During World War II, the United States government limited the use of fabric to 3½ yards per garment, and zippers were not allowed. The dress on the right didn't meet regulations because of the extra trim at the bottom.

U.S. men to battlefields all over the world. In their absence, women took over the factory jobs. Soon the clothing of females began to change. They started wearing pants. Skirts became much shorter because there was not much fabric available for personal use. Can you think of other events in the economic history of our country that have influenced clothing styles?

TECHNOLOGY

The way a society uses its resources to produce things is referred to as its **technology.** The Industrial Revolution brought many changes in technology. You read on page 17 how these affected men's clothing styles. Women's clothing changed also. As more women entered the work force, they looked for clothing that was comfortable

Long-sleeved, high-necked blouses and long, flowing skirts were popular in the 1890s. The style was inspired by the drawings of Charles Dana Gibson and became known as the Gibson Girl look.

and practical. In the 1880s separate blouses and skirts were introduced. These were more practical than one-piece dresses because several outfits could be made by matching different blouses and skirts. They were also easy to mass produce and did not require the custom fitting that dresses of that time needed.

Prior to this century, clothing was made from natural fibers, chiefly cotton, flax, wool, and silk. The invention of polyester, nylon, and other manufactured fibers altered the way clothing looks and performs. Today we have fabrics that our great-grandparents could only dream of. There are fabrics that look like silk but cost much less, that do not wrinkle or shrink, that stretch and then regain their shape. These new fabrics have made possible new styles in clothing. Swimwear made from stretch fabric is one example. Can you think of others?

There is another way technology has affected clothing styles. Mass communication and modern transportation enable people to share ideas quickly. The latest fashions are available across the country within days. It no longer takes months for clothing styles to spread from one country to another. And there are fewer differences in clothing styles. A Japanese man's business suit is the same as that of an American or an Englishman. You can buy jeans in Russia, T-shirts in Africa, and running shoes in Australia. Could these be signs that we are developing a world culture?

Many changes are ahead for our planet. Space travel is becoming more common. Machines and gadgets are plentiful. More and more of our population is involved in service jobs instead of production jobs. What changes in clothing styles do you predict for the future?

—The Way It Was

HOW DID IT BEGIN?

Have you ever wondered how certain clothing styles or customs began? For example, why do men wear ties? If you study the history of clothing, you'll discover some interesting facts about the culture of earlier times. Here are a few examples.

Ties

In the 1600s long wigs became fashionable. At the same time, the starched ruffs that men had been wearing around their necks went out of style. But this was not an age for plain clothing. The ruff was replaced by the cravat (kruh-VAT), a small scarf tied around the neck. Over the next three centuries, the cravat was gradually transformed into the modern tie.

Buttons

Although buttons were invented in prehistoric times, they were not widely used until about A.D. 1500. The earliest buttons were made of bronze or bone. By 1500, there were wooden buttons covered with silk as well as buttons of gold, pearls, and precious stones. Of course, these were expensive. Buttons were a way to show off wealth and status. They were used more often for decoration than for fastening. The French king Francis I (1494–1547) ordered his tailor to make him a black velvet suit with 13,400 gold buttons!

In today's clothing, most buttons are functional, but there are exceptions. For example, men's suit coats usually have a row of buttons on the sleeves. In earlier centuries, when men wore shirts with lace cuffs, these buttons served a useful purpose. The coat sleeves could be buttoned to cover and protect the lace cuffs. Today the buttons are strictly ornamental.

Jeans

In 1850 thousands of people were rushing to California to look for gold. Levi Strauss, a twenty-year-old immigrant from Bavaria, came to San Francisco with the idea of selling canvas for tents and wagon covers to the prospectors. When a miner complained that his work clothes wore out too fast, Strauss had a tailor make trousers from the canvas. Soon Strauss set up a shop to make and sell work pants. He switched from canvas to denim, and blue jeans were born.

Hawaiian Shirts

Vacationers began bringing these colorful shirts back from Hawaii in the late 1940s. The shirts were made of silk or rayon and often had buttons of carved coconut. Many were printed with the names of Hawaiian islands or with slogans about Hawaii.

In 1953 Montgomery Clift wore a Hawaiian shirt in the movie *From Here to Eternity.* That started a fad, one which recently made a comeback.

REVIEW-2

SUMMARY

People wear clothes for protection, modesty, and adornment. The first clothes were made from animal skins. Later, people learned how to spin and weave cloth from natural fibers such as flax, wool, cotton, and silk. Until the Industrial Revolution of the late 1700s, spinning, weaving, and sewing were done by hand. The new machines and mass production methods of the Industrial Revolution changed the way clothes were made and even the styles of clothing. Culture also affects clothing styles. By studying people's clothing, we can learn about their culture.

CHECK YOUR KNOWLEDGE

1. What is culture?
2. *True or False:* Until the Industrial Revolution, clothing was very plain and was worn mainly for protection from the weather.
3. The process of twisting fibers around each other to form long strands is called ______.
4. ______ is the process of interlacing yarns to form cloth.
5. Name the four most widely used natural fibers.
6. The Industrial Revolution began (A) 10,000 B.C.; (B) during the 1700s; (C) in the Middle Ages; (D) in A.D. 1500.
7. *True or False:* The first power loom was run by electricity.
8. Who started the textile industry in the United States?
9. What is custom?
10. The use of polyester for clothing is one example of the influence of ______ on clothing styles.

EXTEND YOUR KNOWLEDGE

1. Write a report describing the clothing of an ancient culture, such as that of Egypt, Greece, China, or Rome.
2. Collect pictures of the native dress of another country. How do the clothes reflect that country's culture? How do they suit the climate?
3. Write a report on the traditional clothing of a Native American Indian tribe.
4. Select an article of clothing worn in a religious ceremony. Research its beginnings and its meaning.
5. Discuss how moving to another state might change the way you dress.

CHAPTER 3

CLOTHES AND YOU

The clothes we wear speak. They tell others who we are. They say we're male or female, conservative or daring, outgoing or reserved.

You can use clothes to express yourself. If you like yellow, you probably wear it often. Yellow is associated with the sun. It communicates warmth, brightness, and light. When you wear yellow often, it tells others that you are a warm, positive, giving, and happy person.

As you read this chapter, think about the following:

- What do your clothes say about you?
- How do clothes affect behavior?
- How do people use clothes to express themselves?

Look for These Terms

impression	emotions
characteristic	job interview

If you saw someone dressed like this, what kind of person would you think he was?

THE MESSAGES OF CLOTHES

What you wear sends out messages. You learned in Chapter 1 about some of the messages clothes can send. They can tell others that you belong to a certain group. They can indicate your role and your status. Clothes send other messages, too. They tell about the inner self—what kind of person you are. What you wear can communicate your mood, personality, and values. The clothes you wear create an impression about you.

FORMING IMPRESSIONS

An **impression** is an image. When you use a rubber stamp, you make an impression on paper. When you meet people, you make an impression, too. The way you look, speak, and act creates an image in people's minds. The image could be good or bad, right or wrong.

Joe had been working on his sister's car. When he saw that it needed a new air filter, he walked to a nearby shopping center to buy one. He was wearing his old clothes, and they were greasy and dirty from the car. Joe didn't know it, but he had some grease on his face, too, and his hair was messy. What impression would Joe make on the people at the shopping center? Would they see Joe as the friendly, helpful person he really was?

We would all like to be judged by the kind of person we are, not by the clothes we wear. Yet the impression others have of us is often based on our appearance. Sometimes we don't mind what impression we make. Joe didn't care about how he looked when he went to the shopping center—until he ran into Cindy. She was in his math class at school, and he had been trying to find a way to meet her. He could just imagine the impression he made on her now. Of all the luck!

WHAT CLOTHES CAN SAY

You've seen that clothes make an impression. They give people clues about the wearer's mood, personality, and values. Joe's clothing, unfortunately, said that he was careless about his appearance. Other kinds of clothing send different messages. For example, people who wear bright colors and relaxed, carefree designs communicate to others that they are happy and cheerful. Some girls prefer to dress in ruffles and lace, while others prefer jeans and T-shirts. Some guys choose school-labeled sweat shirts instead of traditional polo shirts. What personality traits and values are expressed by these choices?

Clothing can show how people feel about themselves. Individuals who feel secure and good about themselves tend to dress in a variety of colors and styles, while a shy person may choose clothes that do not attract attention. The shy person might wear conservative styles and neutral colors in hopes of not being noticed. Outgoing people, on the other hand, enjoy the looks and attention they get from wearing eye-catching outfits.

CLOTHES AFFECT BEHAVIOR

Some people's actions and attitudes vary with different clothing. How do you act when dressed in a shirt and tie or a "special" dress? Are your actions different than when you are dressed in faded jeans and sneakers? Do you think police feel braver in uniform? Do ball players feel more capable when wearing the team colors?

The clothes you wear can affect the way you feel and act.

Dressing differently from others gains people's attention, but not necessarily their approval.

Certain clothing styles cause reactions in other people. Female executives report that when they travel wearing a tailored suit, they are treated more professionally than when they wear slacks. A Brooklyn study found that people obeyed directions more often from a security guard in uniform than from one in a sports coat. When you want to impress a possible employer, you dress neatly and conservatively for your interview.

When carefully selected, clothing can help a person feel more self-confident. Sometimes teens feel that nothing they do is right or okay. Often confidence can be gained by wearing clothing that is in style. Have you ever been in a group in which you were dressed differently from the others? How did you feel? How did the others treat you?

EXPRESSING YOURSELF

You can express yourself—tell the world who you are—by the clothing you wear. But who are you? How can you know what styles are right for you? You'll express yourself best when you choose clothes that suit your characteristics.

YOUR CHARACTERISTICS

A **characteristic** is a trait, feature, or quality that makes someone or something different from others. The combination of all your characteristics sets you apart from others and makes you unique. The way you laugh and smile, the way you think and learn, your appearance—these are some of the characteristics that make you the *you* that you are.

Physical Characteristics

Your height, weight, body type, and the color of your hair and eyes are all physical characteristics. Some physical characteristics can be changed; some cannot. You can change the color of your hair, but you cannot make it thicker. Exercise can develop muscles and change body size, but it cannot make a person shorter or taller.

Clothes can't change your physical characteristics, but they can improve your appearance. A shirt and slacks of the same color will tend to make you look taller. An outfit of several different colors will tend to make you look shorter. Loose clothes can make you look thinner. Stripes that are horizontal (go from side to side) make you look heavier.

Mental Characteristics

These characteristics relate to functions of the mind. How you think, remember, and learn are all mental characteristics.

Do you remember facts easily? Do you like reading and writing, or are you a "numbers person"? Are you interested in computers, or do you prefer working with people? These kinds of abilities and preferences reveal much about your mental characteristics.

A person's clothing choices can reflect mental characteristics. People who are well organized and thorough tend to dress in clothes that are neat and well coordinated. Creative people will try new styles or unusual color combinations. What does your clothing say about your mental characteristics?

Although you have much in common with other people, you also have certain characteristics that set you apart from everyone else.

Is this man an artist or an accountant? What clues about his mental characteristics do his clothes provide?

When your behavior and your looks send different messages, people may get a false impression of you.

Emotional Characteristics

When you laugh or cry, you are showing emotion. **Emotions** are feelings, and feelings determine much of our behavior. Have you been in love? How did you behave when you felt love for someone else? How do you behave when you are happy or when you are sad?

Clothes can indicate emotions. Think about the last time you were unhappy. Did you choose clothes that had bright colors and bold patterns? When you're feeling unhappy, you tend to choose "quiet" clothes.

Your clothing choices are influenced by your emotions. But it can work the other way, too. When you're feeling a little down, wearing cheerful clothes can lighten your mood.

BEING YOURSELF

To be yourself means that the impression you make on others is consistent with your physical, mental, and emotional characteristics. Your behavior and your looks communicate the same message.

The better you understand yourself, the better you can express yourself through clothing. Try this experiment. Write a list of words that describe you, such as "outgoing," "quiet," "casual," or "formal." Now look at the clothes you own. Does your description of yourself fit your clothing style?

Perspective

DRESSING FOR A JOB INTERVIEW

The clothes you wear send messages about you. Naturally you want those messages to be good ones. This is especially true when you are going to a job interview. A **job interview** is a meeting you have with a possible employer to discuss your interest in and qualifications for a job. Whether it's a part-time, "make some spending money" job or one which you expect to make a career of, you'll want to look your best.

What you should wear depends on the job for which you are applying. If it's a job as a grocery store clerk or a gas station attendant, a shirt and slacks would be all right for a male (dress or skirt and blouse for a female). But if you're applying for an office job, a suit is better. No matter what the job, make sure your clothes are neat, clean, and free of wrinkles.

Avoid loud colors and patterns. Simple, conservative clothes are best. Choose navy, gray, or black for a suit, slacks, or skirt. Blouses and shirts can be white or a light color.

Shoes also should be simple and conservative. Sandals or athletic shoes would not be appropriate. Women should avoid open-toed shoes and shoes with very high heels.

Hair should be clean and neatly combed. Face and teeth should also be clean. Women should avoid heavy makeup. Don't wear strong perfume or cologne.

A good general rule to follow is: Do not put on anything that draws attention to itself. After all, it's not your clothes they'll be hiring, it's you.

REVIEW-3

SUMMARY

Our clothes send messages about who and what we are. Other people's impression of us is often based on our appearance. Clothes can give clues about our mood, personality, and values. Clothes can also affect behavior, both the way we act and the way others act towards us. We can express ourselves by the way we dress, and the best way to do that is to choose clothes that suit our physical, mental, and emotional characteristics.

CHECK YOUR KNOWLEDGE

1. *True or False:* The clothes we wear have an effect on the impression we make.
2. *True or False:* People who feel good about themselves pay little attention to how they dress; they don't concern themselves with their looks.

#3-7 are a description of a young person. Tell whether each characteristic listed is physical, mental, or emotional.

3. 5′7″ tall
4. red hair
5. musically talented
6. sentimental
7. friendly and outgoing
8. People who wear clothes that attract attention are likely to be (A) shy; (B) rich; (C) outgoing; (D) unhappy.
9. A shirt and slacks of the same color tend to make the wearer look (A) heavier; (B) friendlier; (C) older; (D) taller.
10. *True or False:* The best way to express yourself through clothing is to dress like the person you most admire.

EXTEND YOUR KNOWLEDGE

1. Collect pictures of clothes that send the following messages: (1) wealth, (2) power, (3) flamboyance (showiness), (4) shyness.
2. Describe two clothing outfits and the behavior that "matches" the clothing.
3. What are you wearing today? How do the clothes suit your characteristics?
4. How do you feel when dressed in jeans and a sweat shirt? How is this different from the way you feel when you're dressed up?
5. Research how clothing is used to portray characters on stage or in the movies.

CHAPTER 4

CLOTHES AND FASHION

Comments such as "This is the current fashion," "That jacket is a fad," and "That style is really 'in' this season" are common. But what do those terms really mean? **Style** is the design of a garment. Pleated pants with cuffs and bell-bottom pants are both styles, but they may or may not be the fashion. **Fashion** is the style that is popular at the present time. A fashion usually lasts more than one season. Blue jeans are a fashion. A **fad** is an extreme fashion that lasts only a very short time. Parachute pants and camouflage fabrics were fads. Can you name a fad that was popular last year but is no longer "in"?

Do you know how fashions and fads start? Who decides what's in and what's out? There are so many different styles of clothes. Do they have anything in common?

In this chapter, you'll learn about fashion and design. Read on to find answers to these questions:

- How do fashions begin?
- What causes fashions to change?
- What are the elements and principles of design?

Look for These Terms

style
fashion
fad
cycle
fashion leaders
elements of design
principles of design

Fashions are never entirely new. They borrow from styles of the past. Compare these clothes with the ones in the photo at left.

FASHION

Why do people follow fashions? One reason is to show they belong to a certain group. With what groups do you associate these fashions: button-down shirt, motorcycle jacket, three-piece suit? Some people like to dress in the latest fashion because they want to be the first ones to have something new. Others want to create an image of success, so they dress in fashionable, expensive clothing.

To understand fashion and its role in society, it helps to know something about the origins (beginnings) of fashion and what causes it to change.

THE ORIGINS OF FASHION

Fashion grows out of the culture. As you learned in Chapter 2, culture—the customs, beliefs, values, economy, and technology of a time—influences the clothing styles. As culture changes, so does fashion. Some cultures change very slowly, and their fashions may stay the same for many years. Other cultures, such as ours, change quickly, and the pace of fashion is faster.

Before the fourteenth century, European fashion changed very slowly. Most people were poor. Their clothes were simple and functional. "Fashion" belonged to the royal class, who could afford costly fabrics and elaborate garments.

Toward the end of the fourteenth century, a new era began. There was increased emphasis on science, art, and exploration. This era is called the Renaissance (ren-uh-SAHNTS), and it is often considered the beginning of modern times.

During the Renaissance, culture began to change more quickly, and fashions reflected the changes. Trade increased, and new fabrics, such as satins and silks from the Orient, became available. The economy changed, and a new class of wealthy people arose. They were not royalty but merchants. One way they displayed their new wealth was by wearing fine clothes.

Fashion became more important. Because they were at the top of the social order, royalty became the style setters. Others imitated them to the extent they could afford to do so.

During the eighteenth and nineteenth centuries, the power of the royal class declined. All over Europe, monarchies (governments ruled by a king or queen) were replaced by other systems of government. The Industrial Revolution brought wealth to new groups. As the royal class lost political and economic power, their fashion leadership ended as well.

Today fashion originates from many sources. Fashion designers create new styles. Famous athletes, politicians, or entertainers may start a new fashion. Some fashions even have their beginnings "on the street." Jeans are a good example. These started out as work clothes. Then students began wearing them. By the 1970s jeans had become so popular that fashion designers began to make them.

FASHION CYCLES

You now know that fashions change because culture changes. There is a pattern to the changes in fashion. It's called the fashion cycle. A **cycle** is a predictable pattern of events. The fashion cycle has three stages:

1. A new style is introduced.
2. The style is accepted and worn by many people.
3. The style is replaced by a newer style.

Fashion Reactions

People will react to the same garment in different ways, depending on where it is in its fashion cycle. Fashion historian James Laver has developed the following:

"Indecent" . . . .10 years before its time	"Dowdy". . . . . .1 year after its time
"Shameless". . . .5 years before its time	"Hideous" . . . . . .10 years after its time
"Daring". . . . . . . .1 year before its time	"Ridiculous" . . . .20 years after its time
"Smart" . . . . .Peak of its popularity	"Beautiful". . . . .150 years after its time

To start a new style takes courage. Someone must be secure enough to wear what no one else is wearing. Those who are the first to wear a new style are called **fashion leaders.**

Other people watch the fashion leaders. They begin to copy the appearance of the fashion leaders. This may happen slowly or very quickly.

Once a style is widely accepted, it stops being new and unusual. The fashion leaders begin to look for a different style. The fashion cycle thus begins again.

DESIGN

Have you ever wondered how fashion designers think up new styles? They are creative people, but they don't pull their ideas out of thin air. They look at what's going on—in world events, the arts, technology, and so on. They observe what other people are wearing, what's in and what's on its way out. From all these things, they get ideas for new designs.

When you look at a finished design, you see it as a whole. But of course the design wasn't created that way. It was put together using "building blocks" called the **elements of design.** These elements were combined according to certain rules, or **principles.** Together, the elements and principles of design present a whole, coordinated "look."

THE ELEMENTS OF DESIGN

The elements of design in clothing are line, space, form, color, and texture. These elements tell you what is included in the clothing design.

Elements of design are much like musical instruments in a rock band. The bass, synthesizer, guitar, and drums are distinct pieces of the total band. Yet all of the instruments can be combined to produce one song.

Just as the instruments are combined to make a song, the elements of clothing design are combined to create garments. And just as the musical instruments are put together to produce different sounds (think of the variety of music in this week's "Top 40" hits on the radio), the elements of design can be put together in a lot of different ways. The overall effect that results from the combination of elements determines whether the garment is a "hit."

Lines

A line is a continuous, narrow mark. Lines in clothing may be formed by seams, edges, or folds in the garment. These lines are called *structural lines* because they are part of the garment's construction. Lines that are applied to the garment to improve its appearance, such as trim or special stitching, are called *decorative lines.*

The lines formed by sewing the garment are called structural lines. Lines added to the basic garment for a better appearance are called decorative lines.

—The Way It Was

GOLDEN OLDIES: FADS AND FASHIONS OF THE PAST

How many of these fads and fashions have you seen in old pictures or movies? Ask your parents or older brothers and sisters whether they wore any of the styles listed here. Do you recognize some that have made a comeback and are popular today?

1950s

blue jeans with the legs turned up
white T-shirts
leather jackets
bobby socks
saddle shoes
monogrammed sweaters
poodle skirts
crinoline petticoats
Hawaiian shirts
sack dresses
ponytails for women
ducktail hairstyles for men

1960s

miniskirts
bell-bottom and hip-hugger jeans
psychedelic prints
A-line skirts and dresses
wide ties
double-breasted coats and jackets
paper dresses
plastic go-go boots
Nehru jackets
granny glasses
false eyelashes
love beads
long hair for women and men

1970s

faded, ragged jeans, often embroidered or studded
the ethnic look, especially Native American Indian, European peasant, and African
patterned stockings and tights
tie-dyed fabrics
flared pants
leisure suits
platform shoes
pantsuits for women
smocked tops
turtleneck sweaters
double-knit fabrics
Afro hairdos
shag haircuts
neck chains

Space

In a garment, space is the area inside and between lines. Spaces may be wide or narrow. Narrow spaces cause the eye to move up and down the length of the space. Wide spaces cause the eye to move side to side along the width of the space.

A pleasing design balances space and lines. If there is too much space within a garment, it will cause the wearer to look like a "blob" and have a very uninteresting appearance. If there are too many lines, the result will be a cluttered appearance.

Form

The form of a garment is its overall shape. Most garment forms resemble basic geometric shapes such as the rectangle, triangle, circle, and square. A rectangular form will make you look taller. In a triangular form, the emphasis is on the base of the triangle. Circles give a soft, full appearance. Square shapes tend to make you look shorter and wider.

Two examples of garment forms. What garments have a rectangular form? A triangular form?

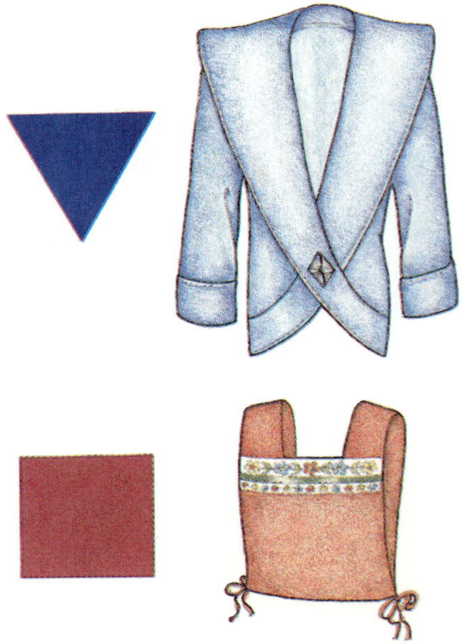

The relationship between the lines of a print and the spaces affects the garment's overall look. Note the difference between the two garments shown here.

Basically there are two kinds of lines: straight and curved. Curved lines suggest movement and softness. Straight lines give the appearance of stability and stiffness. They may be horizontal, vertical, or diagonal. Horizontal lines go from side to side. They tend to make things appear wider and shorter. Vertical lines go in an up and down direction. They make things appear taller and thinner. Diagonal lines slant. If they are slanted more up and down than across, they will act as vertical lines and makes things look taller. If they are slanted more across than up and down, they will act as horizontal lines and make things appear shorter and wider. Use lines to your advantage to make yourself appear taller or shorter.

Color

Color is the first thing most people notice about a garment. Colors communicate moods. Bright colors appear cheerful. Dark ones seem serious. Reds and oranges are warm and exciting, while blues and greens are cool and calm. Colors also affect the apparent size of a garment. Cool colors usually make a garment seem smaller. Warm colors tend to make the garment appear larger.

The color of a garment depends on more than just the color of the dye that is used. Different fabrics absorb dyes differently. Perhaps you have heard a garment referred to as "dull" or "bright." If a fabric is loosely woven, it may absorb more dye than a tightly woven fabric. More dye may cause the fabric to appear duller, even if the color is the same as that in the tightly woven fabric.

Because warm colors seem to move toward us, the red circle appears larger. Actually, both are the same size.

Texture

The other elements of design—line, space, form, and color—can be described by what you see. Texture, however, can be described by what you feel as well as what you see. There are many textures. Surfaces of fabrics may be loopy, fuzzy, soft, crisp, smooth, rough, slippery, or scratchy. Can you think of other words to describe textures? Look around you and identify the textures of clothing and room furnishings.

The texture of your clothing affects your appearance. Smooth surfaces make you look more slender. Fuzzy textures generally add bulkiness. Because crisp textures tend to hang away from the body, they increase size. What look would a loopy fabric create? A slippery fabric?

THE PRINCIPLES OF DESIGN

The principles of design are used to combine the elements in many different ways and achieve different looks. The principles of design are emphasis, balance, proportion, rhythm, and harmony. When these principles are properly used, the total look of a garment or outfit will be pleasing to the eye. Understanding how to use the principles of design will help you create an attractive effect.

Different textures absorb or reflect light in different ways. Therefore we can see texture as well as feel it.

Emphasis

Emphasis is the center of interest on a garment. It is the part that gets noticed. For example, a white collar would be the center of interest on a navy polo shirt.

Each garment or outfit should have a center of interest. For instance, white slacks and a white shirt would be dull and uninteresting. Adding emphasis with a collar, tie, or belt of a different color would create a crisp, more pleasing look.

Color contrasts are one way to create emphasis. Repetition is another. Several buttons in a row create a line that draws attention. Repetition of one color in a plaid shirt provides emphasis. The center of interest could also be in the lines, texture, or shape of a garment. What is the emphasis on the clothing you are wearing today?

Emphasis should draw attention to your best features and away from any figure flaws. Contrasting collars emphasize the neckline. Pleated or gathered skirts and pants emphasize the hips. How would you emphasize long legs? How would you draw attention away from them?

Repetition of lines is one way to create a center of interest on a garment.

Which photo shows formal balance? Which one shows informal balance?

Balance

Remember as a child playing on a seesaw and trying to balance it? You and the child on the other end had to squirm around, shifting your weight forward and back until the balance was right. You were trying to distribute your weight equally on the seesaw. Balance in clothing design is the distribution of visual weight or size.

Balance may be formal or informal. Formal balance occurs when the design is the same on both sides. When texture, lines, and color are the same on both sides of a shirt, formal balance exists. Placing the same size pocket on the left and right of a jacket creates formal balance.

Informal balance is created when the two sides are different but still make a pleasing combination. For example, three narrow lines on the right side of a shirt could balance two wider lines on the left side.

Proportion

Another principle of design is proportion. Proportion in clothing is the relationship of one part to another and of all the pieces to the total look. In a well-proportioned garment, all the parts work well together.

You may have put on a new shirt to wear with your jeans only to find that the two didn't look right together. When you tucked the shirt into the jeans, though, the look improved. That is because you changed the proportion. The new combination gave a more pleasing look.

The ideal body proportion is a 3/8 to 5/8 relationship. This means 3/8 of the total body length should be above the waist. The remaining 5/8 should be below the waist.

If you are 5′ 4″ (64″) tall, the distance from the top of your head to your waist should be 3/8 of 64, or 24″. The distance from your waist to the floor should be 5/8 of 64, or 40″.

Few people fit the ideal body proportions. If your body above the waist is less than 3/8 of your height, you are short waisted. If your body above the waist is more than 3/8 of your height, you are long waisted. How many people in your class are long waisted? How many are short waisted? Does anyone fit the ideal body proportions?

Even if your body proportions are not ideal, you can learn to select clothing that will make your proportions look right. You'll learn how to do this in Chapter 5.

Dividing an outfit exactly across the middle usually does not create pleasing proportions. Note the improvement when the proportions are changed to 3/8 and 5/8.

How is rhythm created in the vest this student is wearing?

Harmony is achieved when all parts of an outfit go together. Note how the necklace, belt, and shoes help to create the total look.

Rhythm

Rhythm in clothing design exists when the eye moves smoothly from one part to another. Each part coordinates with all the other parts. Rhythm contributes to the unity of all the pieces of clothing for a total look.

Rhythm may be created by:

- repetition—using regular repeats of lines, colors, or patterns
- variation—varying the sizes of lines or the fabric color in a regular way
- progression—using tints and shades of a color or moving from wider lines to narrower ones

Harmony

All parts of an outfit or garment should be in agreement with one another. Harmony is the principle of design that ties all the elements together for a pleasing look.

You wouldn't wear a silk tie with a sweat shirt or running shoes with formal clothes. The outfits would not have harmony. On the other hand, the silk tie and formal clothes would be harmonious. Why?

The most harmonious look is achieved when the design of the garment and the shape, coloring, and personality of the wearer all go together. In the next unit, you'll learn how to create that look.

REVIEW-4

SUMMARY

In earlier times, royalty used to set new fashions. Today, fashions might originate with fashion designers, celebrities, or social groups. Fashion follows a cycle. First, a new style is introduced and worn by fashion leaders. Then others follow the fashion leaders and begin wearing the new style. Finally, the style becomes so common it's old. A new style takes its place. Whatever the style, there are certain elements and principles of design which should be followed in order to create a pleasing appearance.

CHECK YOUR KNOWLEDGE

1. What is the difference between a fashion and a fad?
2. *True or False:* Fashions change faster during times when culture changes rapidly.
3. *True or False:* New fashions are always started by famous or wealthy people.
4. What are the stages of a fashion cycle?
5. Those who are the first to wear a new style are called fashion ______.
6. Name the five elements of design.
7. Which element of design can be felt as well as seen?
8. What is the difference between structural and decorative lines?
9. Name the five principles of design.
10. Describe the two types of balance.

EXTEND YOUR KNOWLEDGE

1. Write a report on the fashions of a particular time and place. For example, you might choose Europe in the 1400s, England during the reign of Elizabeth I, France during the reign of Louis XIV, the French Revolution, or the Victorian Age.
2. Name some current fads. How did they start? What groups follow them? How long do you think they will last?
3. Select a fashion designer and research his or her career. Possible subjects include Paul Poiret, Coco Chanel, Elsa Schiaparelli, Christian Dior, Mary Quant, Yves St. Laurent, and Calvin Klein.
4. Cut out fashion pictures from magazines, newspapers, or catalogs that illustrate the elements and principles of design. Label each picture to indicate which elements and principles are shown.
5. Talk to a middle-aged or elderly adult. Ask him or her to describe clothing fads of the past.

CHOOSING CLOTHES

Choosing clothes is a process that involves many decisions. Would you look better in dark colors or light ones? Should you wear what you already have or get something new? If you decide to get new clothes, should you buy them or make them? These are just some of the decisions you may need to make.

Making decisions about clothes can seem hard. With so many things to consider, how can you make the right choices? There's a simple method that can help you make good decisions. It's called the decision-making process, and it is made up of five steps.

Step 1: Define the problem or set the goal.

Step 2: Consider your resources. What do you have that can help you solve the problem?

Step 3: Consider your alternatives. In what ways could you solve the problem? What are the advantages and disadvantages of each way?

Step 4: Choose one of the alternatives. Select a plan of action and carry it out.

Step 5: Evaluate the results. Did you solve your problem or reach your goal? If not, what could you do differently?

As you read this unit, think about the decision-making process. How could you apply it to choose clothes that are right for you?

Unit 2

CHAPTER 5

THE RIGHT CLOTHES FOR YOU

meant that what you wore and how you looked influenced the impression you made on others. Do you think this is still true? Research shows that clothing and personal appearance *do* have an effect on your success at work or in school. Why do you think this happens?

As you have already learned, clothes send a message about you. Part of that message has to do with how attractive you are and what your personality is like. When your clothes fit well and flatter you, you send a message of well-being. Your clothes say that you care about your appearance, that you do things carefully and not sloppily.

As you study this chapter, think about the following:

- Can you recognize the different face and figure types?
- What design elements and principles can help you choose clothing?
- How can your clothes reflect your personality?

Look for These Terms

hue	secondary colors
value	tertiary colors
intensity	color schemes
primary colors	self-image

The basic figure shapes. There are, of course, many variations. A stout person, for example, might be tall, short, or of average height. Also, most people have a combination of shapes. For instance, you may have a short trunk and long legs or a long trunk and short legs.

FIGURE SHAPES

By studying your shape, you can become aware of your figure's special features. You can recognize what you should call attention to and what you should play down.

You can determine your figure shape by comparing your figure to those shown on this page. These are the basic figure types, and most people's figures come close to one or the other.

To make the best comparison, put on your bathing suit and stand in front of a full-length mirror. Another method is to stand in front of a blank wall with a strong light behind you. Which figure type does your shadow resemble?

Is your body well-proportioned? Proportion has to do with how your height, weight, and body parts relate to your figure in general. For example, some people's arms or legs seem long in relation to their height. Look at the figures on this page. Notice how the body proportions of each are different.

The distribution of weight is also important. Look at the figures again. On the ideal female figure, the shoulders and hips are about the same width and the waist is narrow. The ideal male figure has shoulders that are wide. The body gradually tapers toward narrow hips. Most of us, however, do not have ideal body proportions or shape.

Look at your own figure. Are you short, tall, or average height? Is your shape thin, stout, or average? What would you have to point up or play down to look more like the ideal? Write this information about your figure on a piece of paper.

FACE SHAPES

Faces resemble geometric shapes. Look at the chart on page 47. Then look at the people sitting around you or those pictured in magazines. What face shapes do you see? Can you find examples of each of these shapes: oval, round, heart, triangle, diamond, square, and oblong? The oval is the ideal face shape. Yet, many very attractive people have faces with other

Which shape is closest to that of your own face? Place this book, opened to the face shape chart, next to a mirror. Pull back your hair. Which of the seven basic shapes do you see? Heart-shaped faces, for example, have wide foreheads and narrow chins. Add your face shape to your list of characteristics.

THE RIGHT DESIGNS FOR YOU

Few of us possess the ideal shapes. If we want to come closer to an ideal figure or face, we must use the elements and principles of design to help us. We draw attention to our best features and away from those less than ideal.

USING DESIGN ELEMENTS

Take out the notes you made about your figure type and face shape. As you read on, think about how lines, spaces, form, texture, and color can be used to make you appear either shorter or taller, smaller or larger. Think how they can make you look more in proportion. What can you use to help your face appear more oval in shape?

Lines and Spaces

Horizontal lines or spaces make you appear wider and shorter. Vertical lines or spaces make you appear taller and slimmer. Look at the pictures on this page. Identify the type of lines or spaces found in each garment. Notice how the direction affects the appearance of the person pictured.

What effect do the lines and spaces in these garments have on the apparent size of the wearer?

—Perspective

WHAT'S RIGHT FOR YOU?

Shown below are the common face shapes. Which one most closely resembles your own? Note the hairstyles and the clothing styles for each face shape. How do they help emphasize good features? How do they minimize less attractive features?

OVAL

- Any style. Scooped necklines will accent the oval shape. Other necklines will make the oval less obvious.

ROUND

- V-shaped or deep necklines
- Pointed collars
- Narrow lapels
- Medium-wide neckties

HEART

- Square, scoop, or wide and round (boat) neck-lines
- Spread collar or rounded collar on shirts

TRIANGULAR

- Rounded collars and lapels
- Scoop and boat necklines

DIAMOND

- Rounded collars and lapels
- Frilly collars
- U-shaped necklines

SQUARE

- Rounded collars and necklines or frilly ruffles
- Deep necklines or U-shaped necklines
- Curved design in neckties
- Rounded lapels
- Long scarves or necklaces

OBLONG

- Medium-wide collars and ties
- Round necklines
- Round collars
- Horizontal pattern in neckties

LONG NECK

- High collars and necklines
- Turtlenecks
- Scarves or ascots
- Wide lapels
- Accessories that create horizontal lines

SHORT NECK

- V-shaped or scoop necklines
- Narrow lapels
- Necklines set away from neck
- Accessories that create vertical lines

The lines at the neck of a garment influence the appearance of your face and neck. Necklines can be horizontal, V-shaped, round, or vertical (turtlenecks). Horizontal necklines add width to the face and neck. The depth of the V-shaped neckline adds length to the face and neck. Round necklines can soften the sharp lines of diamond, square, triangular, and oblong faces. Close-fitting turtlenecks can emphasize a small face. Loose turtlenecks can balance a large face.

Form

Form, or shape, is the general outline of clothing. It can make you appear taller and thinner or wider and shorter. Form-fitting clothes add height and help reduce apparent weight. A bell shape, such as that created by flared pants and skirts, is good

—Perspective

CLOTHES FOR YOUR FIGURE

Figure Shapes	Characteristics	Do Wear	Don't Wear
Tall/Thin	■ Men: 6′0″ or taller Women: 5′8″ or taller ■ Height may not be in proportion to rest of figure ■ Very little fatty tissue ■ Bones may "stick out"	■ Horizontal lines in fabric or clothing construction ■ Two-piece outfits of different colors ■ Flared skirts or pants and full sleeves ■ Bright colors and plaids	■ Tight, high turtlenecks, clingy fabrics, or very short shorts ■ Too-tight pants or pipe-stem or leg-hugging looks
Tall/Stout	■ Men: 6′0″ or taller Women: 5′8″ or taller ■ Height may not be in proportion to rest of figure ■ Body is well rounded, although padding may be heavier in some areas	■ Soft cowls and tailored collars ■ Belts of same color as garment ■ Tailored clothes ■ Lightweight, soft fabrics	■ Colors with light values or high intensity ■ Clothes that show figure "bumps"

for tall, slim people. The fullness of the bell fills in their lean bodies. Full shapes are also good for thin people. The more fullness, the wider the form. Look at current pattern books and fashion magazines. Find examples of each general outline. Which one is best for you?

Color

Color is very helpful in playing features up or down. Color is discussed in depth starting on page 51.

Texture

Fabric texture affects the power of color. Fabrics that have a slick, shiny surface, such as satin, reflect light. They make bright colors appear even brighter.

HELPFUL HINT: If you want to play up a feature, such as your waistline, wear bright, shiny fabrics in that area.

Fabrics with rough textures absorb light. Bright colors do not appear as bright when the fabric texture is rough. Rough-textured fabrics include linen, muslin, and woolens.

Figure Shape	Characteristics	Do Wear	Don't Wear
Average (If weight is above or below average, follow the guidelines in whatever category is closest to your height. If you're 5′5″ and overweight, look under the category "Short/Stout.")	■ Men: 5′9″ to 5′11″ Women: 5′4″ to 5′7″ ■ Body proportion and weight evenly distributed ■ Weight that covers bones and hollow places, but person is not overweight	■ Colors that play up the skin and hair tones ■ Accessories to complement best features	■ Clothes that are too tight ■ Prints or plaids that are too large or too small
Short/Thin	■ Men: 5′8″ or under Women: 5′3″ or under ■ Very little fatty tissue ■ Bones may be prominent	■ Bright colors ■ Designs in fabric (in proportion to body size) ■ Some fullness in skirts or slacks	■ Long turtlenecks, narrow sleeves, or leg-hugging pants ■ Heavy horizontal stripes ■ Pants with cuffs
Short/Stout	■ Men: 5′8″ or under Women: 5′3″ or under ■ The body is well rounded, although padding may be heavier in some areas	■ Outfits of one color ■ Belts which match the garment ■ Vertical lines in garment construction or fabric design ■ Soft colors, dull textures	■ Large prints, bulky fabrics, or pleated pants ■ Shiny textures or bright colors

Texture also determines the bulk of a fabric. Bulky fabrics add weight to your figure. A thick wool sweater is bulky and heavy looking. It can make a slim man appear wider and shorter. Often, fabrics that are loosely woven also are bulky. A pleated skirt made from a loosely-woven wool will make a slim girl's hips appear larger. This added width may draw attention away from height if the skirt and top are in contrasting colors.

USING DESIGN PRINCIPLES

The principles of design can also be used to emphasize your good points and play down your less desirable features.

Balance

Informal balance draws attention to one area. For example, a pin worn on one shoulder draws attention to that spot. Formal balance is harmonious because both sides are the same. On a jacket with lapels, the two lapels are an example of formal balance.

Proportion

Most bodies do not have ideal proportion. You may be long- or short-waisted. Your height could be in your torso (trunk) or your legs. By raising or lowering a waistline or jacket length, you can create a sense of better proportion. If you are long-waisted, shorten the jacket length. If you are short-waisted, wear longer jackets and tops.

Sleeve length influences how long your arms look. Long sleeves or no sleeves make short arms appear longer. Three-quarter or short sleeves make long arms appear shorter.

What uses of proportion can you find among your classmates' clothing? How can proportion help your own figure?

Rhythm

Rhythm draws attention to the area where it occurs. A series of stripes on a sweater will focus attention on the torso and away from the legs. Such emphasis would be good for people whose height is in their legs.

Find pictures that show other examples of rhythm. Would any of the examples be helpful for you?

Emphasis

Emphasis attracts the viewer's eye. You notice bright or light colors, prints or plaids, and jewelry, belts, or other accessories. Wearing a red tie or scarf with a navy suit and white shirt emphasizes your face and upper body. Plaid slacks and a solid-color shirt emphasize the lower part of the body.

HELPFUL HINT: Place eye-catching details near your best features to emphasize them.

Harmony

A harmonious look means that the parts of an outfit blend. The outfit and the body also complement each other. Blue polka dots and red stripes usually are not harmonious. Blue polka dots and blue stripes, however, may be.

COLOR

To understand how color can work for you, it is important to fully understand the basics of color. Color has hue, value, and intensity. Each can be used to affect how you look.

Hue (HYOO) refers to a color family. For instance, red is a hue. All colors that have red as their major part belong to the red family. However, there are many types of red. Red changes from its pure form when other colors are added to it. For example, it becomes brighter when yellow is added. When this mixed color is given a name, its main hue is its "last" name, such as "yellow-red."

Hues may be warm or cool. The warm colors are those with red or yellow in them. Cool colors have blue or green in them. The warmth or coolness of a color influences the appearance of size. Warm colors seem to come forward. You notice them first. An orange shirt appears closer to you, and the wearer appears bigger. Cool colors tend to draw back. They make the wearer look smaller.

Value tells how light or dark a color is. When white is added to a color, its value becomes lighter. Adding black produces a darker value. Instead of calling these colors white-red and black-red, we give them nicknames. In this case those nicknames are pink and maroon.

Values affect how large or small an object appears. Dark values make an object look smaller. Light values make it look larger.

Helpful hint: If you are thin, wearing light-colored clothing can make you appear heavier. If you are heavy, dark colors can help you look slimmer.

Intensity (in-TEN-sih-tee) is the brightness or dullness of a color. Lime green is a bright color, and forest green is a dull color. What other bright or dull colors can you identify?

Colors of full intensity are striking. They call attention to themselves. If you want to emphasize broad shoulders or an attractive face, you may add a bright-colored scarf or necktie. Dull shades of any color make you appear smaller than you are. A dull color, such as rust or navy, will make large body areas less noticeable.

THE COLOR WHEEL

The color wheel is a circle of different colors. The basic colors are red, yellow, and blue. These are **primary colors,** the colors from which the other colors are made. When two primary colors are mixed together in equal amounts, **secondary colors** are created. Mixing red and yellow produces orange. Yellow and blue produce green, and blue and red produce purple. The secondary colors are placed between the primary colors on the color wheel.

More colors are made when primary and secondary colors are mixed. These colors are called **tertiary** (TUR-she-air-ee) **colors.** For example, when violet and red are mixed, the new color is red-violet.

The outer circle shows the primary colors (names in bold type), the secondary colors (capitals), and the tertiary colors (capital and lowercase letters).

COLOR SCHEMES

Color schemes are clusters of colors used together. The types of color schemes are analogous, complementary, monochromatic, and triad.

An analogous (uh-NAL-uh-gus) color scheme is formed by selecting colors that are next to each other on the color wheel. Blue slacks and a green shirt make an analogous color scheme.

Complementary (kahm-pluh-MENT-uh-ree) colors are opposite each other on the color wheel. Blue slacks worn with an orange shirt make use of complementary colors.

A monochromatic (mahn-uh-kroh-MAT-ik) color scheme uses different values of one color. For example, blue slacks might be teamed with a light blue shirt.

The three colors forming a triad (TRY-add) color scheme are equally distant from one another on the color wheel. Red, yellow, and blue are triad colors. A red, yellow, and blue plaid shirt represents a triad color scheme.

THE PSYCHOLOGY OF COLOR

Colors are often linked to emotions. People "see red" when angry or "feel blue" when depressed. Studies show that the color red can actually raise blood pressure and speed up heartbeat. Blue can bring them down.

A French airline once painted the interior of its passenger planes bright yellow-green, a popular color of the day. However, sunlight reflected inside the planes gave passengers greenish complexions. They looked and felt sick. Cases of airsickness increased. The airline soon figured out what was causing the problem and repainted the planes.

The color of your clothing can change your mood. If you feel down in the morning, try wearing orange or yellow. The day may seem not quite so bad if your clothes are cheerful. Blue and green suggest quiet or calm and are helpful when you feel nervous. You may choose your clothing colors by how they make you feel or how you want to make others feel.

YOUR PERSONAL COLORING

When you choose clothes, consider your personal coloring—your skin tone, eyes, and hair. The colors of your clothes should enhance your personal coloring. People with medium skin tones can achieve a pleasing appearance with a broad range of colors. People with pale skin tones generally look best in medium color values. Dark values tend to drain color from the face, and light values provide too little contrast. If you have dark skin, dark values may help balance your personal coloring.

Helpful hint: If you want to emphasize your eyes, choose a color of the smae hue as your eyes. Hues that are lighter or darker than your hair will emphasize the color of your hair.

Drape fabric or clothing of different hues, values, and intensities around your shoulders. Do some colors look unbecoming with your skin tone? Which colors complement your eyes and hair? Ask other people to give you their opinions, too. If they compliment you on a particular color, chances are it is a good choice for you.

YOUR PERSONALITY AND SELF-IMAGE

Your personality and self-image affect your clothing decisions. They help determine what you buy as well as what you choose to wear each day.

PERSONALITY

Your personality is created by all the characteristics that make you unique. It is your likes and dislikes, your abilities, the way you act and feel.

Clothing is one way people express their personalities. Athletic people might choose comfortable, casual clothes. Outgoing people often wear bright, warm colors such as red, yellow, or orange. Shy people often select clothing that does not attract attention. They choose conservative styles and quiet colors. People who care about being "with it" wear very fashionable clothing. Can you name other examples of clothes that express personality traits?

SELF-IMAGE

Self-image is the mental picture that you have of yourself. It is important that you have a good self-image. Having a good self-image means that although you realize you're not perfect, you try to focus on your good points. You keep a positive attitude.

Your clothing choices should reflect a good self-image. They should show you at your best. If you are not pleased with how you look, work to change it. When your clothes help you keep a good self-image, you tend to be more confident and relaxed. You are also usually more successful in achieving your goals.

Clothes that match your personality and reflect a good self-image will help you feel good about yourself.

REVIEW-5

SUMMARY

Your body and face can be classified according to their shape. Using design elements and principles when you choose clothing can bring your face and figure closer to an ideal shape. Clothes should enhance not only your appearance but your personality and self-image as well. The picture you have of yourself should be a good one.

CHECK YOUR KNOWLEDGE

1. In deciding which clothes are best for you, why is it necessary to study your figure type?
2. Name the three basic figure shapes.
3. Name the seven basic face shapes.
4. Do V-shaped necklines make the face and neck appear longer or shorter?
5. *True or False:* Thin people should wear form-fitting clothes to appear heavier.
6. How does a smooth, shiny surface affect color?
7. Three properties of color are hue, value, and ______.
8. Name the primary colors.
9. Name and describe the three types of color schemes.
10. Explain what is meant by the statement, "Color affects the way you feel."

EXTEND YOUR KNOWLEDGE

1. Draw three different figure types or use pictures from magazines. Select two garments appropriate for each figure type. Tell how the elements of design in the garments are used to bring the figure closer to the ideal.
2. Make a chart to show how color can be used to enhance the features of a face or figure.
3. Put an outfit together and wear it to class. Tell the class how you used the elements and principles of design to choose the garments.
4. Use paints or markers to show examples of the three types of color schemes. Prepare at least three examples of each type.
5. Visit a fabric or clothing store. Compare one color in several different textures. Note the effect on the power of the color. Make a list of the colors and textures that look best on you.

CHAPTER 6

FEELING WELL, LOOKING GOOD

If you just bought an expensive new car, how would you treat it? You'd probably wash and wax it until it gleamed. You'd keep the upholstery vacuumed and the windows shiny. Would you change the oil regularly and use the proper fuel? Would you take it in for tune-ups and a good going-over once in a while? You would if you didn't want to walk. Who wants a car that breaks down all the time or that's falling apart from rust?

Your body is a lot like an expensive car, but with one big difference: you only get one. You can't trade it in every few years for a new model. It has to last you for a long, long time. The better the care you give it—both inside and outside—the better it will work for you all your life.

In this chapter you'll find the answers to these questions:

- What can you do to maintain good health?
- What does your posture tell about you?
- How can you make your skin, hair, nails, and teeth look their best?

Look for These Terms

aerobic exercise
nutrients
posture
grooming
manicure
pedicure
plaque

Choose a type of exercise you enjoy so you'll be encouraged to stick with it.

GOOD HEALTH FOR GOOD LOOKS

Looking good starts with feeling good, with being healthy and energetic. However, that "great to be alive" feeling doesn't just happen. It takes exercise, the right foods, and plenty of rest to keep your body working well for you.

EXERCISE

Daily exercise helps your body run smoothly. A good exercise program strengthens muscles and body organs, such as the lungs and heart. It improves blood circulation, digestion, and other body functions.

Exercise also provides an outlet for tension. It clears the mind and relaxes the body. The next time you feel tense, try jogging for fifteen minutes or riding your bike for half an hour.

Fitness can be simple to achieve and maintain. Follow the P.E.P. formula:

- Participate in some physical activity daily. Start with a few stretching exercises to loosen tight muscles. Then you can do traditional exercises such as push-ups, situps, sidebends, and leg lifts. You should also include an **aerobic** (air-RO-bik) **exercise.** Aerobic activity makes your body use oxygen as you exercise. It gives your heart and lungs a good workout, strengthening them. Types of aerobic exercise include aerobic dancing, jumping rope, bicycling, jogging, swimming, and brisk walking. If you are not used to exercising, start slowly and gradually increase your level of activity. It's a good idea to have a medical checkup first.
- Enroll a partner or partners in your exercise program. Working out with others can make exercising more fun.
- Personalize your fitness program. In addition to general exercises, you should choose some activities to fit your body frame and needs. For example, if you have weak ankles and legs, do special exercises to build them up. Ask your physical education teacher to help you plan a personalized exercise program.

NUTRITION

Food is what your body uses to operate. Does it matter what kind of food you eat? Yes. Although most foods will keep you going for a while, you need the right combinations to maintain good health.

Food supplies **nutrients** (NOO-tree-unts). These are chemicals the body needs in order to function, grow, repair itself, and provide energy. Carbohydrates (kar-bo-HIGH-drates)—sugars and starches—are one kind of nutrient. Others include fats, proteins, vitamins, and minerals.

For good health, you need the right amount of each nutrient daily. How can you make sure you are eating foods that supply the nutrients you need? Scientists have developed the Daily Food Guide to help people make wise food choices.

In the Daily Food Guide, foods are divided into five groups according to the nutrients they contain. These include the Milk-Cheese Group, the Fruit-Vegetable Group, the Meat-Poultry-Fish-Beans Group, the Bread-Cereal Group, and the Fats-Sweets Group. All the nutrients needed for good health can be obtained from the four main food groups. The fifth group, Fats and Sweets, contains foods that are high in calories and low in nutrients. Foods in this group are not needed for good health.

The Daily Food Guide lists the number and size of servings needed daily from each of the four main food groups. Use the Guide in planning your daily food choices. It will help you select the right fuel for your body.

SLEEP AND REST

Most motors do not run nonstop. They must shut off now and then to "cool down." Your body must also rest regularly. Periods of rest and sleep give the body a chance to build new cells, fight bacteria, and remove wastes.

How much sleep do you need? The amount varies from one person to another. Most teenagers and adults require 6 to 10 hours of sleep during each 24-hour period. Droopy eyelids, irritability, and lack of concentration are symptoms of too little sleep. Be sure to plan your activities so that you get enough sleep.

Dietary Guidelines

Most Americans eat too much fat, sugar, and sodium and too little fiber. To help people improve their eating habits, the United States government has developed these guidelines:

- *Eat a variety of foods.* Each day, select foods from the four major food groups. (See the Daily Food Guide on p. 59.)
- *Maintain ideal weight.* Eat in moderation—neither too much nor too little. Exercise will help use up excess calories.
- *Avoid too much fat and cholesterol.* Choose lean meats, fish, and poultry. Limit your intake of butter, cream, and eggs. Eat baked or broiled foods rather than fried.
- *Eat foods with starch and fiber.* Good sources include whole-grain breads and cereals, fruits, vegetables, beans, peas, and nuts.
- *Avoid too much sugar.* Cut down on sweets. Limit your use of sugar, honey, and syrup.
- *Avoid too much sodium.* Avoid salty foods, such as pickles, chips, soy sauce, and cured meats. Cut down on your use of salt in cooking and at the table.

The Daily Food Guide

Milk-Cheese Group

4 servings daily for teenagers
Sample servings:

- 1 cup milk
- 2 slices American or Swiss cheese
- 1 cup yogurt

Fruit-Vegetable Group

4 servings daily (at least one daily serving of a vitamin C food, such as citrus fruit; at least one serving every other day of a vitamin A food, such as dark green or deep yellow fruits or vegetables)
Sample servings:

- 1 medium fruit
- 10-12 grapes or cherries
- ½ cup fruit juice
- ½ cup cooked vegetables
- 1 medium potato

Meat-Poultry-Fish-Beans Group

2 servings daily
Sample servings:

- 3 ounces lean cooked meat, poultry, or fish
- 2 medium eggs
- 1 cup dried peas or beans
- 4 tablespoons peanut butter

Bread-Cereal Group

4 servings daily
Sample servings:

- 1 slice whole-grain or enriched bread
- 1 whole-grain or enriched roll, muffin, or bagel
- ½ to ¾ cup cooked cereal, cornmeal, grits, rice, or pasta
- 1 cup ready-to-eat cereal

Fats-Sweets Group

Limit to small amounts

WHAT YOUR POSTURE SAYS ABOUT YOU

Posture refers to the way you carry your body when walking, standing, and sitting. Posture affects the appearance of the clothes you wear. It also tells others how you feel.

Try this experiment. Stand in front of a full-length mirror. Bend your back a little, hunch your shoulders forward, and stick out your stomach. How do you look? Pretty bad, right? Poor posture makes people look heavier, and it causes clothes to hang wrong. Poor posture also creates a poor image. It tells the world "I'm tired," "I'm a failure," or "I don't care about myself."

Now stand up straight. Tuck in your stomach, hold your spine straight, and pull back your shoulders. Don't exaggerate. Stand naturally, but make sure your posture is good. Now how do you look? Much better, right? Good posture makes your clothes fit better, and it makes you look more alert and self-confident. It also provides better support for your internal organs and helps prevent back problems. Develop the habit of good posture. You'll look and feel better.

GROOMING: HOW TO LOOK YOUR BEST

Imagine a fashion model wearing the latest designer clothes. What if the model had dirty hair, broken fingernails, yellow teeth, or bad skin? The clothes would not look nearly as attractive, would they?

Taking care of your skin, hair, nails, and teeth is part of **grooming,** the general cleaning and care of the body. Grooming is very important. A well-groomed person makes carefully chosen clothes look even better. But even the best clothes won't disguise poor grooming.

TAKING CARE OF YOUR SKIN

Skin is very sensitive. It dries out in cold, windy weather and is more oily in hot, damp weather. Both dry and oily skin are more likely to become infected. When overexposed to the sun, skin becomes damaged. This damage can cause skin disease or early signs of aging. For these reasons, it's important to take good care of your skin.

Clean, healthy skin helps you look your best. As with the rest of your body, your

How to Improve Your Posture

- *Standing.* Stand with your back straight and your head centered over your body. Pull your stomach in, lift your chest, and tuck your hips under. These three actions will help straighten the spine. Bend your knees a little. Keep a relaxed, not stiff, body. Remember to "stand tall."
- *Walking.* Hold your body as you should when standing. Move your legs from the hips. With your knees flexed, keep your toes pointed straight ahead.
- *Sitting.* Again, keep your back straight and your head centered over your body. Your legs should be parallel, with both feet flat on the floor. If you are working or studying at a desk, lean forward from the hips, not the shoulders.
- *Stooping.* If you need to pick up an object off the floor, don't bend from the waist. Bend at your knees, pick up the object, and then raise your entire body.

You'll look your best and feel more confident when you are well groomed.

skin benefits from good nutrition, exercise, and rest. A regular routine of skin care will keep that healthy glow.

Wash your face at least once a day. If your skin is oily, you'll need to wash more often. Wash your body often enough to remove dirt and odor. Usually, this means a daily shower or bath. After bathing, the use of deodorants (dee-ODE-uh-runts) or antiperspirants (AN-tee-PUR-spur-unts) will help reduce body odor. Deodorants stop odor but do not prevent wetness. Antiperspirants prevent both odor and wetness.

Some areas of the skin may become dry and chapped. This often happens to the feet, hands, elbows, and face, especially in cold weather. Apply a lotion after washing to return moisture to the area and protect the skin from drying out. If you will be out in the sun a lot, use a sunscreen or sunblock on exposed skin to prevent damage.

Acne

Acne—pimples—is a skin disorder that affects many people, especially in their teen years. Keeping your face clean and using medicated lotions can help control the problem. Never squeeze pimples. You could make the infection worse or cause scars to form.

Pimples can be covered up. The best way to do so is with a dab of a benzoyl peroxide (BEN-zuh-will puh-ROCK-side) product on top of the pimple. Most such products are available in shades that blend with skin tones.

If you have severe acne, consult a dermatologist (dur-muh-TAHL-uh-jist). A dermatologist is a doctor who specializes in treating skin.

Shaving

Attitudes about facial and body hair vary, depending on the culture and fashion. Today in the United States most women shave their legs and underarms. In Europe, they usually don't. In the 1960s and 1970s it was fashionable for men to wear beards or moustaches. Today the clean-shaven look is more common.

If you shave, here are some tips:

- Use warm water to soften the hairs. Soft hairs are easier to cut.
- Before using a blade razor, lubricate your skin with shaving soap or cream. Before using an electric shaver, apply a preshave.
- After you've selected the best preparation for your skin type and applied it, wait for at least two minutes.
- Now it's time to shave. For a blade shave, use smooth strokes in the direction of hair growth. Blade shaving "against the

grain" roughens the skin and increases the chances of ingrown hairs and infection. Use a light touch. Too much pressure will irritate the skin. When using an electric shaver, move the shaver in a circular motion against the grain.

HELPFUL HINT: After shaving, use a moisturizer to soothe and soften the skin.

Closed-style shoes made from synthetic materials may trap air around the feet and cause the feet to perspire. Foot odor and infections, such as athlete's foot, may develop. Changing socks or stockings daily, allowing shoes to air between wearings, and using a foot deodorant help reduce the problem.

TAKING CARE OF YOUR HANDS AND FEET

Grooming for hands and feet is important, too. A **manicure** refers to the special care given to hands. A **pedicure** refers to the care given to feet. See the chart on this page for tips on manicures and pedicures.

TAKING CARE OF YOUR HAIR

The secret to great looking hair is to keep it clean and healthy and to find a hairstyle that suits your face and lifestyle. You don't need to spend a lot of money, but you do need to choose the right products for your hair type.

Five Steps to Well-Kept Nails

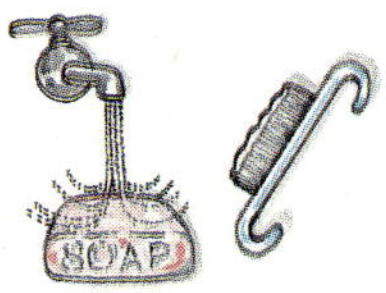

Step 1 Wash hands and feet with soap and warm water.

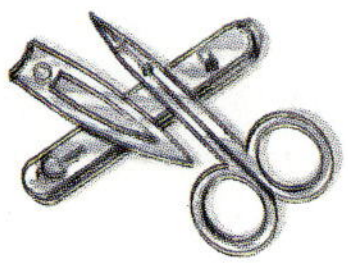

Step 2 Remove hangnails with a cuticle nipper. Use nail clipper to trim nails. Start at one corner and work around to the other. To prevent ingrown toenails, always clip them straight across.

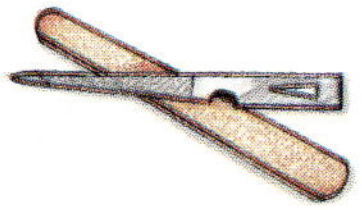

Step 3 Use a nail file or emery board to smooth any rough edges. Long fingernails are not clipped at all, just filed to shape.

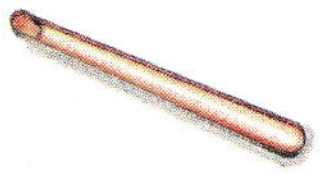

Step 4 Clean up cuticles. Push gently against the base of the nail with a towel, an orange stick, or other blunt instrument. Using a cuticle cream or soaking in warm water will make the cuticle softer and easier to move.

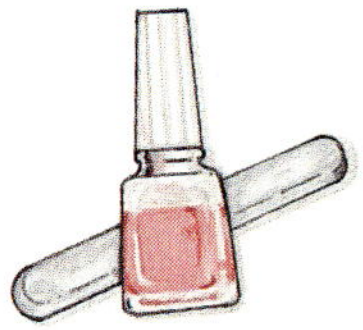

Step 5 Buff nails or apply polish, if you wish, for a finished look.

Shampooing

If you want to keep it looking great, your hair should be washed whenever there is a buildup of dirt or oil.

Normal and dry hair can usually go several days between washings. If your hair is oily, you may need to shampoo daily.

Choose a shampoo for your hair type: dry, normal, oily, or problem hair. Some people have a problem with dandruff (flaking of the scalp). Mild dandruff can be controlled with a dandruff shampoo. People with a serious dandruff problem should see a doctor.

Dry, damaged, or over-processed hair needs special care. If your hair lacks shine, tangles easily, and is difficult to manage, then you have problem hair. Try using a conditioner after each shampoo. Twice a month, give your hair a longer, deep-conditioning treatment.

To make hair clean and shiny, shampoo it, rinse, shampoo again, rinse thoroughly. Use your fingertips, not your nails, to work the shampoo gently into your hair and scalp.

Styling

Wet hair is easily damaged, so it should be treated gently. Blot dry. Gently comb the hair with fingers or a wide-tooth comb. Never brush your hair when it is wet.

If you use a blow dryer, curling iron, or other styling tool, be sure to follow the manufacturer's instructions. Be careful not to burn your hair or scalp.

Safety Tip

Water and electricity can be a deadly combination. Never use an electrical appliance where it could fall into water.

Brushing

Brushing your hair stimulates the scalp and distributes natural oils. Daily brushing helps your hair stay clean by removing dirt, dust, and dead cells. It brings out the natural luster of hair.

Choose your brush carefully. Most experts recommend a natural bristle brush. Fine hair needs a gentle brush. Coarse hair needs a stiff-bristle brush with wide spacing. The bristles of all brushes should be rounded at the ends so that you do not scratch your scalp or break your hair.

HELPFUL HINT: Remember, your brush needs to be washed, too. If your hair is oily, it's a good idea to wash your brush at every shampoo.

Hairstyles

Hairstyles for both males and females change with fashions. Today there is enough variety that you can choose a hairstyle that's in fashion and is still uniquely "you." You can select your hairstyle to fit your lifestyle, your hair type, and your facial features.

Follow these five basic steps to choose the right style for you.

1. Find a "look" you like. From fashion, beauty, or sports magazines, clip photos of hairstyles that appeal to you.

2. Compare face shapes and features of the people in the photos with your own. Discard those photos of hairstyles that would not suit your features. For example, if one model has a wide jaw and your face is heart shaped, the hairstyle will not look the same on you.

3. Consider the nature of your hair. If your hair is straight and you have chosen a straight style, you're OK. If your hair is curly, you may never be able to get the same straight look as the model.

4. Consider the amount of time you wish to put into maintaining the style. Will you have time to set or blow dry your hair

Choosing the Best Hairstyle for You

Basic Face Shape	Hairstyles to Wear
Oval 	■ Almost any style, since face has good proportions
Round 	■ Side part ■ Center height ■ Hair at sides kept away from face ■ No fullness below ears ■ No heavy sideburns
Heart 	■ Less height at top of head ■ A side part and hair swept over part of forehead to decrease width ■ Hair length at or below jawline, using curls to add width to lower face
Triangle 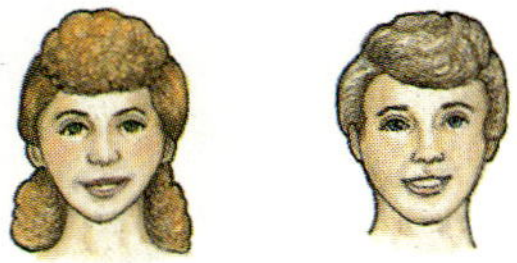	■ Long, curly, or fluffy hair that fills in space under chin ■ Hair lifted over center of forehead, but flat at sides of forehead
Diamond 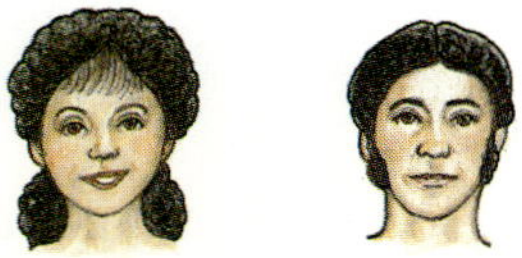	■ Center part ■ Full, curly, or fluffy styles that create fullness at temples or chin ■ Styles close to the head at cheekbones ■ Full sideburns

Basic Face Shape	Hairstyles to Wear
Square 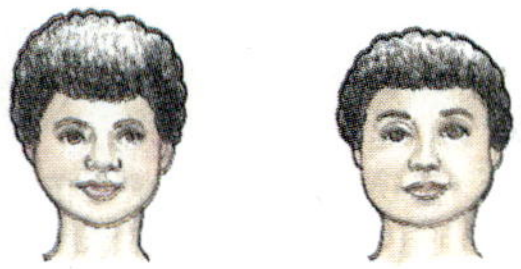	■ Waves or curls around ears to soften angles of face ■ Height at top of head to give more length ■ No jaw-length styles, since they call attention to the jaw ■ Side parts worn high to make face look longer ■ No heavy sideburns
Oblong 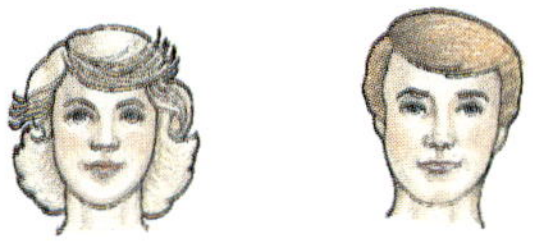	■ Medium-length hair ■ Side part ■ Curls or fullness at sides or behind ears ■ No height on top ■ Waves over sides of forehead to soften angles at temples ■ Bangs across forehead to add width ■ Sideburns short and full

every day or two? If not, then a wash-and-go style is probably a better choice.

5. Talk to a hairstylist about the styles you have chosen. Discuss what you like and do not like about each style. Find out what will be necessary to achieve the look you want.

TAKING CARE OF YOUR TEETH AND GUMS

Everyone responds to the warmth of an attractive smile. That smile is brightened by clean, shiny teeth and healthy gums. Daily care and regular visits to a dentist keep teeth and gums in good condition.

It is best to brush your teeth after every meal. If that is not possible, then be sure you brush at least twice a day. Always brush before you go to bed. Brushing helps remove **plaque** (PLAK), an invisible sticky film. Bacteria grow on plaque and cause cavities. Also, plaque that builds up on teeth forms tartar, a hard deposit that can cause gum disease.

Use a toothbrush with soft bristles. They're easier on your gums than hard bristles. Choose a toothpaste with fluoride to help prevent cavities.

Do you floss your teeth? Dental floss is a special kind of thread that is used to remove plaque and food particles between teeth. Dentists recommend daily flossing to keep teeth and gums healthy.

Regular brushing and flossing also help control bad breath. When you brush your teeth, brush your tongue as well. After brushing and flossing, use a mouthwash.

HELPFUL HINT: Be sure to visit your dentist every six to twelve months. Having regular checkups keeps minor problems from becoming major ones.

Tips for a Healthy Smile

- Snack on fresh, raw vegetables, hard cheeses, nuts, popcorn, and whole-grain breads. Their chewiness and texture stimulate, clean, and massage gums.
- Avoid sugar-rich snacks. Sugar clings to teeth, mixing with plaque to form an acid that eats away tooth enamel.
- If you cannot brush after eating, rinse your mouth with water. The rinsing action tends to flush out food particles lodged between teeth. Rinsing also helps prevent plaque buildup.
- Protect your teeth with a mouth guard if you are involved in contact sports.

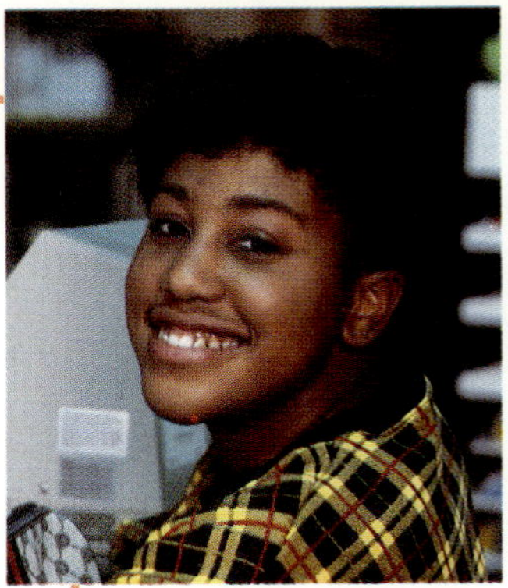

Getting Your Money's Worth

CHOOSING GROOMING PRODUCTS

Walk into any drugstore or department store and you'll see that there are hundreds of grooming products available. The ingredients vary widely, depending on what they are designed to do. The cost depends on the brand, size, and type of product you purchase. The cost also may vary from store to store. How can you choose the right product for you?

- Determine your particular use or need for a product. For example, do you need a special conditioning shampoo for damaged hair or just a mild shampoo to clean normal hair? Know your hair, skin, and nail characteristics and choose products made for these characteristics.
- Read consumer magazines to learn whether products really do what they claim.
- Compare products by reading labels. If two products contain the same ingredients but one is less expensive, which would you buy?
- Compare stores. A drugstore, supermarket, and discount store may all carry the same product, but at very different prices.
- Buy trial-size packages. They give you a chance to try a new product without spending a lot. You can always purchase the large, economy size after you're sure you like the product.

REVIEW-6

SUMMARY

Good health and grooming habits are as important as clothing selection in determining how you appear to others. Exercise, nutrition, and rest are basic to good health. Good grooming habits require very little time and energy, yet they add much to your success with people. The many products available should be chosen to meet your special skin, hair, and nail conditions.

CHECK YOUR KNOWLEDGE

1. Activity that makes your body use oxygen as you exercise is called ______ exercise.
2. Name the five food groups in the Daily Food Guide.
3. *True or False:* For good health, you need one serving daily from each of the five food groups.
4. *True or False:* Everyone needs eight hours of sleep at night.
5. Define posture.
6. Define grooming.
7. How often should a person wash his or her face?
8. When shaving with a blade razor, why should you shave in the direction of hair growth?
9. Why should toenails be clipped straight across?
10. What causes tooth decay?

EXTEND YOUR KNOWLEDGE

1. Do a research report on various kinds of aerobic exercise. Compare the benefits, the calories used up, and the cost or convenience of doing the exercises.
2. Plan a day's menu (including three meals and one snack) based on the Daily Food Guide. Be sure to include the recommended number of servings from each group.
3. Complete the following in 75–100 words: "Good grooming is important because . . ."
4. Research the sun's effects on skin. What precautions should be taken when you are going to be in the sun for long periods of time? Why? What is sunburn? What effect does sunburn have on the skin (immediate and long-term)?
5. Identify a grooming goal. Develop a one-month plan to achieve the goal. Keep a progress journal.

CHAPTER 7

CLOTHES AND THE LIFE CYCLE

While you're in school, you move from one grade to the next. What grade you're in usually depends on your age. In each grade you learn different things because your needs and abilities change as you grow older. Something similar happens as you grow from a tiny baby to an elderly person. You pass through certain life stages. Together, these are called the **life cycle.**

A person in each of the life stages has different clothing needs. Your needs are not the same now as they were when you were a baby. They will change again as you grow older.

This chapter will discuss clothes and the life cycle. You'll learn answers to the following questions:

- What are the differences in clothing needs between babies and toddlers?
- How do clothing needs of toddlers differ from those of school-age children?
- What special clothing needs do adolescents have?
- How do the clothing needs of young adults differ from those of middle-aged and older adults?

Look for These Terms

life cycle
flame-retardant
toddlers
adolescents

Babies are happier when their clothes are comfortable.

BABIES

Perhaps you have younger brothers and sisters, or maybe you plan to have children of your own someday. You will need to know their special clothing needs.

Babies are children up to one year old. The first year of life is a time of rapid growth. Many babies triple their birth weight by the time they reach their first birthday.

CHARACTERISTICS

During the first six months, babies spend most of their time sleeping and eating. They depend completely on others for their care. Someone must feed them, dress them, change their diapers, and even move them from place to place.

By the time they are from six to twelve months old, babies begin to sit, crawl, and stand. They even move around when they're asleep.

CLOTHING NEEDS

Diapers can be bought in washable cloth or paper disposable form. Cloth types should be of absorbent cotton. Some disposables are made to draw moisture away from the skin. Waterproof pants (worn over cloth diapers) are usually made of rubber or plastic. They should not bind at legs or waist.

The clothes worn by babies should be soft, lightweight, absorbent, and washable. They should allow plenty of room for growth and have snaps, elastic waistbands, and front openings so they are easy to take off and put on. Pants should have a snap crotch for ease in diaper changing. Babies often need several changes of clothes each day to keep them clean and dry.

Babies who are crawling need pants with padded knees. The padding protects the baby's knees and makes the garment last longer. Socks and shoes should be ½″ longer than the feet. Shoes should fasten securely.

Sleepers help wiggly babies stay covered on cool nights. A blanket sleeper is a one-piece sack that reaches from neck to foot. It is usually made of a blanket fabric. Other sleepers are made like pajamas with feet. The top should open from neck to waist. Sleepers for older babies should have rubber-soled feet to aid in standing without slipping.

Safety Tip

Clothing for children should be *flame-retardant.* This means the fabric has been treated so that it will not catch fire easily or burn quickly. The label will state whether or not the garment is flame-retardant and whether special care is needed to maintain the finish.

TODDLERS AND YOUNG CHILDREN

At ages one and two, children are usually called **toddlers.** They got this name because they're unsteady on their feet—they toddle. Children who are three and four years old are called "young children" or "preschoolers."

CHARACTERISTICS

From one to four years is an important period for growth and learning. People change from babies unable to care for themselves to children ready for school. Never again in life does so much take place in such a short time.

Think about the toddlers and preschoolers you have seen. They run and jump and play with zest. They're eager to be "big kids" and independent. They want to do things for themselves. They ask questions about everything. Their shapes change from that of chubby toddlers to that of leaner, more upright children.

CLOTHING NEEDS

Toddlers and young children need clothes that are loose and can take a rough-and-tumble life. Fabrics that resist soil and wrinkles and are easy to clean are best. Sturdy fabrics and pants with reinforced knees help add to length of wear. Children prefer soft, comfortable fabrics. Stretch fabrics and cotton knits allow easy movement.

Before long children want to dress themselves. "Self-help clothing" has features a young child can handle alone. Such features include:

- front openings
- wide openings

Toddlers and young children need clothes that allow them to move freely.

- large buttons, zippers with large tabs, or Velcro® fasteners
- elastic waistbands
- marks to distinguish front from back and left from right
- stretch fabrics

Children grow so rapidly during this stage that they often outgrow clothes before the clothes are worn out. Selecting clothes that can "grow" with the child means the clothes can be worn longer and make a better investment. Look for:

- buttons that can be moved to add room
- garments without definite waistlines
- two-piece outfits
- adjustable straps for adding length
- deep hems that can be let down
- wide seam allowances that can be let out
- stretch fabrics
- items that can be worn for more than one season, such as coats with zip-out linings

Clothing should fit properly. Straps that are too long will slide off the shoulder and down the arm, getting in the way of arm movement. Pants that are too long can trip a running child. Some children take off clothes that bother them. Others become irritable.

Shoes that are too big cause stumbling. Shoes that are too small hurt children's feet. Shoes should be ½″ longer than the feet. Socks should be loose enough so toes can wiggle but not so loose that the socks bunch up.

Young children take an interest in their clothes. Often, they have a favorite garment that they want to wear all the time.

SCHOOL-AGE CHILDREN

School-age children are still growing physically, although growth in other areas is easier to see. They develop friendships. They also develop a feeling about themselves and who they are.

CHARACTERISTICS

School-age children have a lot of energy. They are always ready to play. Kindergarten and grade school give them many new learning experiences. At school, they must be members of a group. They learn the feeling of belonging. The more they are away from home, the more they must be able to do things for themselves.

CLOTHING NEEDS

Since school-age children are still growing and are very active, they need clothes that grow with them and hold up under rough wear. Clothing that is loose fitting or stretchy makes it easier for arms to swing and legs to run.

Children at this age like bright colors and special designs. A yellow shirt with a cartoon character on it or a dress with pink rosebuds might be appealing.

These children tend to select garments like those worn by their friends. They want to feel they belong.

ADOLESCENTS

Adolescents (add-ul-ES-unts) are people in the period between childhood and adulthood, like you. It is a time of many changes.

CHARACTERISTICS

Between ages ten and twelve, physical growth occurs in spurts. These bursts of growth seem to take place overnight. For some adolescents, growth spurts cause pain in their legs. The active, growing muscles become tense and cramped. Also, parts of the body grow at different rates. Arms and legs may mature before the trunk of the body. Shoulders may broaden before the waist slims.

During this time the body begins to mature sexually. Some adolescents develop early. Others maintain their childhood build for a while longer. Maturing early or late can be difficult when your friends are changing at a different rate. Changing bodies and changing feelings often make adolescents moody.

CLOTHING NEEDS

For adolescents, clothing takes on a new meaning. More than ever, individuals want to dress like other members of the group. Leaving one group for another may mean that this month's favorite shirt will stay in the closet next month.

Sometimes, clothing choices are influenced by what a famous person, such as a rock singer, wears. The wearer wants to be like the famous person. Then style becomes more important than fit. The feeling the garment gives is more important.

When body growth happens in spurts, choosing clothing becomes a challenge. Late-developing adolescents may not want clothes too young or childish in design. Early developers may feel shy of things that look too grown-up. Preteen and student sizes designed to fit a developing body help solve this problem. They are shorter from shoulder to waist and are cut narrower in the shoulders and flatter across the chest. The designs are similar to adult styles.

Buying separates such as skirts, shirts, pants, sport coats, and sweaters may be easier than finding dresses and suits that fit. Separates can be bought in different sizes and worn together to make a complete outfit. If one part of the body grows faster than another, that half of the outfit can be replaced.

Other clothing that helps allow for uneven growth includes:

- garments with raglan sleeves to disguise broad shoulders
- shirts and other garments with set-in sleeves and horizontal stripes that add width to a small body
- padded bras to increase bust size
- loose or full-cut shirts that hide large or early breast development
- jackets with padded shoulders to increase shoulder size
- shirts with fullness at the waist to allow for waists with less taper.

A sense of belonging is important to school-age children. What do you think would happen if one of these children wore an outfit that was very different from the others' clothing?

Clothes you buy in the last years of high school may still be in your wardrobe when you start a career or continue your education. Which outfit would be a better investment for the future?

During your teen years, try to spread out clothing purchases. You may outgrow them sooner than expected. Also, if your clothing budget has been spent before school starts, you may not be able to buy the latest fad item.

YOUNG ADULTS

The adult stage of the life cycle begins when physical growth is complete. For most people, this happens when they are between twenty and twenty-two.

CHARACTERISTICS

Most young adults have found a general clothing style they like that fits the way they live. They have completed their education and have begun a career. Some may have started families. Others, because they are just getting started, may be on a limited budget.

CLOTHING NEEDS

Young adults need clothing for their jobs. Some jobs require uniforms. Others may require a style of dress that creates a particular image. Workers in banks and business firms are often asked to wear tailored clothes. This gives an impression of success and confidence. A clerk in a sporting goods store may be expected to dress casually. In each case, the clothing is suitable for the type of business.

Adults also need leisure-time clothes. These are usually styles that would not be acceptable on the job. Special clothing may also be needed for some sports and other activities.

In general, clothing should allow room for bending and sitting and for shoulder movement. Sleeve lengths should cover the wrist. Women's long coats should cover skirt or dress hems. Men's jackets should cover the hips.

Dressing appropriately can help people be successful at their jobs. This young woman is a sales representative. Because she is dressed in an attractive, businesslike way, clients are willing to listen to her.

Adults do not outgrow their clothes if they control their weight. Also, they may not be able to afford many outfits. New additions may be a part of the wardrobe for a long time. Therefore each new item should be carefully chosen. New clothes should be wearable with those already owned.

MIDDLE-AGED ADULTS

Middle age covers the years between ages forty and fifty-nine. It is a time when most people enjoy success in a career and families that have grown up.

CHARACTERISTICS

During the second half of the adult stage of the life cycle, the body begins to show signs of aging. Those who have gotten enough rest, exercise, and a proper diet when they were younger usually stay in good health. Because of lifestyle or inherited traits, however, some people will appear to be older or younger than their age.

Physical signs of increasing age include a variety of body changes. The face and neck area become thinner and lines appear. Often, the shoulders become rounded, the chest or bust begins to sag, the waistline thickens, and the hips broaden. Muscle tone is lost, leaving the thighs and upper arms flabby. Skin may grow paler; hair color grays. There is a tendency to gain weight easily.

The lifestyle of the middle-aged adult also changes. Although most are still employed, any children may be self-supporting and living away from home. Leisure time is often spent traveling or developing hobbies that can carry over into retirement.

Middle-aged people tend to dress more conservatively, but they wear many of the same styles as younger adults.

CLOTHING NEEDS

Middle-aged adults usually have more time and money to spend on their wardrobes. Having clothing that suits their activities and that helps them feel attractive is important.

Middle-aged adults often choose clothing that hides figure changes. Outfits with vertical lines, for example, make the figure seem more slender. Accessories or garment details can be used to draw attention away from undesirable features.

Clothing color should be given special consideration. For those with light skin, colors should be darker than the skin tones to prevent a pale, washed-out appearance. Colors that are rich and radiate excitement and vitality are usually best.

OLDER ADULTS

This is the last stage of the life cycle. It begins around age sixty and continues through the remainder of a person's lifetime.

Advances in medicine mean people are enjoying better health during old age. Many older adults lead active lives. Attractive clothing is as important at this stage of life as at any other.

CHARACTERISTICS

Some people show advanced age at sixty, while others show few physical signs of aging by seventy. In most older adults, however, physical changes are easy to see. These include drying and increased sensitivity of the skin, deeper lines, and a stiffening of joints. A decrease in height and rounded shoulders alter the shape of the upper body. A shift in weight may leave the shoulders narrower and the waist and hips thicker.

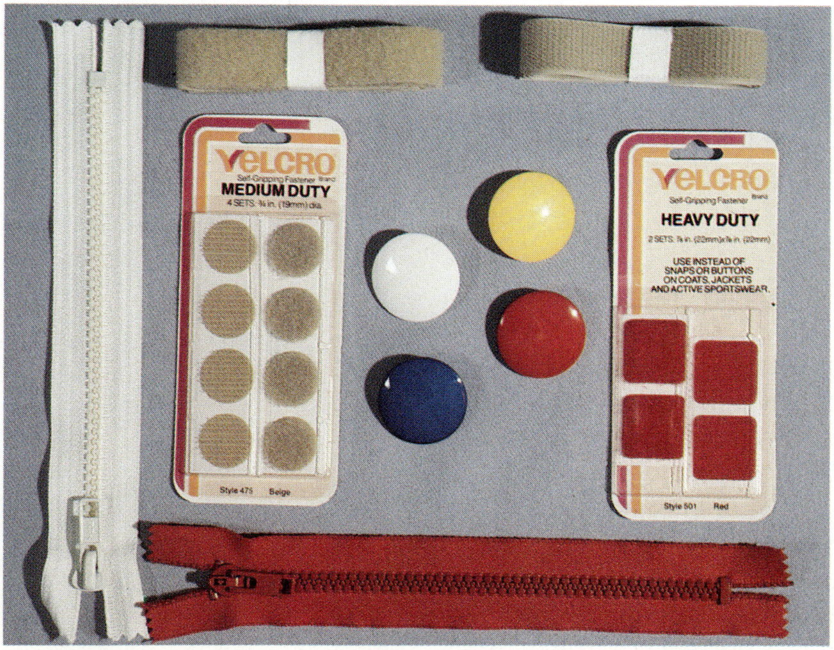

Larger zippers, Velcro® closures, and bigger buttons are some of the features that make clothing easier to put on and take off.

What special clothing needs might these older adults have?

CLOTHING NEEDS

Senior citizens need clothes that suit their lifestyles, fit their figures, and are comfortable. For women, designs with additional fullness in the back and no waistline are most comfortable. Men have fewer problems with fit, but they may need a different size than before. Garments with loose collars and sleeves are often preferred by both men and women.

The right colors will improve appearance and make people feel more attractive. Bolder colors are often a good choice.

Fabrics that are soft do not irritate delicate skin. Sheer fabrics protect skin from sunburn while keeping the body cool. Warm fabrics are especially important in cold weather. Because they are less active, older people have trouble staying warm.

Many elderly persons lose some of their ability to move and do things. For example, arthritis may cripple their hands. This can make dressing a challenge. Garments that open down the front are easier to handle. Velcro® fasteners, zippers, and medium-to-large buttons make it easier to fasten garments.

Getting Your Money's Worth

BUYING CLOTHES AS GIFTS

A gift of clothing can be a special way of showing that you care about someone. A pair of warm gloves for your father, that sweater your sister has been wishing for—gifts like these show that you're thinking about the other person's comfort and happiness. But most people don't know how to shop for others. Too often the gift must be exchanged, or it's left in the closet and never worn.

When you shop for someone else, do you keep in mind how the other person dresses, or do you think about what *you* like? Everyone's tastes are a little different. Don't assume that the other person will like what you like. Do a little research. Try to learn:

- the correct size
- any favorite clothing colors
- any style preference—for example, if it's a woman, does she like tailored or frilly garments? Would she prefer classic clothes or trendy ones?
- any fabric preferences—for example, is the person allergic to wool?

Sometimes people like a garment that's a little bit different from what they usually wear. But don't stray too far unless you know for sure the person is ready for a change. And if you want to be extra safe, look for something that goes with a garment the person already owns and likes.

Some people, such as children or the elderly, have special clothing needs. Before you choose a garment for them, re-read Chapters 7 and 8. Make a note of any special requirements you must watch for.

When you shop for someone else, make sure that the garment can be returned. Even if you are careful about colors and sizes, they may vary from item to item. If the garment doesn't match or fit, you do not want your money wasted. And the person who receives the gift will certainly want to be able to exchange it if necessary.

REVIEW-7

SUMMARY

Each stage of the life cycle has special characteristics. These characteristics affect clothing needs. Finding suitable clothing is more of a problem in some stages than in others. Clothing selection seems easiest for infants, young adults, and the middle aged. The other stages have special needs that require more careful consideration.

CHECK YOUR KNOWLEDGE

1. Define life cycle.
2. *True or False:* By the time they are 6 to 12 months old, most babies begin to sit, crawl, and stand.
3. Why is it better to buy children's clothes that are washable than ones that must be dry-cleaned?
4. Toddlers are children between the ages of 1 and ______.
5. Why should clothing for young children be able to "grow" with them?
6. *True or False:* School-age children like to dress in clothes that are different from those of their friends so they can attract attention.
7. People between childhood and adulthood are called ______.
8. Between what ages is physical growth usually completed?
9. *True or False:* Adults should choose their clothes carefully because they may have to keep them a long time.
10. Why should clothing for the elderly be easy to put on and take off?

EXTEND YOUR KNOWLEDGE

1. Compare prices. Is it cheaper to buy and launder cloth diapers, use a diaper service, or buy disposable diapers? Make a set of guidelines for when each might be useful.
2. Observe young children. What items of clothing are they wearing? Do their clothes seem appropriate for their age and activities?
3. What styles of clothing are popular for school-age children? Cut out pictures from catalogs or advertisements showing these styles.
4. Interview two elderly people about the types and colors of clothing they prefer. What factors influence their clothing decisions (need, cost, style, etc.)? What changes would they like to see in clothing (more designs that are easy to put on, more variety in styles, etc.)?
5. Plan a basic wardrobe for one of the stages of the life cycle. Tell the reasons for your choices. How much would the wardrobe cost?

CHAPTER 8

CLOTHES FOR SPECIAL NEEDS

At one time or another, most people have special clothing needs. It may be for a special occasion, such as a Halloween costume party, or for a special job, such as digging in the garden. Many times, regular clothing can be adapted for the occasion. Some people, however, have needs for which special clothing must be made or bought. Such needs include those resulting from sports activities, work conditions, physical handicaps, and pregnancy.

This chapter tells about special clothing needs and answers these questions:

- What features should you look for when buying sportswear?
- What kinds of special clothing may be needed on the job?
- What can be done to make clothing more attractive and comfortable for people with physical disabilities?
- What features are important in maternity clothes?

Look for These Terms

sportswear
paralysis
durability

ANATOMY OF A RUNNING SHOE

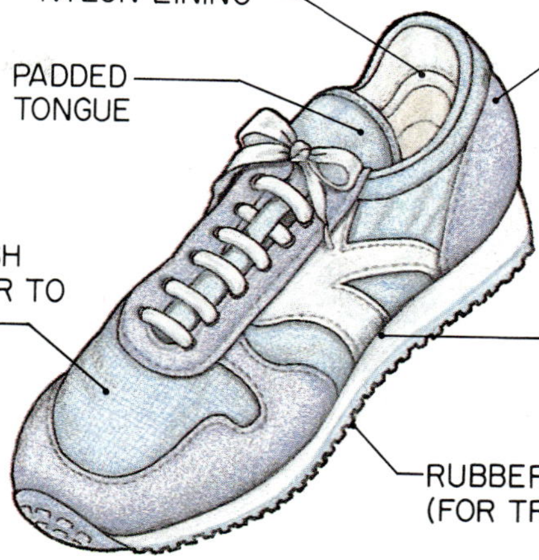

SPORTS CLOTHES

Sportswear is clothing designed for physical activity. Today almost everyone owns sportswear of some kind. With the emphasis on physical fitness, more people are buying it than ever before.

When choosing sportswear, freedom of movement is especially important. The garment should be fitted to the body so that arms and legs can move without pulling or binding. Sportswear should be well made to withstand wear and tear. Look for straight, reinforced seams that hold up when pulled or stretched.

There are many types of sportswear. Choose clothing that is right for your activities.

JOGGING, RUNNING, AND WALKING

For warm weather, shorts are usually worn along with a T-shirt. Sweat suits are popular during cold seasons for more vigorous exercise. The legs should be loose enough for easy movement. Waistbands and armholes should not bind.

Shoes are the most important item when jogging, running, or walking. A running shoe that fits well helps prevent injury. Running shoes should be flexible at the front, yet stiff enough in the heel to keep the foot stable and centered. Stability and support are more important than softness. At the same time, there should be enough cushioning to protect the foot from hard pavements.

Your feet may swell slightly during the day. You should try on shoes at the same time of day that you plan to do your running and with the same socks. You will then get a better idea of how they will fit when you are actually using them.

At the front of the shoe, there should be from ¼ to ½ inch of space beyond your toes. There should be enough room for you to wiggle your toes. The shoe should be snug in the middle and rear portions for stability. When you lace the shoes, there should be about an inch of tongue showing between the eyelets. The arch should press against your foot to prevent muscle fatigue.

Choosing the right socks is important also. Cotton, wool, or polypropylene socks prevent blisters and absorb perspiration. Socks should be soft and roomy enough for you to wiggle your toes.

TENNIS

Both the arms and legs should be free to move when you play tennis. Short sleeves, cap sleeves, or no sleeves at all are best. Pants may restrict bending and can get in the way of the racket, so shorts are usually preferred.

Fabrics should be lightweight. Can you imagine playing tennis in a bulky knit sweater? The fabric should also absorb perspiration and thus help cool the body.

As with running shoes, support and cushioning are important in a court shoe. The feet need to roll and twist more than when jogging or running. The right shoes can help your game and prevent tiredness.

Tennis shoes should have a well-made upper. The upper is the part of the shoe above the sole. A leather and nylon mesh combination is lightweight, gives support, and allows air to circulate. Stitching should be sturdy.

Before you try on the shoes, squeeze the heel; it should feel fairly rigid. After putting on the shoes, move your feet from side to side. Then go up on your toes. If your heels stay firmly in contact with the soles of the shoes, you have a good fit. There should be room in the front of the shoe to wiggle your toes.

Tennis shoes should have a padded tongue and padding around the ankles. The lacing system should support the foot and be easy to tighten.

What features make these clothes appropriate for tennis?

Clothes for aerobics should be lightweight and stretchable.

CYCLING

Cyclists need to move their legs freely. Also, clothing on the legs should not get caught in bike chains or wheel spokes. Pants should be made of stretch fabric and should fit the legs snugly.

Windbreakers and helmets give protection when cycling. The Windbreaker jacket prevents windburn, scrapes, and too rapid a loss of body fluids. Helmets protect the head from falls and flying objects.

Shoes for cycling should support the feet and be lightweight. The collar of the shoe should fall below the anklebone so that the ankle can move without rubbing. The heel should hug the foot gently without friction.

AEROBICS

Tights, leg-warmers, leotards, and sweat suits can be worn for aerobics. Clothing should be loose or stretchable so that the body can move freely. However, clothing should not be so loose that it gets in the way of movement.

Aerobic dancers move in many directions, much like tennis players. The shoes for both are similar. Since many aerobic movements are performed on the ball of the foot, the shoe should be cushioned. There should also be enough cushion to absorb shock from jumping. The heel of the shoe should be rigid. Your heel should not slide when you move. The shoe should be reinforced across the upper arch for stability. Padded ankle collars and tongues add comfort.

SWIMMING

Swimsuits should not create a drag on the body or make it difficult for the swimmer to move. Stretchable garments with a smooth surface are best. Swimsuits should be made of a fabric that does not absorb water. A suit that absorbs water adds weight. The fabric should also dry quickly, for comfort out of the water. Spandex has these features and is often used for swimsuits.

Men's swimsuits should have a drawstring waist. The chlorine in swimming pools makes elastic waistbands lose their stretchability.

Swimmers should choose garments that are smooth and stretchable. The smooth surface reduces drag, and the stretch fabric makes movement easier.

What safety features can you identify in this person's clothing?

WORK CLOTHES

Some people need special clothing for their work. Some employers, such as the post office, fire department, and food services, usually require uniforms. Sometimes the job itself may create a need for safety clothing.

UNIFORMS

Some uniforms are provided by the employer. The employee has no choice of style. Other employees may select designs that appeal to them. Medical uniforms, for example, come in a wide range of styles.

Uniforms should be durable and comfortable. Uniforms worn every day go through much wear and tear. They need to be of sturdy fabrics and construction. Comfort is especially important in an active job. Clothes that bind or get in the way make the workday unpleasant. A uniform that is washable is more economical to keep clean than one that must be dry-cleaned.

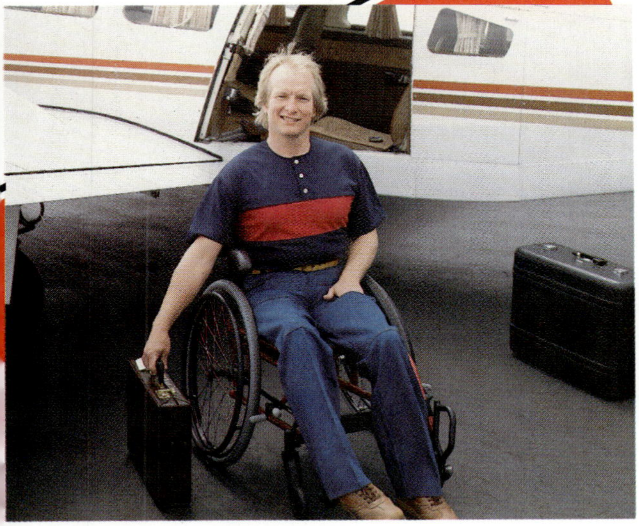

People with disabilities want clothes that are comfortable and easy to manage as well as attractive. How could the elements and principles of design be applied to accomplish these goals?

SAFETY CLOTHES

Some work requires special clothing to protect the worker. Safety clothing is needed on construction sites, in chemical labs, in coal mines, and in some factories. Hard hats, helmets, and fireproof suits and aprons are examples of clothing that is worn for protection. Crossing guards at school intersections wear yellow or orange safety vests so that they can be seen clearly.

Safety clothes should in general be heavier and of sturdier construction than everyday clothes. Safety shoes should have steel toes to protect the feet from falling objects. Do not try to get by with safety clothes of poor quality. You might be injured as a result.

Another reason for wearing special work clothing is to protect others. Doctors and nurses wear gloves to protect patients from infection. Workers in food processing plants wear special tunics and head coverings. Cooks, waiters, or waitresses also must wear garments that ensure cleanliness when handling food.

CLOTHES FOR PEOPLE WITH DISABILITIES

People with physical handicaps may find that regular clothing presents problems. For example, people in wheelchairs may find it difficult to dress. Some styles of clothing are uncomfortable for them because they must remain seated most of the time. People with limited hand and finger movement find small buttons and snaps hard to manage.

Like everyone else, people with disabilities want to feel attractive. Thus, appearance as well as function must be considered. Clothing styles should be chosen which meet physical requirements, are becoming, and are basic in design. Current fashions may not always be workable. Instead, creativity can be shown in the choice of fabric, colors, and patterns.

These garments have special features which make them easier to put on and take off.

APPEARANCE

As you have already learned, clothing can be used to highlight a person's best features and play down others. In general, the face and upper body should be emphasized. For example, a person on crutches might wear a collar of a contrasting color. This would draw attention to the face and away from the crutches.

Some ways in which braces or other features can be played down include the following:

- Sweaters, vests, or loose shirts hide irregularities of the upper body.
- Raised or lowered waistlines add fullness.
- An unfitted dress or jump suit creates a sleek figure outline.
- Extra fullness at shoulders, waist, or in sleeves makes movement easier and hides figure problems.
- Elastic waistlines add fullness and increase comfort.
- Wide pant legs conceal leg braces.
- Long skirts give a graceful appearance.
- Bright colors draw attention to good features and away from disabilities.

FUNCTION

Many physical handicaps call for special clothing. Others require only the careful choice of standard clothing. The key is to remember that not all conditions are alike. The disability could be severe, such as a complete **paralysis** (puh-RAL-uh-sus)—inability to move. Or it could be minor, like a stiff shoulder. Each person's special needs must be considered. Generally, clothing should meet four requirements: comfort, safety, durability, and ease of care.

A gusset is a piece of fabric inserted in a seam to provide extra room for movement.

Comfort

Have you ever had to sit through a long class in an outfit that cut your waist or legs or pulled under the arms? Comfort is even more important when you must sit in a wheelchair or manage with braces all day.

Clothing design can vary, but loose styles are often most comfortable. Pay attention to proper fit. One-piece garments are often easier to put on but may be strained at the waistline and armholes. Separates allow for more movement. One disadvantage, however, is that shirts may not stay tucked in. Tops worn outside look neater. Step-in or wrap-around styles may also be good choices.

Garments that open in the front are easier to handle. The openings should be large enough to allow safe and easy dressing.

Pleats, gussets, and gathers make movement easier and decrease the strain on the fabric and seams. Raglan rather than set-in sleeves are a good feature because they have larger armholes and no shoulder seams.

Well-designed pockets can be a real plus. Large pockets on pants, skirts, or aprons allow several items to be carried easily. Pockets can be lined with plastic so

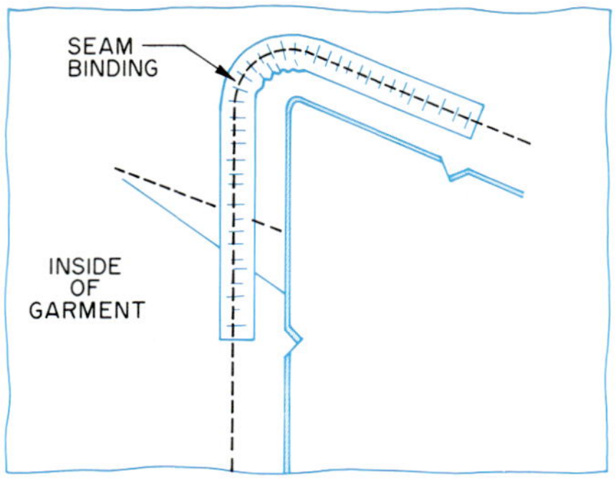

Areas of strain, such as underarm seams, can be reinforced with seam binding or tape. Note that the curve is clipped. This is done so the seam will bend more easily when the garment is worn.

things like a damp cloth, medicine, and snacks can be carried without damage to the fabric.

Fasteners should suit individual needs. Zippers, for example, are easy to work. But a larger pull tab may be needed for those whose hands or arms are weak. Small buttons are difficult for some people to manage. Large ones make this task easier. Velcro® fasteners are easy to close, but require some strength to pull apart.

Knit fabrics are often a good choice. Knits stretch, making dressing and movement easier. Cottons or cotton blends are cooler in hot weather. Woolens are more comfortable in cold weather. Also, look for fabrics that do not wrinkle easily.

Safety

Safety is especially important for people with disabilities. Because movement may be limited, poorly-designed clothing may get in the way and cause accidents.

If a person is in a wheelchair, the length and fullness of sleeves must not hinder the operation of the chair. Pants and skirts should be full enough to be comfortable and long enough to cover the body when seated. Yet they should not be so full or long that they get in the way. Belts should be attached to the garment so that they don't slip or slide.

Persons who wear braces should choose clothing that is loose and full enough to cover the brace without getting in the way. When crutches are used, pant length and skirt width are important. Pants that are too long may be caught underfoot and trip the person. Very wide skirts hinder movement.

Shoe styles can affect how steady a person is. Shoes with a wide, flat heel are safest.

Durability

Durability, or toughness, of fabric and construction must be considered by people using braces or crutches. The armpits, elbows, and knees of garments are strained and rubbed as the person moves. A suede or leather patch may be added to the underarm area in order to prevent wear from crutches or armbands. Garments made from closely-woven fabrics may be reinforced with seam tape at seams and pressure points. An extra layer of fabric inside a sleeve or pant leg protects the fabric from rubbing.

Ease of Care

People with physical handicaps may exert more energy when moving about and thus perspire more heavily. They may also have more accidents that soil clothing. Therefore their garments should be stain-resistant. Cleaning should be easy and economical.

Garments made of no-iron fabric are good choices. Look for cotton blended with nylon or polyester. Knit fabrics usually don't need ironing, and their stretchiness gives greater freedom of movement.

ADAPTING CLOTHING

Sometimes ready-made garments or home-sewn garments can be adapted to a person's handicaps. Seams may be let out or tucks taken in. Sleeves may be shortened. Hems may be taken up or let down. Look for matching or coordinating fabrics to help make changes. See the chart below for more suggestions.

What to Do When . . .

Here are some tips on adapting clothing for people with physical disabilities. For directions for making common alterations, see Chapter 22.

Garment is tight across shoulders

- Cut up the center back and insert a pie-shaped piece of complementary fabric.
- Use the same fabric somewhere else on the garment (cuffs, collar, etc.) to tie the look together.

Blouse or shirt comes out of waistband

- Add fabric to lengthen hem.
- Finish hem edge and wear outside.
- Remake into body shirt by adding darts.

Sleeves pull up when person uses crutches

- Make short sleeves out of long sleeves.
- Add a gusset under the arm.

Jacket bunches up when person is seated in a wheelchair.

- Cut a half circle of fabric from the lower front or back and finish the edge.
- Make slits in the jacket sides.
- Adjust length so it's even with the chair seat.

Skirt is too narrow for easy movement

- Add fullness by inserting several box pleats made from a complementary fabric. Use the same fabric as a trim at the neck and sleeve.

Buttons on cuff are difficult to button

- Sew button with elastic thread; button the cuff before dressing.
- Use Velcro® fastening tape instead of a button.
- Cut the cuff off just above the seam line and add a stretchy knit cuff.
- Make short sleeves.

Garment is difficult to put on and take off

- Open the inside seam of pants and insert a pressure-type closure.
- Insert a zipper in the leg seam.
- Move skirt zippers to the front.
- Place larger pulls on zipper tabs.

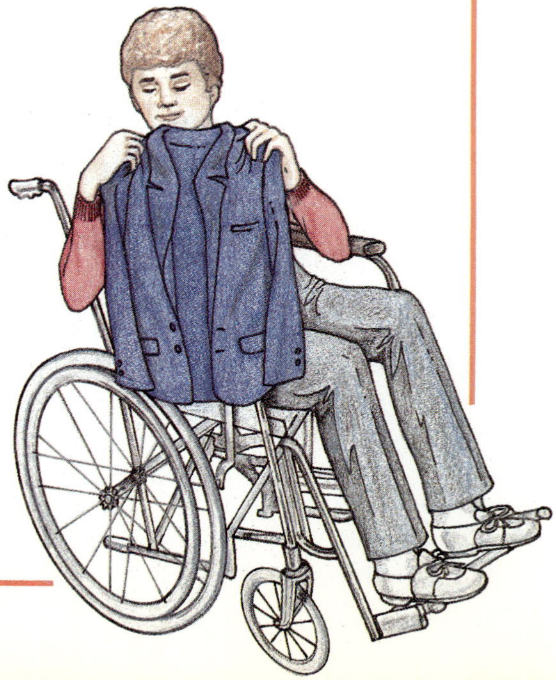

MATERNITY CLOTHES

Toward the end of a pregnancy, a woman's size increases and movement is more limited. Maternity clothes are designed for her special needs. She also wants to feel attractive. The principles and elements of design should be used to play down her size and highlight her face.

Skirts, slacks, or shorts cut larger or made of knit fabrics allow room for the growing baby. They may also include a pouch, or stretch panel, that can expand.

Comfortable shoes are also needed. In later months the mother's posture changes to adjust for the weight of the growing baby. Shoes that have low and wide heels are more stable and secure.

HELPFUL HINT: Feet may swell, so shoes that don't have binding straps and that are not too tight may feel more comfortable.

Special underwear will be needed for the latter part of the pregnancy. Maternity bras, slips, and underpants allow for size changes and provide a comfortable fit.

After delivery, the mother's body gradually returns to its normal shape. For a while she may want to wear loose clothing in order to feel comfortable and attractive. Some maternity clothes can be worn after the baby is born. Blouses can be tucked in, and dresses may be belted at the waist to take in extra fullness.

Jumpers are a good choice for maternity clothes. They are comfortable and can also be worn after pregnancy.

—Perspective

ASTRONAUTS' CLOTHING: OUT OF THIS WORLD!

No one has more special clothing needs than an astronaut. The suit astronauts wear while "walking" in space has been called "the world's smallest manned spacecraft." Everything they need is built right in!

To make the suit, a new fabric was created—Teflon®-coated fiberglass. It is nonflammable in temperatures up to 1200°F. The suit itself has 14 layers. One layer cools the wearer and equipment, another controls air pressure, a third adds insulation. The outer layer is so strong it can protect the wearer against a very tiny meteor traveling 30 times faster than a rifle bullet!

The space suit must provide life support when the astronaut is outside the spacecraft. Oxygen and water are stored in a backpack and brought into the suit through tubes. Other tubes carry away body wastes. The helmet protects eyes from radiation. Special wire mesh gloves guard the hands. The boots worn on planet surfaces can resist temperatures reaching 250°F above or below zero.

For long voyages inside the spacecraft, astronauts wear more ordinary clothing that provides both comfort and safety. Trousers, shirts, and jackets are made of fire-resistant fabric. Boots and gloves are lined with fire-resistant materials. Shoes are fitted with metal plates for safer climbing on the gridwork of the walls and ceiling.

Skylab's three crews of three astronauts carried a total of more than 700 items of clothing, including: 39 jackets, 69 pairs of trousers, 126 shirts, 30 pairs of boots, 18 pairs of gloves, 201 T-shirts, 45 half-union suits, 85 jockey shorts, 112 boxer shorts, 54 knee shorts, 286 pairs of socks, and 24 constant-wear garments. How would you like to pack all that for a trip?

NASA has made available to manufacturers the details about the new space fabrics. Fibers used in space can also be used to make safer draperies, upholstery materials, mattresses, and clothing. For example, fireproof Beta cloth is now being used for city firefighter suits. Pressure suits have been used to help stop bleeding in patients during medical emergencies.

REVIEW-8

SUMMARY

Many people have special clothing needs brought about by their activities or physical condition. Sports, certain jobs, physical disabilities, and pregnancy all require special types of clothing. Clothing for special needs should be comfortable, durable, and safe. It should also be attractive. Apply the elements and principles of design to enhance good features and minimize figure problems.

CHECK YOUR KNOWLEDGE

1. What is the most important clothing item for jogging?
2. Why are short sleeves good for a tennis outfit?
3. Why should the pants cyclists wear fit snugly around the legs?
4. Why should swimsuits be made of fabrics that don't absorb water?
5. Why should work uniforms be made of washable fabrics?
6. One reason for wearing safety clothing is to protect yourself. What is another reason?
7. Why are knit fabrics a good choice for people with physical disabilities?
8. In addition to attractiveness, what are four requirements for the clothing of people with disabilities?
9. Why are shoes with low, wide heels a good choice for a pregnant woman?
10. How can maternity clothes be adapted for wear after pregnancy?

EXTEND YOUR KNOWLEDGE

1. Find articles about running shoes or other sportswear in consumer magazines. Which brands are highly rated? Why?
2. Write a research report on the development of sports clothes during the nineteenth century. You could focus on one aspect, such as the connection between the popularity of sports and the increased freedom of women.
3. Visit a store that sells work uniforms. What fabrics are used for the uniforms? How does the cost of uniforms compare with the cost of ordinary clothes?
4. Find out what safety clothing is worn by the following: welders, construction workers, surgeons, police officers, workers exposed to nuclear radiation.
5. Interview a disabled person about his or her special clothing needs. How does the person find clothing that meets those needs?

CHAPTER 9

PLANNING YOUR WARDROBE

"I have nothing to wear!" How many times have you said that? Of course, you didn't mean that there were no clothes in your closet. You meant that you had nothing that seemed right for the occasion.

Your **wardrobe,** or collection of clothes, is always changing. New clothes are added to meet new needs or to keep in style. Old clothes are removed because they are worn out, no longer needed, or out of style. You could update your wardrobe in a hit or miss way. But if you plan your wardrobe, you'll have one that better meets your needs. You won't have to worry that you'll have "nothing to wear."

When planning your wardrobe, you should think about the following:

- How can you determine which clothes you need?
- How can you use the clothes you already own to meet your needs?
- How can you obtain new clothes?

Look for These Terms

wardrobe
inventory
budget

Hiking is one activity that requires special clothes. For what other activities could the shoes and jacket be worn?

MAKING DECISIONS

To build and maintain your wardrobe, you will make many decisions. These decisions must take into account your figure, activities, current clothes, new fashion trends, and your clothing budget. The information helps you decide what you need, how much, and where to find it. If you make the right decisions, you will get the most use from what you buy, and you'll look more attractive in it.

Look again at the information about making decisions on page 42. Once you have decided what clothes you need and how much you can spend, you can consider alternatives. This chapter will suggest several ways to use what you already have or to add to your wardrobe. After you have chosen alternatives and carried them out, you will have a well-planned wardrobe.

IDENTIFYING YOUR NEEDS

The first step in wardrobe planning is deciding what type of clothes you need for your lifestyle. To do this, you need to think about your activities and surroundings.

LIST YOUR ACTIVITIES

As a teenager, you will probably take part in many activities. Make a list of them. Attending school would be one activity. Do you play any sports? Do you have other interests that might require special clothes, such as hiking or ballet? You might have a part-time job or chores to do at home. Perhaps your family is planning a special trip. All these activities should be added to your list.

Now look at your list. How many regular activities require the same type of clothes? Most of your school clothes will probably work for art, music, scouts, or computer camp. School clothes, with a few changes, may also work for dressy occasions such as religious services or parties.

HELPFUL HINT: Clothes you no longer wear to school because they are old or out of style could be worn for doing chores at home.

How many of your activities require special clothing? Basketball, swimming, and skiing all require some special clothes. If you have a part-time job, you may need a uniform or clothes that are dressier than your regular school clothes. Can the special clothing be used for other activities?

List the kinds of outfits that you'll need for your activities. Keep this list in a convenient place because it will help you make other decisions about your wardrobe.

CONSIDER CLIMATE AND SEASON

Clothing must also be suitable for the climate in which you live. Does the temperature remain within a certain range all year long, as it does in most parts of California? Or does it change a lot between winter and summer, as it does in Chicago?

If you live in the South or the Far West, you will probably not need many heavy winter clothes. You will, however, want more lightweight clothing for the warmest seasons. Instead of snow gear you will probably need rainwear.

If you live in the North, you will probably need clothes for both hot and cold months. Cold weather will require at least one heavy coat or jacket, boots, gloves, and a hat.

USING WHAT YOU HAVE

The second step in wardrobe planning is to take a look at what's in your closet. Then you can compare what you have to your lists of activities and needs. Much of what you need may already be a part of your wardrobe.

MAKE AN INVENTORY

An **inventory** (IN-vun-tore-ee) is a list of what you have. To make an inventory of your clothes, begin by trying on each garment. Note the fit, color, whether it is still in fashion, and how well you like it. As you review each garment, place it in one of three stacks. Label the stacks:

- use as is
- repair or remodel
- give away

If you have clothes you can no longer use, give them away. Be sure to clean them first and make any needed repairs.

COORDINATE OUTFITS

The second step allows you to experiment and be creative. While your clothes are out of the closet, try grouping them together in outfits. For example, an outfit may include slacks, shirt, belt, shoes, socks or hose, jewelry, scarf or tie, and a jacket or sweater. Or it may consist of only shorts, shirt, and shoes.

Experiment with different combinations of colors and textures. Do not be afraid to try combinations you did not consider in the past. Experimenting with new combinations is the way many designers get ideas for new styles. Write a brief description of any outfit you like and its uses so you won't forget how you planned to wear it. These descriptions will also help you plan additions to your wardrobe.

Count the number of different outfits you put together. The more combinations in which a garment can be used, the more valuable that garment is to your wardrobe.

Some outfits may not be complete. One or more items may be missing. Make note of the missing items. These may be things you will need to get.

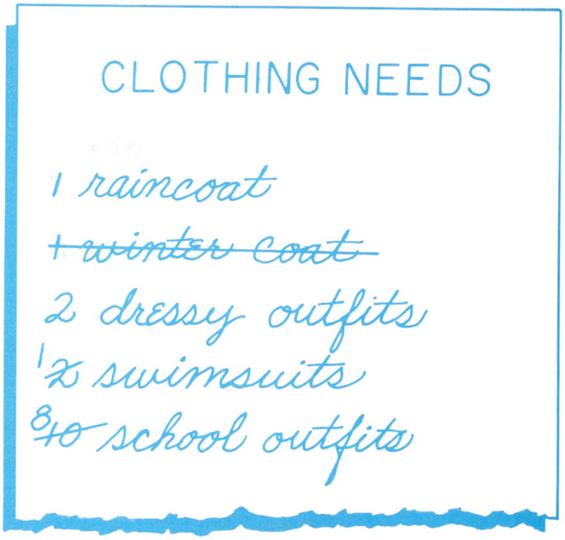

ADDING TO YOUR WARDROBE

Now you are ready to determine what new clothes you need. Compare your lists of outfits, activities, and clothing needs. On the clothing needs list, cross off needs you can take care of with the outfits you already have. Add to the list those items needed to complete an outfit. This new list tells you the things you need to add.

RESOURCES

You have now identified your new clothing needs. The next step in the decision-making process is to consider your resources. In this case your resources are time, money, and skills.

Time

Do you have a lot of free time to shop or sew? How many new things you need will affect how long it takes. Also, if you plan to sew, the type of garment and fabric will make a difference. It usually takes less time to make a vest than to make a shirt. It also takes less time to make a solid-colored garment than one from plaid.

Money

Very few people can afford to buy everything they need and want. Most of us have a **budget**—a spending plan that matches expenses to income. How much money does your budget allow for clothes? How much do you think the new garments will cost? Note on your list which things you need right away and which can wait. If your money is limited, buy only what you need now and save for the rest.

Time and skill can substitute for money. This young woman saved money by making her skirt and buying her blouse at an outlet store. She bought the vest at a yard sale.

Skills

Can you sew or knit? If so, perhaps you can make some garments. How well you sew or knit will affect which kinds of garments you should attempt. Even if you don't plan to make your garments, a knowledge of the techniques will help you judge the quality of ready-to-wear clothing. You'll also be able to make alterations.

Perhaps you are creative and have a good eye for style and color. These abilities will help you to mix and match garments to make complete outfits.

ALTERNATIVES

Once you've considered your resources, you are ready to think about your alternatives. How could you obtain the clothes you need? One alternative is to buy them. Sewing is another. You could also share, trade, or rent clothes. Which alternative is best for you depends on your resources.

Buying

Clothing is sold in many places. You can buy it at specialty shops or boutiques (boo-TEEKS), department stores, discount stores, outlet stores, variety stores, and even some supermarkets. Used clothing can be found at yard sales, flea markets, bazaars, and second-hand stores. Many people like to order clothes from catalogs. Where you shop depends on your personal preferences, the sources available, and the time and money you have to spend.

When you go shopping for clothes, be sure to take your list of wardrobe additions. It will help you resist buying things you don't really need. However, be somewhat flexible. The clothes you find may be different from what you expected.

HELPFUL HINT: If you are looking for a garment to go with clothes you already have, take along swatches of fabric from those clothes. They'll help you to match colors and textures.

One way to stretch your clothing budget is to buy as many items on sale as possible. Keep in mind that an item on sale is a good buy only if you need it. Buying clothes will be discussed in more detail in Unit 4.

Sewing

Sewing can stretch your clothing budget. For some, it is also the only way to get the style, color, and fit they want. The time you have available and your skill make a difference. When do you need the items? How easy (or hard) are they to make?

Accessories such as scarves, ties, and some belts are much cheaper to make than to buy. They are also easy to make. On the other hand, tailored jackets and shirts require both time and skill.

Trading or Sharing

If you are the same size as a friend or another family member, you might consider trading or sharing clothes. You both get a new item at no cost. Hand-me-downs also are a kind of sharing.

Renting

Some clothing, such as that for formal dances and weddings, can be rented. A variety of styles is usually available. Clothes that can be rented also include party costumes and some uniforms. If you need the garment for a limited time, renting may be the answer.

When you share clothes, be considerate. Always return your friend's clothes clean and in good condition.

Getting Your Money's Worth

DRESSING FOR ENERGY SAVINGS

In recent years high energy costs have meant less heat or air conditioning in many buildings. Careful wardrobe planning can help you stay comfortable.

In the summer, dress to let body heat escape. The loss of heat helps you stay cool. Loose, lightweight clothing and light, bright colors will help. Loose knits that let the air pass through are also comfortable.

The key to keeping warm in cold weather is insulation. Clothing traps body heat, and layered clothing traps it best. Several thin but warm layers of clothing with air sandwiched in between keep you warmer than a single, heavy piece of clothing. Start with something lightweight, such as a cotton shirt. Cotton helps absorb body moisture, keeping you dry. Each layer of clothing should be heavier than the last. The final layer might be a heavy sweater or parka.

Include covering for your head, ears, hands, and feet. About 50 percent of body heat loss is through the head alone. A wool knit hat or cap will help you stay warm. Mittens are better than gloves. Loose pile or silk-lined leather gloves tend to be warmer than knitted styles. Warmest of all are knitted gloves worn *under* oversized leather mittens.

When you shop for outerwear, the following tips will help you get the most warmth for your dollar:

- Pay careful attention to garment design and construction. Look for knit cuffs on sleeves and pants. They prevent cold air from entering the garment. Also good are snap or Velcro® closures that can be adjusted.
- Check the garment's outer shell. A tightly woven material such as nylon or polyester-cotton keeps out the wind.
- If you choose a quilted style, look for one that has widely spaced sewing lines. Sewing squeezes the insulation, reducing its effectiveness.
- Be careful about fit. If the garment is too tight, air will not be trapped. Too loose a fit lets cold air enter.

Getting Your Money's Worth

STRETCHING YOUR WARDROBE

Most people can't afford a different outfit for every occasion. Neither can they afford a whole new wardrobe every time the fashion changes. To make their wardrobes more versatile and to keep them up to date, they use "wardrobe stretchers" such as multi-use garments and accessories.

Multi-use garments are those that can be used for more than one activity or in more than one outfit. Jeans are a good multi-use item. They can be worn to school, for roller skating, or on a date. A corduroy blazer is another example. In cool weather it can be worn as a jacket. If it is a neutral color, it can be used to coordinate different outfits.

Accessories are items worn in addition to the basic outfit. Shoes, belts, ties, scarves, hats, and jewelry are accessories. Accessories add variety to a wardrobe. They can make a basic or small wardrobe seem bigger than it really is. Dark blue slacks and a light blue shirt can look formal with a red, white, and blue striped tie or scarf, black shoes, and a black belt. A more casual look can be created by leaving the shirt open at the neck and wearing tan or plaid accessories. Thus you can make one basic outfit suitable for two different occasions. Also, as you mix tops and bottoms of different colors, multi-colored scarves, ties, or belts help bring these pieces together into an outfit.

Try using accessories to bring clothes up to date. They usually cost less than garments. You'll feel as though you have a new outfit, and you won't have to spend a lot of money. Here are some suggestions:

- A silk scarf tied ascot-style into a shirt neckline or a V-neck sweater. Some scarves come with matching handkerchiefs for a pocket.
- An angora muffler loosely tied to one side, or tucked in at the neckline of a jacket. Some of these come with matching hats.
- A paisley or flowered shawl tied at the shoulder or waist over a plain knit dress.
- A bow at the collar or tied high at the neckline.
- A very long scarf tied at the waist as a belt.
- A buckled or sash belt over a sweater.

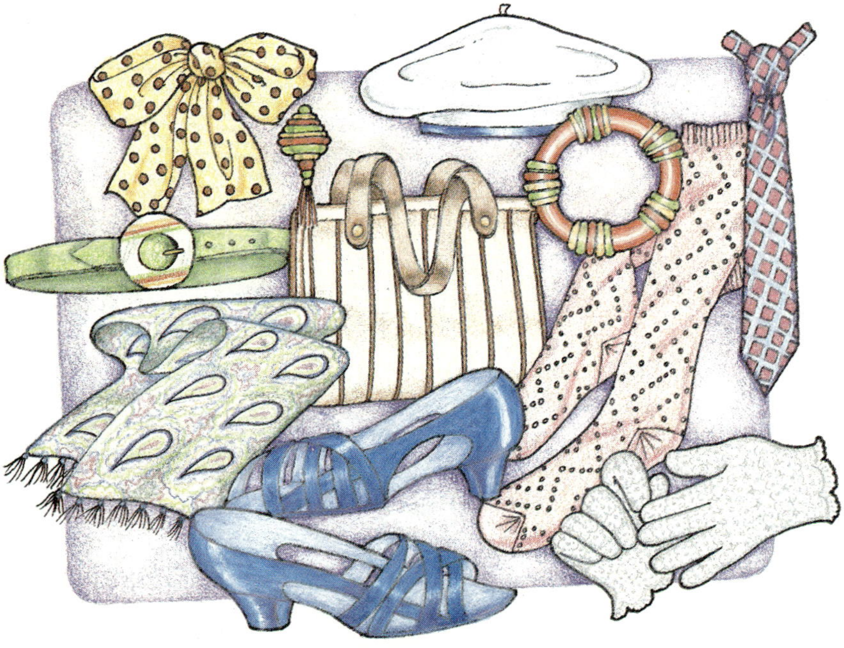

REVIEW-9

SUMMARY

Building your wardrobe is an on-going process. You must make many decisions about your needs and how to meet those needs. Using a plan for adding to your wardrobe helps you obtain the right clothes. Make an inventory. Coordinate outfits. Make the most of what you have. Then use your resources to add the clothes you need.

CHECK YOUR KNOWLEDGE

1. What is the first step in wardrobe planning?
2. What effect would the climate of the South have on a person's wardrobe selections?
3. How should you make a clothing inventory?
4. *True or False:* An *outfit* consists of the basic garments plus the accessories that are worn with them.
5. In wardrobe planning, your resources include money, skills, and ______.
6. How can sewing skills help you when you are buying clothes?
7. Besides buying or sewing them, how can you add clothes to your wardrobe?
8. When dressing for cold weather, why are several layers of clothing better than a single, heavy garment?
9. What is a multi-use garment?
10. How can accessories stretch your wardrobe?

EXTEND YOUR KNOWLEDGE

1. Make a list of the types of clothing needed for the climate in which you live. Which types of clothes are needed most? Which are needed least?
2. What organizations in your town collect used clothing? Are there any consignment shops? How do they operate?
3. Besides giving them away or throwing them out, what can you do with old clothes?
4. Make an inventory of your clothes. What can you do to repair or remodel the clothes that are no longer in good condition or that are out of fashion?
5. Select a garment, such as jeans or a sweater, and compare the cost of that garment at a department store, specialty shop, outlet store, and discount store. If you were going to buy the garment, where would you shop? Why?

FABRICS FOR CLOTHES

Suppose you were going to buy a summer shirt. Should you choose cotton or polyester? Which would be more comfortable? Which would be easier to take care of? What about a blend of cotton and polyester?

To make wise clothing decisions, you need to know something about textiles (fabrics). The fabric used to make a garment will affect the way that garment looks, feels, and wears. This unit will tell you about fabrics. You'll find out how they are made and used. You'll learn the advantages and disadvantages of various fabrics. And you'll learn about special treatments that can change a fabric to make it more useful.

Unit 3

CHAPTER 10

FIBERS

Can you imagine clothes being made from trees, grass, cocoons, oil, or coal? It may sound strange, but these are the raw materials for some of our most widely used fabrics. The materials are processed to obtain hairlike strands called fibers. The fibers are combined, usually by twisting, to make yarns. The yarns are then made into fabrics.

In this chapter, you'll learn about the first step—the making of fibers. Read on to find the answers to these questions:

- What are the sources of fibers?
- How are fibers produced?
- What are some of the common fibers, and how are they used?

Look for These Terms

natural fibers
manufactured fibers
generic name
trade name
cellulosic fibers
noncellulosic fibers

HOW FIBERS ARE CLASSIFIED

Fibers are divided into two basic groups: natural and manufactured. **Natural fibers** grow in plants or on animals. Cotton and wool are examples of natural fibers. **Manufactured fibers** are made in factories from materials that are not in fiber form. For example, nylon fibers are made using petroleum (oil) or natural gas, air, and water.

Within each group, there are families of fibers. All the fibers within a family are similar. They are called by a generic (juh-NAIR-ik) name. A **generic name** is a name given to a whole class of similar items. "Wool" is a generic name. It usually refers to the fleece of sheep, but it also includes goat, camel, and other animal fibers. Nylon, rayon, and polyester are generic names of manufactured fibers.

Manufactured fibers may also have a trade name. The **trade name** is the name given to a fiber by the company that produces it. For example, Dacron® is a polyester made by DuPont. Kodel® is a polyester made by Eastman.

The Textile Fiber Products Identification Act of 1960 requires manufacturers to list fiber content on their labels. The generic name of the fiber and the percentage of the fiber used must be included. For example, the label might state, "55% cotton, 45% polyester." The trade name of the fiber may also be listed, although that is not required by law.

NATURAL FIBERS

Thousands of years ago, people learned to make fabrics from natural fibers. They learned that some fibers were better than others for making fabric. Fibers used to make fabric must be long enough to be spun into yarn. They must be strong yet able to bend without breaking. They should also be able to stretch at least a little.

Natural fibers come from plants or animals. The two major plant fibers are cotton and flax. The two major animal fibers are wool and silk.

COTTON

Cotton was used in ancient times. People in India were growing cotton as early as 3000 B.C. It was probably Alexander the Great (356–323 B.C.) who brought this "vegetable wool" to Europe. Long before Columbus came to the New World, cotton was being grown in what is now the southwestern United States.

Today cotton is the world's major natural fiber. It can be grown wherever there are at least six to seven months of warm weather. The largest producers of cotton are the United States, the Soviet Union, China, and India.

Cotton fibers grow from the seeds of the cotton plant. The seeds are inside green pods called cotton bolls. When the cotton boll ripens, it bursts open and the fluffy white fibers are exposed.

Cotton grows best in a mild, warm climate such as that of the southern United States.

The cotton fibers are cleaned to remove seeds and leaves. Then the cotton is carded. Carding is a process much like combing. It straightens the fibers. Spinning machines twist the fibers and form the yarn. Yarns are wound onto bobbins or spools and then woven into fabric.

Cotton may be blended with other fibers. This is done to take advantage of the best characteristics of both fibers. Check the label of one of your shirts. You may find that the fabric is a blend of cotton and polyester. Cotton absorbs moisture and is comfortable to wear, but it wrinkles easily. Polyester neither wrinkles nor absorbs moisture. Since it doesn't absorb body moisture, pure polyester can be uncomfortable to wear. However, a shirt made from a blend of cotton and polyester doesn't wrinkle and it absorbs moisture. Therefore it is comfortable to wear.

Flax

The fibers of the flax plant are used to make linen. Flax, a type of grass, was grown in Egypt thousands of years ago. The Pharaohs (rulers) wore beautiful linen robes made from the flax plant. The mummies in ancient Egyptian tombs were wrapped in strips of linen.

For many years linen was used to make tablecloths, sheets, and towels. These items are still called "linen" today, even though they are usually made from other fabrics.

Ireland became the world's linen manufacturing center in the seventeenth century. The Irish brought the linen industry to the United States in the early 1800s. However, today Ireland is still known for its fine linen cloth.

The flax plant is adaptable. It can be grown in the cool climate of Russia as well as in the warm temperatures of Egypt and India. The leading producers of flax are the Soviet Union and eastern Europe.

Linen is made from the stalks of flax. The seed pods are used to make linseed oil, an ingredient in many paints and varnishes.

When seeds form in the blossoms of the plant, it is time to harvest the flax. Threshing machines remove the seeds and their pods. The stalks are bundled and tied. They are then soaked in order to loosen the tough outer part. Only the inside of the stalk is used to make linen yarns.

Linen is strong and comfortable to wear. It wrinkles easily, but it can be treated with chemicals or blended with other fibers to make it wrinkle-resistant.

WOOL

Thousands of years ago people discovered that the fleece of sheep was warmer than animal skins. Today about forty different breeds of sheep are raised for wool. Almost every country produces wool, but the leaders are Australia, New Zealand, and South Africa. Sheep are sheared about once a year after the cold season is over. The mass of fibers, which resemble hair, is called fleece.

Sheep being sheared. "Lamb's wool" is the first fleece to be sheared from the animal. The lamb is six to eight months old, and its fleece is fine and soft.

After the fleece is removed from the sheep, it is washed and carded. Next, the fibers are spun into yarn. The spinning process varies according to the type of fabric desired. Some yarns are thick and nubby, while others are thin and smooth.

Unlike cotton or linen fibers, wool fibers can be reused. However, reused wool is usually of lesser quality. The Wool Products Labeling Act requires wool to be identified as new or reused. "Virgin wool" is wool that has never been made into yarn or fabric before. "Recycled wool" has been reprocessed from used or unused fabric.

Wool is comfortable to wear. It is warm and resists wrinkling. However, it may shrink when washed. For this reason, most wool must be dry cleaned or gently hand washed in cool water. Wool can be treated with finishes or blended with nylon to make it washable.

SILK

The Chinese discovered silk as early as 2600 B.C. They found that the cocoon spun by the silkworm could be unwound. The fibers could be spun into yarn, and the yarn woven into fabric. Their secret was closely guarded until about 300 A.D. when refugees smuggled cocoons into Korea. The Japanese learned about silk production from the Koreans. The "secret" spread through Asia into Europe.

The silkworm is actually a moth caterpillar. It spins a cocoon around itself in a figure eight. In only three days the cocoon is finished. It is about the size and shape of a peanut shell. After two weeks, the fiber is strong enough to detach from the animal.

The cocoons are placed in a series of hot and cold water baths until they are soft enough to unwind. The unwound fibers are dried and twisted into yarn.

Silk is strong and wrinkle-resistant. It is comfortable to wear because it absorbs body moisture. Because making silk takes time and quite a bit of hand work, it is an expensive fiber.

The silkworm spins its cocoon from one continuous strand of silk. The strand may be 800 to 1500 yards long.

OTHER NATURAL FIBERS

Many other natural fibers are used to make fabrics. *Specialty hair fibers* include fibers from the camel family (such as camel and llama), the goat family (mohair, cashmere), and the fur-bearing animals. *Down,* the soft, fluffy growth under the feathers of birds, is used as filling for coats and jackets. *Ramie* (RAY-me) comes from the stalks of China grass. It is a strong, durable fiber which may be combined with other fibers for use in sweaters or scarves. *Natural rubber,* which comes from trees, may be used in elastic waistbands and stretch fabrics.

Angora goats are raised in the southwestern United States. Their wool, called mohair, is the strongest wool fiber.

MANUFACTURED FIBERS

Throughout most of history, clothing and other textile products were made from the natural fibers. From prehistoric times until the end of the nineteenth century, cotton, linen, wool, and silk were the most widely used fibers. However, natural fibers had some drawbacks. High demand, a poor growing season, or a war could cause a shortage. A shortage meant high prices. The labor involved in growing natural fibers and making them into yarn also added to their cost. People looked for ways to make fibers by easier, less expensive methods.

In the late 1800s artificial silk, later known as rayon, was developed. This was the first breakthrough in what was to become a huge industry. By 1980, 75 percent of all fibers were manufactured fibers.

The first rayon was too shiny and had little strength. Improvements were made, and today rayon is a popular fiber for clothing and household fabrics such as table linens.

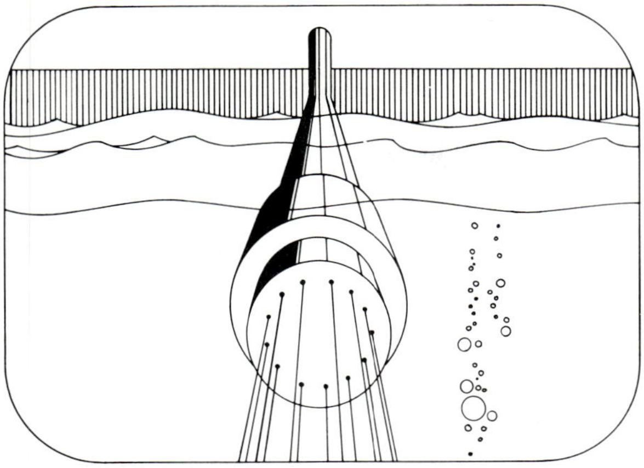

Wet Spinning

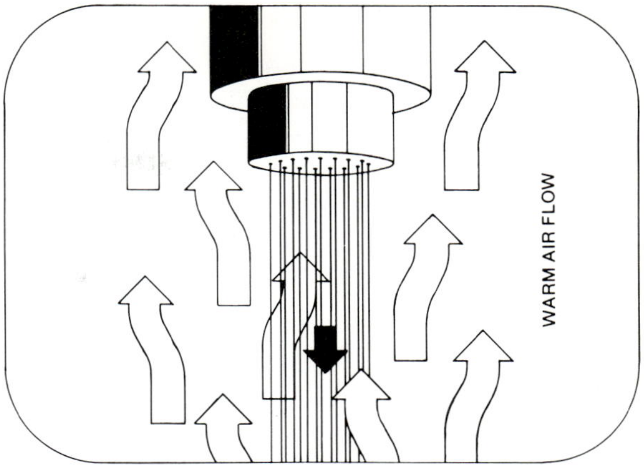

Dry Spinning

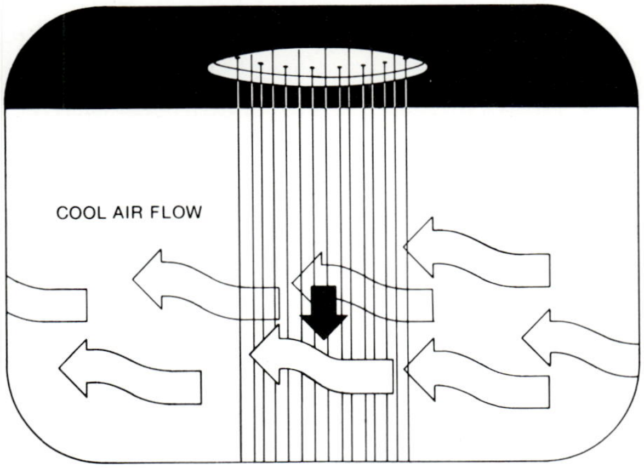

Melt Spinning

To harden the fibers as they emerge from the spinneret, one of three processes is used. In *wet spinning*, the fibers pass through a chemical bath. In *dry spinning*, the fibers harden by drying in warm air. In *melt spinning*, cool air hardens the fibers.

The first manufactured fibers used cellulose (SELL-you-lows). Cellulose is the major ingredient in the cell walls of plants. Later, fibers were made entirely from chemicals. Today we have two types of manufactured fibers:

- **Cellulosic fibers** are made using the cellulose of a plant (usually wood).
- **Noncellulosic fibers** use chemical ingredients derived from coal, petroleum, or natural gas.

While the ingredients used are different, the basic process for production is much the same for all manufactured fibers. The materials are dissolved or melted into a liquid about as thick as honey. The liquid is then forced through tiny holes of a spinneret, a device which resembles a shower head. Different shapes and thicknesses can be produced. As the liquid passes through air or a chemical bath, it turns into solid fibers. The fibers are stretched and twisted into yarns.

CELLULOSIC FIBERS

Common cellulosic fibers include rayon, acetate, and triacetate. These are described in the chart on page 111.

NONCELLULOSIC FIBERS

The noncellulosic fibers are made from air, water, and petroleum, coal, or natural gas. About one percent of the nation's total petroleum supply is used to produce noncellulosic fibers. When there are shortages of petroleum or any of the other resources, there may also be a shortage of noncellulosic fibers, or the price of the fibers may increase.

There are many different noncellulosic fibers, but they share some important properties.

- They are heat sensitive. This means heat can cause the fibers to soften or melt. They should not be washed in hot water or pressed with a hot iron. Heat sensitivity has some advantages. It allows pleats and creases to be permanently heat-set into a garment. Products such as sweaters and hosiery can be heat-set into a particular shape. They will retain this shape during wearing and washing.
- Noncellulosic fibers have low moisture absorbency. This means they dry quickly because they do not hold moisture. But their low moisture content results in a tendency to build up static electricity. Static electricity causes dirt and lint to stick to the surface of the fabric. Clothes may also cling to the wearer.
- Noncellulosic fibers are very resilient (rih-ZIL-yunt). This means they regain their original size and shape after being bent, stretched, or twisted. Garments made from these fibers do not wrinkle easily. They are also easy to care for.
- Noncellulosic fibers readily absorb oil and grease. Frequent washing is needed.
- Noncellulosic fibers pill. Pilling means the fiber ends ball up on the surface of the fabric.

There are currently eighteen families of noncellulosic fibers. The most widely used are acrylic, metallic, modacrylic, nylon, polyester, and spandex. These are described in the chart on pages 111–112.

Here are three common noncellulosic fibers (left to right): nylon, Dacron polyester, Orlon acrylic.

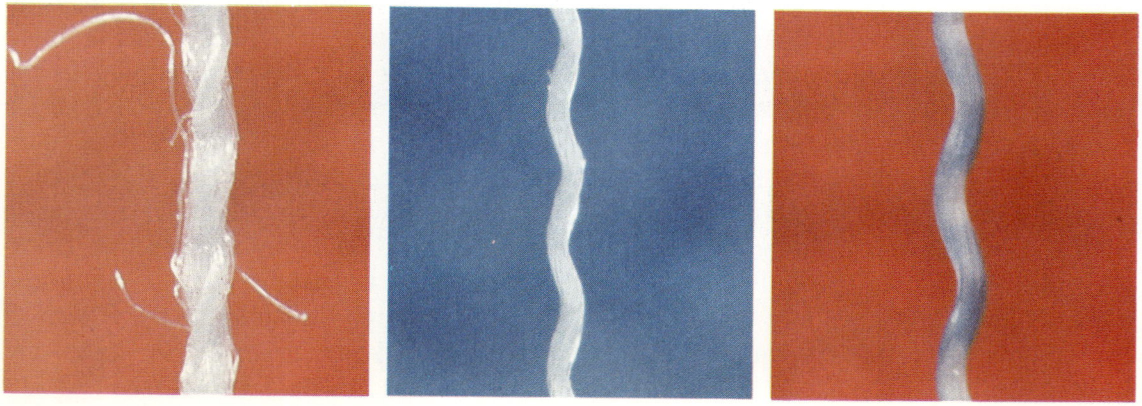

-Perspective

NEW USES FOR MANUFACTURED FIBERS

Manufactured fibers are widely used in clothing. They are also found in nearly every other aspect of modern life. Here are a few examples:

- Tires for all kinds of vehicles are made from manufactured fibers. Nylon, polyester, and aramid (AIR-a-mid) now account for two-thirds of the tire market. The tires last longer than rubber ones and give better gas mileage.
- Soft body armor (such as the bulletproof vest) made from aramid is standard equipment in most police departments today. An aramid undervest weighing only 2½ pounds can stop a .38-caliber bullet fired from 10 feet away.
- Disposable surgical products made from rayon, aramid, polyester, olefin, or nylon are playing a major role in modern hospitals. Throwing away hospital clothing, sheets, face masks, and hair coverings is less costly than washing and sterilizing them. It also helps stop the spread of germs.
- Polyester is used for artificial blood vessels.
- Bubble-shaped domes made of manufactured fibers are coverings for swimming pools, restaurants, stadiums, and theaters.
- The points on felt-tip pens are made of rayon or nylon.
- Spun bonded olefin is used to make waterproof children's books.
- Hollow aramid fibers can be used to filter the salt out of seawater, turning it into fresh water.

Can you add other uses of manufactured fibers to this list? Be alert to newspaper articles which mention the use of manufactured fibers.

Disposable surgical gowns, masks, and sheets are used in many hospitals.

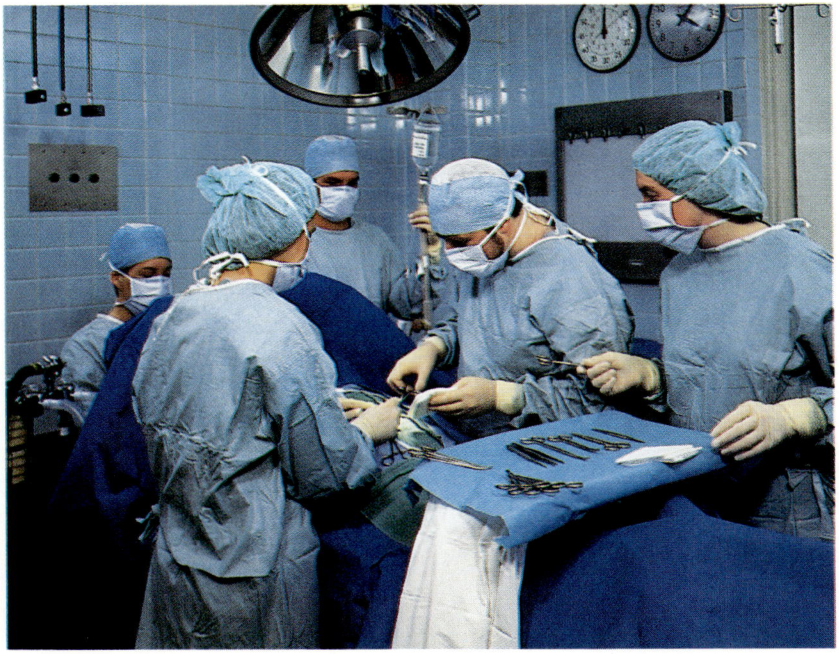

Natural Fibers

Fiber and Uses	Advantages	Disadvantages*	Care
Cotton shirts, blouses, undergarments, work clothes, jeans, sheets, towels	Absorbs moisture Dries quickly Strong, durable Easy to dye	Wrinkles easily Shrinks easily Damaged by sunlight and mildew Burns easily	Machine wash Iron while damp Chlorine bleach may be used on whites
Linen suits, blouses, tablecloths	Strong Does not build up static electricity Resists heat Absorbs moisture Resists sunlight, moths, and other insects Does not lint	Wrinkles easily Shrinks somewhat Burns easily	Machine wash for softness; iron at high temperature Dry-clean for crispness; do not press in sharp creases
Wool sweaters, skirts, pants, suits, dresses, outerwear, blankets, carpeting, upholstery	Holds body heat Sheds wrinkles Easy to dye Flame resistant	Shrinks easily Damaged by strong soaps and detergents Attacked by moths and carpet beetles Builds up static electricity Dries slowly	Dry-clean, or hand wash in cool water Never use chlorine bleach Steam with a pressing cloth at medium temperature; high temperatures stiffen wool Store with mothballs to protect from moths and beetles
Silk suits, dresses, blouses, skirts, scarves, neckties, formal wear, draperies, upholstery	Very strong Good wrinkle recovery Retains shape well Does not conduct heat Absorbs moisture Easy to dye Burns slowly Resists mildew	Shrinks somewhat Sensitive to heat Weakened by sunlight Can be damaged by perspiration and deodorants	Dry-clean, or hand wash Never use chlorine bleach Press while damp with a moderately warm iron Protect from long exposure to sunlight Finishes and soil may attract insects; store with mothballs

*Many of the disadvantages can be overcome with special treatments or by blending with other fibers.

Manufactured Fibers

Fiber and Uses	Advantages	Disadvantages*	Care
Cellulosic Fibers			
Rayon suits, dresses, blouses, work clothes, lingerie, scarves, hats, ties, disposable diapers	Inexpensive Easy to dye Absorbent Comfortable to wear Can be made to look like cotton, linen, wool, or silk	Wrinkles easily Shrinks easily Melts when overheated Burns readily Attacked by mildew	Dry-clean, or machine wash and dry at warm temperatures Do not twist or wring when wet Press at low to medium temperature while damp, on the wrong side of the garment
Acetate blouses, dresses, lingerie, draperies, upholstery	Inexpensive Lightweight Drapes well Dries quickly Does not shrink Resists mildew and moths Not easily damaged by sunlight	Sensitive to heat May be damaged by acetone (an ingredient in some nail polishes and polish removers) Builds static electricity Melts at high temperatures	Dry-clean, or hand wash Do not twist or wring when wet Press at very low temperature
Triacetate children's clothing, sportswear, household goods	Resists wrinkles Dries quickly Resists heat-set pleats Resists moths and mildew	Does not absorb Lacks strength Builds static electricity Melts at high temperatures	Dry-clean, or machine wash and dry at warm temperatures Press at medium high temperature
Noncellulosic Fibers			
Acrylic knitted garments (such as sweaters), snow and ski wear, socks, work clothes, carpets, draperies, upholstery	Resists wrinkles Not easily damaged by sunlight Lightweight	Does not absorb moisture Builds static electricity Tends to pill	Dry-clean, or machine wash and dry at low temperatures Press at medium temperature

*Many of the disadvantages can be overcome with special treatments during fiber production or finishing.

(continued on next page)

Manufactured Fibers (continued)

Fiber and Uses	Advantages	Disadvantages*	Care
Noncellulosic Fibers (continued)			
Modacrylic deep pile coats and trims, artificial furs, wigs, hairpieces, blankets, carpeting	Easy to dye Resists abrasion Dries quickly Resists wrinkles Lightweight	Does not absorb moisture	Dry-clean, or machine wash and dry at low temperatures Press at very low temperature
Metallic decorative trim, ribbons, table linens, upholstery, carpeting	Does not tarnish if coated with a finish Used in carpeting to reduce static electricity	Sensitive to bending and abrasion Stiff	Some trims can be washed or dry-cleaned; others should be removed before cleaning garment. For garments with metallic yarns in them, follow care instructions on label
Nylon hosiery, lingerie, outerwear, bedspreads, carpeting, draperies, upholstery	Strong Resists wrinkles Resists abrasion Elastic Resists mildew and insects Dries quickly	Does not absorb moisture Builds static electricity Damaged by sunlight Sensitive to heat	Follow label instructions for dry-cleaning or washing Press at low temperature
Polyester shirts, blouses, dresses, suits, slacks, children's wear, home furnishings	Strong Easy to dye Dries quickly Resists wrinkles Retains pleats and creases	May pill Does not absorb moisture Sensitive to heat	Machine wash Dry at low temperature Press at low temperature
Spandex bathing suits, golf jackets, ski pants	Highly elastic Resists abrasion Resists body oils Lightweight	Sensitive to heat	Machine wash at warm temperature Dry at low temperature Do not use chlorine bleach

*Many of the disadvantages can be overcome with special treatments during fiber production or finishing.

REVIEW-10

SUMMARY

Natural fibers come from plants or animals. Manufactured fibers are made in factories using ingredients derived from petroleum, coal, or natural gas. Natural and manufactured fibers can be combined to take advantage of each one's best properties. Both natural and manufactured fibers are used in a wide variety of clothing and household goods.

CHECK YOUR KNOWLEDGE

1. In the name *Kodel® polyester,* which is the generic name and which is the trade name?
2. Name the two major animal fibers.
3. Name the two major plant fibers.
4. *True or False:* Cotton fibers are obtained from the stalk of the cotton plant.
5. From what plant is linen made?
6. What is "recycled wool"?
7. What is the source of silk fiber?
8. Name the two basic types of manufactured fibers and tell what they are made from.
9. Name three cellulosic fibers.
10. What properties do the noncellulosic fibers have in common?

EXTEND YOUR KNOWLEDGE

1. Do a research report on the origins of one of the natural fibers. Where and when was it first used?
2. Check the labels of the clothes in your wardrobe. How many garments are made from natural fibers? From manufactured fibers? From blends? Which do you think are the most comfortable?
3. Write a report about the invention of rayon, nylon, or any other manufactured fiber.
4. If there were no manufactured fibers, how do you think our clothing would be affected? Would styles be different? What about cost and variety?
5. Make a flow chart which shows the steps in the making of a manufactured fiber or the processing of a natural fiber.

CHAPTER 11

FABRICS

The suit and sweater in the pictures are both made of wool. Yet they are very different in weight, feel, and appearance. Why? The differences are due to the type of yarn and the method by which the yarn is made into fabric.

Whether you buy ready-made clothes or sew your own, a knowledge of yarns and fabrics will help you select the right material for your needs.

In this chapter, you'll learn the answers to these questions:

- How are yarns made?
- How are fabrics made?
- What should you look for when selecting a fabric?

Look for These Terms

filaments
staple fibers
warp
filling
plain weave
twill weave
satin weave
weft knit
warp knit

YARNS

All fibers, whether natural or manufactured, must be made into yarn before they become fabric. Yarn can be thick, like the knitting yarns used to make sweaters. Most yarns, however, are about the size of sewing thread. How the yarn is made depends on what fibers are used and what characteristics are desired.

Fibers may be long or short. Long fibers are called **filaments.** Silk is a filament, and so are manufactured fibers. They may be many yards long. Short fibers are called **staple fibers.** Cotton, flax, and wool are staple fibers. Manufactured fibers can be cut to desired lengths to make staple fibers.

Filament yarns may consist of a single filament. More often, they are made of a bundle of filaments that may or may not be twisted together. To make staple yarns, the fibers are twisted together into a continuous thread. The amount of twist and the length of the fibers being twisted affect the final appearance of a fabric. Low-twist yarns produce soft fabrics. High-twist yarns produce hard-surface fabrics.

Staple yarns are not as smooth as filament yarns, and they are more bulky.

FILAMENT YARN

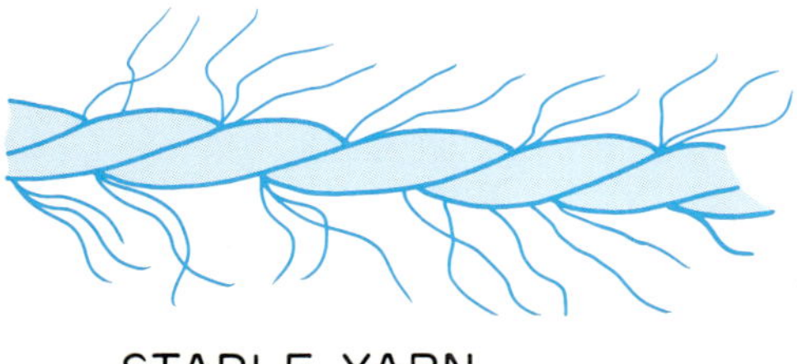

STAPLE YARN

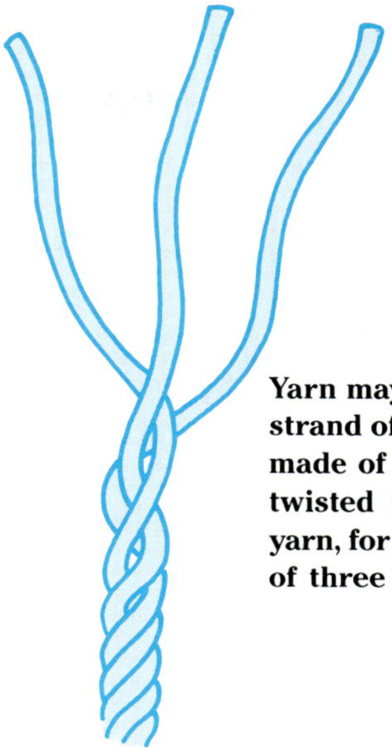

Yarn may consist of a single strand of fibers, or it may be made of two or more yarns, twisted together. Three-ply yarn, for example, is made up of three yarns.

Different fibers may be combined as they are made into yarn. These yarns are called blends. They are designed to bring together the best characteristics of each fiber. Cotton-polyester is a blend often used for clothing fabric.

The type of yarn used determines certain characteristics of the fabric:

- *weight*—light to heavy
- *texture*—smooth, rough, fuzzy, nubby, dull, shiny
- *hand* (the way a fabric feels and drapes)—soft, hard, crisp, stiff
- *comfort*—cool, warm, scratchy, silky, stretchy
- *performance*—strength, resistance to abrasion, ability to keep its shape, type of care required

HOW FABRICS ARE MADE

Yarn can be made into fabric in a variety of ways. The most common are weaving and knitting.

WEAVING

Weaving is done by interlocking yarns at right angles to each other. The lengthwise yarns are called the **warp.** Crosswise yarns are known as the **filling.** (Sometimes the crosswise yarns are called the weft or woof.) A loom is used to interlock the warp and filling yarns. Fabrics are usually woven in one of three basic ways:

- **plain weave**—filling yarns go under and over alternate warp yarns. Weaving the yarns close together gives a dense, strong fabric. Weaving the yarns loosely gives a more open, lighter weight fabric. Percale (pur-KALE), a cotton cloth often used for bed linens, is a plain woven fabric.
- **twill weave**—filling yarns go over one warp yarn, then under two or more warp yarns. Each filling yarn dips under a warp yarn to the right or left of the previous filling yarn. This creates diagonal ridges of yarns on the surface of the fabric. Twill weaves are heavier and sturdier than plain weaves. Denim is an example of a twill weave.
- **satin weave**—filling yarns go over one warp yarn, then under groups of warp yarns, as in twill weave. However, the filling yarns go under the warp yarns in a random pattern. Fabrics woven in this manner have a smooth, shiny surface. Satin fabric is popular for formal wear, blouses, and bed linens.

These workers are monitoring an air-jet loom, a state-of-the-art weaving machine.

Woven Fabrics

Type of Weave	Fabric Name	Characteristics
PLAIN WEAVE  	broadcloth chambray (SHAM-bray) duck gingham organdy oxford cloth percale poplin seersucker shantung taffeta	Vary, depending on the weave. Fabric may be sheer or heavy, fragile or sturdy, soft or rough, shiny or dull.
TWILL WEAVE  	denim flannel gabardine serge tweed	Diagonal lines on the surface of the fabric. Firm and durable.
SATIN WEAVE  	satin sateen	Smooth, sometimes shiny. Not as durable as plain or twill weave.

Perspective

DICTIONARY OF FABRICS

batiste (buh-TEEST): A soft, sheer fabric, usually made of cotton and used for blouses, dresses, and nightwear.

bouclé (boo-KLAY): Knitted or woven fabric with small spaced loops on the surface. Used for sweaters and dresses.

broadcloth: Closely woven fabric with a smooth, soft surface. Made from wool, silk, cotton, or manufactured fibers. Comes in various weights. Used in many types of clothing.

brocade: Fabric jacquard-woven with elaborate, raised designs. Used in upholstery and evening dresses.

calico (KAL-i-koh): Lightweight, coarse cotton fabric often printed with small designs. Used in summer clothes.

canvas: Heavy, closely woven, stiff fabric. Made from cotton, linen, or manufactured fibers. Used for sportswear, sails, awnings, and home furnishings.

cashmere: Soft, lightweight, expensive fabric knitted or woven from hair of Kashmir goat.

challis (SHALL-ee): Lightweight, soft fabric of cotton, wool, or manufactured fibers. Often printed with small flowers. Used for blouses, shirts, dresses, and draperies.

chiffon (shif-AHN): Very sheer, soft, light fabric of silk or manufactured fibers. Used in dressy clothes.

chino (CHEE-no): Mediumweight, sturdy fabric of cotton or cotton blend. Used in pants and sportswear.

chintz: Glazed cotton fabric, brightly printed or solid colored. Used in clothing and home furnishings.

corduroy: Sturdy fabric with "ribs" of cut pile. Made of cotton or cotton blends. Used in sportswear and upholstery.

crepe (KRAYP): Light, crinkled fabric of natural or manufactured fibers. Used in blouses, dresses, and linings.

damask: Fabric with jacquard-woven design. Unlike brocade, the design is flat. Used for table linens, clothing, draperies, and upholstery.

denim: Sturdy cotton or cotton-blend fabric. Often blue. Used for jeans and sportswear.

dotted swiss: Sheer, crisp, lightweight cotton fabric with woven or flocked dots. Used in dresses, blouses, and curtains.

double knit: Sturdy fabric of wool or polyester knitted with two sets of needles to produce a double thickness. Used for dresses, suits, and sportswear.

duck: A heavy closely woven fabric, usually cotton. Used for awnings, beach and lawn umbrellas, upholstery, and sportswear.

faille (FILE): Slightly shiny, ribbed fabric of silk, cotton, or manufactured fibers. Used in dresses, suits, and draperies.

felt: Nonwoven fabric made of wool fibers that have been moistened, heated, and pressed together. Used in hats and craft items.

flannel: Napped fabric of cotton, wool, or manufactured fibers. Used in suits, shirts, sleepwear, and sheets.

gabardine (GAB-ur-deen): Firm, durable twill fabric of natural or manufactured fibers. Used for sportswear, coats, and suits.

georgette: Thin, loosely woven fabric similar to crepe. Made of natural or manufactured fibers. Used for dressy clothes.

gingham (GING-um): Closely woven, plain-weave cotton fabric. Usually yarn-dyed and woven into stripes, plaids, or checks. Used for dresses, shirts, and home furnishings.

jersey: Lightweight knit of cotton, wool, silk, or manufactured fibers. Used for dresses, shirts, and sportswear.

khaki: Light yellowish brown fabric, usually cotton or wool. Used in military uniforms and sportswear.

madras: Plain- or jacquard-woven fabric, usually cotton, in stripes, checks, or plaids. Used for sportswear.

muslin: Strong, plain-weave cotton fabric. Made in various weights. Used for sheets, draperies, dresses.

organdy (OR-gun-dee): Sheer, crisp, lightweight cotton fabric used for dressy clothes.

organza (or-GAN-zuh): Similar to organdy, but made of silk, rayon, or nylon.

oxford cloth: Cotton or cotton blend fabric with a colored warp and white filling. Used for shirts, dresses, and sportswear.

percale: Smooth, tightly woven cotton or cotton blend used for dresses, shirts, and sheets.

poplin: Mediumweight fabric of natural or manufactured fibers. Finely ribbed. Used for dresses and sportswear.

satin: Any one of many smooth, slippery fabrics of natural or manufactured fibers. Used mainly for dressy clothes.

seersucker: Cotton or cotton blend with woven-in, crinkled stripes. Used for sportswear, dresses, blouses, and home furnishings.

serge: Sturdy, twill-weave fabric with a diagonal rib on both sides. Made of wool, silk, or rayon. Used in suits.

suede: Leather with a napped surface. Used for shoes, purses, jackets, and coats.

taffeta (TAF-ut-uh): Crisp, tightly woven fabric with a dull luster. Made of natural or manufactured fibers. Used for linings and dressy clothes.

terry cloth: Absorbent fabric, usually cotton, with uncut loops on one or both sides. Used for beachwear, robes, towels, and bedspreads.

tweed: Sturdy fabric, usually wool or wool blend, with a nubby texture. Used for suits, skirts, coats, and upholstery.

velour (vuh-LOOR): Soft fabric with a pile surface similar to velvet. Made of cotton, wool, silk, or manufactured fibers. Used for sportswear, robes, and upholstery.

velvet: Soft lustrous fabric with a short pile. Made of silk, wool, or manufactured fibers. Used in dressy clothes.

velveteen: Similar to velvet, but made of cotton.

voile (VOYL): Soft, sheer fabric of wool, cotton, silk, or manufactured fibers. Used for summer dresses, blouses, and for home furnishings.

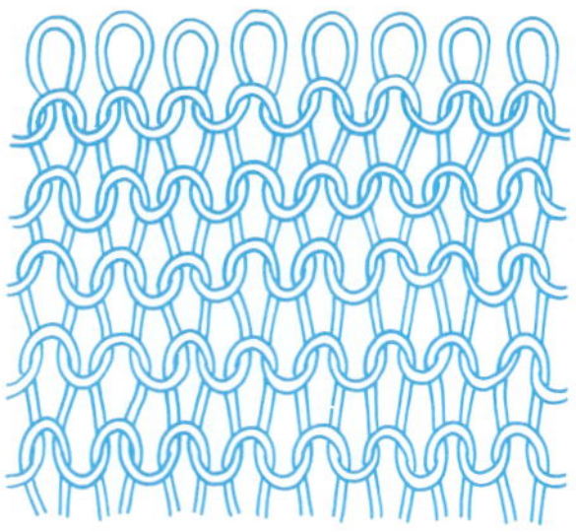

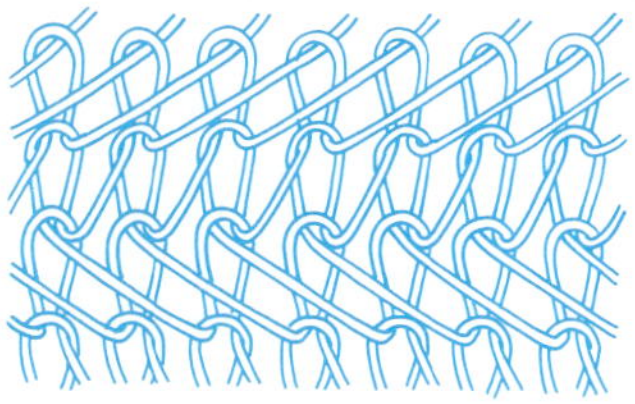

The two basic categories of knits are weft and warp. Within each category are many variations.

KNITTING

Knitted fabric is made by interlocking loops of yarn. When only one yarn is used, the fabric is called a **weft knit,** or filling knit. A **warp knit** is made using several yarns.

Both weft and warp knits can be made on flat knitting machines. Many sweaters are produced on flat knitting machines. Sheer flat fabrics such as tricot (TREE-koh) are also produced on a flat knitting machine.

Weft knits can also be made on a circular knitting machine. This machine produces a tubelike fabric which can be used for scarves and hosiery or slit to form a flat piece of fabric.

The unique construction of knitted fabrics gives them special characteristics:

- Knitted fabrics stretch more than plain woven fabrics. For this reason they should never be hung on a hanger. They will "grow" in length, and the hanger will leave marks.
- Knitted fabrics wrinkle less than woven fabrics.
- Some knitted fabrics may ravel or "run."

OTHER METHODS OF MAKING FABRICS

Nonwoven, or "bolted," *fabrics* are made by interlocking fibers together without weaving or knitting. Felt, made from wool, is an example. Wool fibers have tiny scales on their surface. When the fibers are moistened, heated, and pressed together, the scales interlock and form a solid fabric. Today, many manufactured fibers are made into nonwoven fabrics. An adhesive or solvent may be used to bond the fibers together.

Nonwoven fabrics are inexpensive to produce, do not ravel, and therefore need no hemming. They also may tear or pull apart easily. They cannot be mended. Because they can be molded and heat-set to hold a permanent shape, these fabrics are often used for hats, trims, and interfacings.

These workers are spraying insecticide. Their protective coveralls are made of Tyvek, a nonwoven fabric made from olefin fibers.

Stretch fabrics may be woven or knitted. The "stretch" comes from the method of weaving or knitting and the nature of the yarn. All stretch fabrics contain heat-sensitive fibers, so they should not be exposed to high temperatures.

Bonded fabrics are actually two fabrics which have been permanently attached to each other with an adhesive. For instance, tricot fabric may be bonded to loosely woven or knitted fabrics. The tricot provides a soft, stable backing for the loose, unstable fabric.

To make *laminated fabrics,* a layer of foam is sandwiched between two layers of fabric. The foam provides warmth without adding a lot of bulk.

Coated fabrics are made by applying a substance, such as vinyl, to fabric. Simulated leather is a coated fabric. The base fabric may be woven or knitted. A coating of vinyl is added to give the look of leather. Rubberized coatings may be applied to the backs of drapery fabrics for insulation. Rainwear is coated to make it waterproof.

Quilted fabrics are produced by stitching together two fabrics with a layer of batting (padding) between them. They may be bulky or light, depending upon the amount and type of batting used. Some quilted fabrics are reversible. This means they have no "right" and "wrong" sides. Quilted fabric in a garment often eliminates the need for a lining.

CHOOSING FABRICS

Have you ever bought clothes that looked great in the store but ended up unused and forgotten in your closet? Chances are you were disappointed with the fabric. Perhaps it was uncomfortable to wear. Or maybe it shrank when you washed it. Knowing about fabrics can help you avoid these problems and get more use out of your clothes. Whether you are shopping for ready-made clothes or for fabrics to sew, consider what your needs are, how the fabric will perform, and what your budget will allow.

Quilted fabrics may be used for jackets, coats, pillows, and bedspreads. Can you think of other uses?

WHAT DO YOU NEED?

Suppose you're shopping for a cool-weather jacket. The one with the fur lining may look good to you, but is it practical? If you live in an area where it seldom gets very cold, you may not have many chances to wear such a jacket. A Windbreaker or a waterproof jacket might be a better choice.

When shopping for fabric, consider what you will be sewing. A heavy wool may be fine for a pair of pants, but you would not want it for a tailored shirt.

HOW WILL THE FABRIC PERFORM?

Is the fabric strong? Will it keep its shape? Does it "breathe"—allow air or body moisture to pass through? What sort of care does it need? Knowing the answers to these questions can help you decide if a fabric is right for you.

Look at the label on the garment or on the end of the fabric bolt. It will tell you about fiber content and methods of care.

Helpful hint: Refer to the charts in Chapter 10 to review the advantages and disadvantages of common fibers.

WHAT CAN YOU AFFORD?

Some fabrics are expensive. Unless you plan to wear the garment many times, you may not get your money's worth from it. It might be better to choose a similar but less costly fabric. A scarf or a tie doesn't have to be silk to look good. On the other hand, the expensive fabric may have qualities you need. An acrylic sweater will cost less, but you'll stay warmer in wool.

Remember, fabric care adds to the cost of a garment. In the long run, an inexpensive garment that has to be dry-cleaned can cost you more than an expensive one that is washable.

Note the label on this sweater. Do you think the sweater will be warm? Will it be easy to care for?

REVIEW-11

SUMMARY

Fibers are made into yarn and then into fabric. The most common methods of making fabric are weaving and knitting. Fabrics made by other means include nonwoven, stretch, bonded, laminated, coated, and quilted fabrics. When choosing fabrics, consider your needs, the fabric's performance, and your budget.

CHECK YOUR KNOWLEDGE

1. Give an example of a filament.
2. Give an example of a staple fiber.
3. How is a staple yarn made?
4. What fabric characteristics are determined by the type of yarn used?
5. What are the three most common methods of weaving fabrics?
6. What is the difference between a weft knit and a warp knit?
7. *True or False:* Knitted fabrics wrinkle less than woven fabrics.
8. Name the advantages and disadvantages of nonwoven fabrics.
9. *True or False:* Stretch fabrics must be woven.
10. When you shop for fabrics, what should you consider?

EXTEND YOUR KNOWLEDGE

1. Write a report on how cotton, linen, silk, or wool fibers are made into yarns and fabrics.
2. Make a chart of fabric characteristics and list examples of each. For example, under "weight," light fabrics could include organdy and chiffon; heavy fabrics could include canvas and duck.
3. Find examples in your wardrobe of woven and knitted fabrics. Bring some of them to class.
4. Do a research report on nonwoven fabrics made from manufactured fibers. Include information on how the fabrics are made and used.
5. Visit a fabric store and look at ten different bolts of fabric. Note the fiber content of each. Name some possible uses for each.

CHAPTER 12

COLORING AND FINISHING FABRICS

Most newly made fabrics do not look at all like the colorful, beautiful fabrics you see in stores. They may be gray or off-white. Instead of being soft and smooth, they are likely to be stiff and fuzzy. Newly made fabrics are called **greige** (GRAY) **goods.** If greige goods were made into garments, they would be unattractive and uncomfortable to wear. They might wrinkle badly or shrink when washed. To solve such problems, textile manufacturers color and finish greige goods.

This chapter describes how fabrics are colored and finished to make them more durable, comfortable, and attractive. You'll learn the answers to these questions:

- How is color added to fabrics?
- What are the functions of finishes?
- What are some of the typical finishes applied to fabrics?

Look for These Terms

greige goods
roller printing
screen printing
heat transfer printing
colorfastness
sizing

COLORING FABRICS

Color adds interest and emphasis to fabrics. Fabrics can be colored in many ways. Adding color to fabrics was first done by painting designs on cloth. Today some fabrics are machine painted. This process is called printing. Fabric is also colored by dyeing the fabric after it is woven or by dyeing the fibers or yarns before they are made into fabric.

PRINTING

Printed fabrics are easy to identify. The design is clearer and brighter on the front (right side) than on the back (wrong side). The back of the fabric appears dull or muted. Three types of printing are done in today's textile factories: roller printing, screen printing, and heat transfer printing.

Roller printing, also known as direct printing, uses a series of engraved rollers. Each roller prints a different color on the fabric. Today's technology can print sixteen colors on a fabric at a rate of two hundred yards per minute.

Screen printing is similar to stenciling. Fabric is placed under a framed screen which contains the desired design. The color is then forced through the screen with a roller or squeegee. This process is slow and therefore more expensive than roller printing.

Rotary screen printing is a recent development. In this process, the screen is a metal cylinder. Color is forced into the cylinder under pressure. It comes out through the screen as it is rolled over the cloth, leaving the design. This method is quicker and cleaner than flat screen printing.

Heat transfer printing can be used only on fabrics that can withstand high temperatures. A paper pattern containing the desired color and design is placed on the fabric. Heat is applied to transfer the color and design to the fabric. Perhaps you have ironed a transfer design onto a T-shirt. If so, you have done heat transfer printing.

Rotary screen printing.

DYEING

Dyeing is another way to add color to fabric. Unlike printing, which colors the surface of fabric, dyeing makes the color seem to be part of the fabric itself.

Dyeing is an ancient art. As early as 2500 B.C. the Egyptians were dyeing fabric yellow, green, red, or blue. The first dyes were natural. They were made from such things as flowers, leaves, berries, shellfish, and insects. In 1856 an English chemistry student, William Henry Perkin, discovered how to make a dye from coal. This was the beginning of synthetic dyes. Today there are over 7,000 different synthetic dyes or combinations of dyes.

—The Way It Was

THE ROYAL COLOR

Have you ever heard the expression "born to the purple"? It refers to someone of royal birth. The color purple is associated with royalty because, in ancient times, purple dye was rare and expensive.

The making of purple dye was perfected by the people of Phoenicia (fi-NISH-uh), a country on the eastern shore of the Mediterranean Sea. By 1400 B.C. the Phoenician city of Tyre had become famous for its purple dye, which was not only beautiful but also colorfast.

Tyrian purple was obtained from a small pouch in the body of the murex snail, a shellfish which lived in great numbers along the shores of the eastern Mediterranean. Obtaining the dye was slow work. The shells had to be broken one at a time and the pouches removed by hand. It took 3,880,000 murex snails to make one pound of dye. It's no wonder that only royalty and other very wealthy people could afford purple clothing!

Today, not even royalty can obtain natural Tyrian purple. The secret for making the dye was lost sometime in the fifteenth century A.D. Modern Tyrian purple is a synthetic dye.

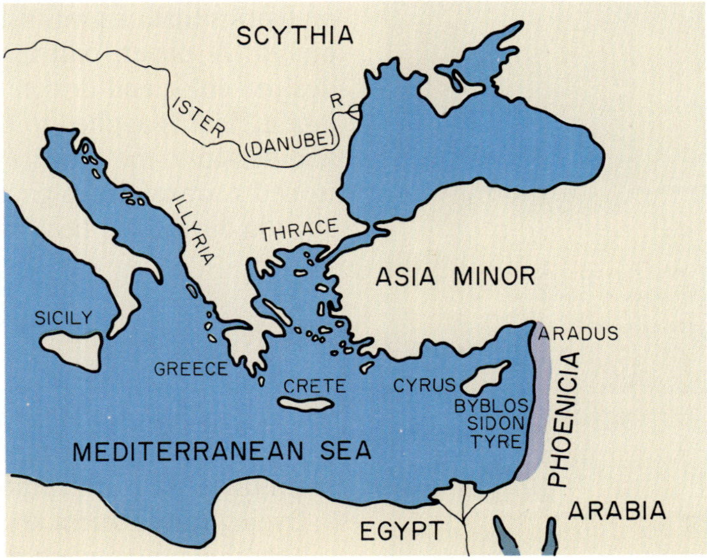

Jet-beck machines such as these are used to pressure-dye synthetic and blended fabrics.

There are four methods of dyeing. Each method is used at a particular stage in fabric construction.

- *Solution dyeing*—color is added to chemicals before they are made into manufactured fibers. These colors are the most resistant to fading.
- *Stock dyeing*—the fibers are dyed before they are spun into yarn.
- *Yarn dyeing*—the yarns are dyed after they are spun but before they are woven or knitted. Most checks, stripes, plaids, and herringbone designs are yarn dyed.
- *Piece dyeing*—the fabric is dyed after it is woven or knitted. Fabrics that are to be a solid color are usually piece dyed.

Dyeing has always been a complex craft requiring a high degree of skill. Today computers help take the guesswork out of making dyes. They can match colors and determine the right proportions for color mixes. Therefore manufacturers can maintain consistency and quality in their dyes.

COLORFASTNESS

All dyes and prints do not have the same degree of colorfastness. **Colorfastness** is the ability of color to remain the same after wear, cleaning, or storage. Some colors fade when exposed to sunlight. Others are affected by deodorants or perspiration. Some dyes rub off onto other materials or "bleed" when washed. Chlorine bleaches will remove color from most dyed fabrics.

The importance of colorfastness depends on the use of the fabric. If a garment will be washed many times, it is important that it be colorfast to washing. If you are buying a shirt, you want to purchase one that will not lose color or change color under the arms due to deodorants.

Manufacturers include colorfast information on labels. Generally, labels will describe the conditions under which the fabric is colorfast. "Colorfast to laundering" and "colorfast to sunlight" are two terms sometimes found on labels. Labels may also state, "Do not use chlorine bleach." Be sure to read labels to learn about colorfastness.

HELPFUL HINT: If you're unsure about a fabric, ask the salesperson.

Some garments are labeled "Wash separately." This means they are not colorfast, and the dye will "bleed" into the wash water. Other garments washed in the same water would pick up some of the color.

Getting Your Money's Worth

COLOR IT YOURSELF

You can add color to white, light colored, or faded fabrics, and you don't need a textile mill to do it! Fabric dyes and paints let you add your own designer touches to your wardrobe.

Fabric Dyes

Fabric dyes are used to color an entire garment. They are available in liquid and powder form. The dyes can be bought at most supermarkets and discount stores. Always read the package directions carefully before you start. Here are some general guidelines:

- The best fabrics for dyeing are washable ones of cotton, linen, wool, silk, rayon, nylon, and acetate. Do not use fabric dyes on 100 percent polyester, 100 percent acrylic, or fiberglass. Some fabrics have a water-resistant or stain-resistant finish. These will not take the dye well.
- Before you dye the entire garment, test dye a small piece that you have cut from the garment's seam allowance. That way, you can see whether the dye works on the fabric and the color is right.
- Remove any stains or spots and wash the garment before dyeing.
- Wear rubber gloves to avoid staining your hands.
- Clean all equipment, such as the washer or sink, immediately after use.
- The first few times you wash a dyed garment, some of the color may bleed into the wash water. Therefore you should wash the garment separately to avoid coloring other items.

Fabric Paints

To draw a design or write words on a garment, use fabric paints. These come in tubes that have a ball point. They are sold in many craft shops and discount stores. Complete instructions for use are on the package. Here are some basic guidelines:

- Wash and dry the garment before painting. Test the paint on a hidden part of the garment, such as a seam allowance, to make sure the fabric will absorb the paint.
- The paint may soak through the fabric. Put something under the fabric layer you're working on to protect the rest of the garment and the tabletop. You could use a paper grocery sack.
- When you have finished, wait at least two days before washing or dry-cleaning the garment.

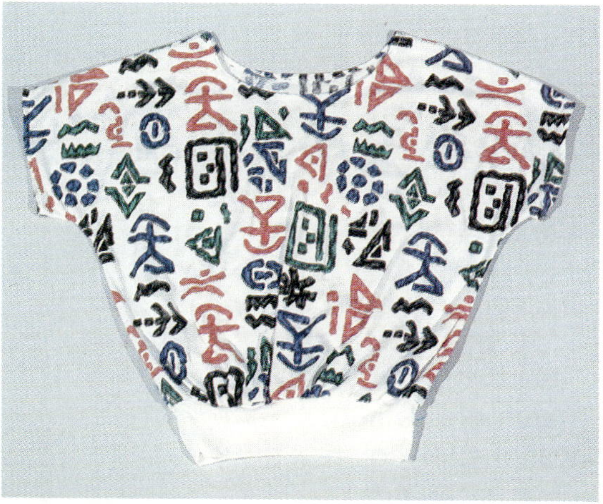

FINISHING FABRICS

Fabric finishes are treatments applied to the fabric. All fabrics are routinely given some type of finish. Some finishes are permanent. They last the lifetime of the fabric. Others are removed as the fabric is washed or dry-cleaned. Finishes do one or more of the following:

- improve appearance
- improve performance
- make it easier to take care of the fabric
- improve the safety of the fabric

One example of a fabric finish is mercerizing (MUR-suh-RISE-ing). In this process a chemical, sodium hydroxide, is applied to cotton fabric. Mercerizing strengthens the cotton and makes it easier to dye.

Many other finishes can be applied to fabrics. Some of these are described here.

- An acid solution may be applied to produce stiffness.

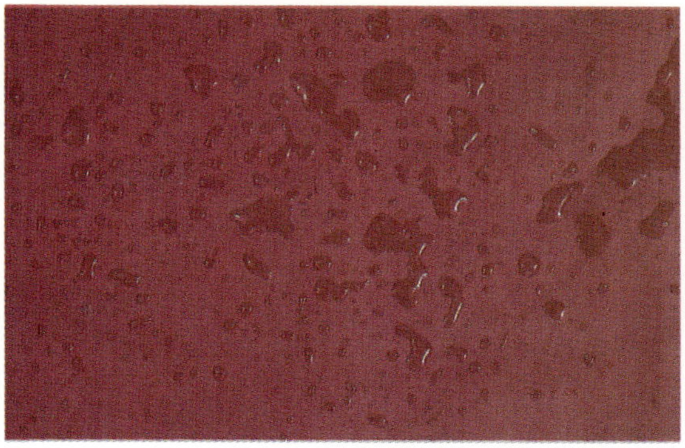

This fabric has been treated with a water-repellent finish. What uses, other than rainwear, might there be for water-repellent fabric?

- Wool fabrics are fulled. This process uses moisture, heat, friction, and pressure to soften the yarns and make them lie closer together. The result is a denser, softer fabric.
- Singeing is a process in which the fabric is passed over a flame or a heated copper plate. This burns off the fiber ends and produces a smoother fabric surface.
- A form of starch, resin, or gelatin may be applied to fabric to add body. This process is called **sizing.**
- A puckered effect is achieved for some fabrics by touching portions of the fabric with chemicals which cause these portions to shrink. The result is called a plissé (pli-SAY) print.
- Chemicals are often added to wools to repel moths.
- Chemicals may be added to fabrics to inhibit (restrain) the growth of bacteria.
- Fatty or oily substances combined with other chemicals are applied to fabrics to produce a water-repellent finish.

Plissé printing is usually done on cotton, rayon, or nylon. Plissé fabrics should not be ironed because that would flatten the puckered surface.

- Certain finishes are designed to help fabrics repel soil.
- Most cellulose-based fabrics are treated with synthetic resins to increase their wrinkle resistance.
- Some finishes provide resistance to fire. These flame-retardant finishes are required by law for some wearing apparel, especially children's sleepwear.

The fabric on the left was treated with a flame-retardant finish. The one on the right was not.

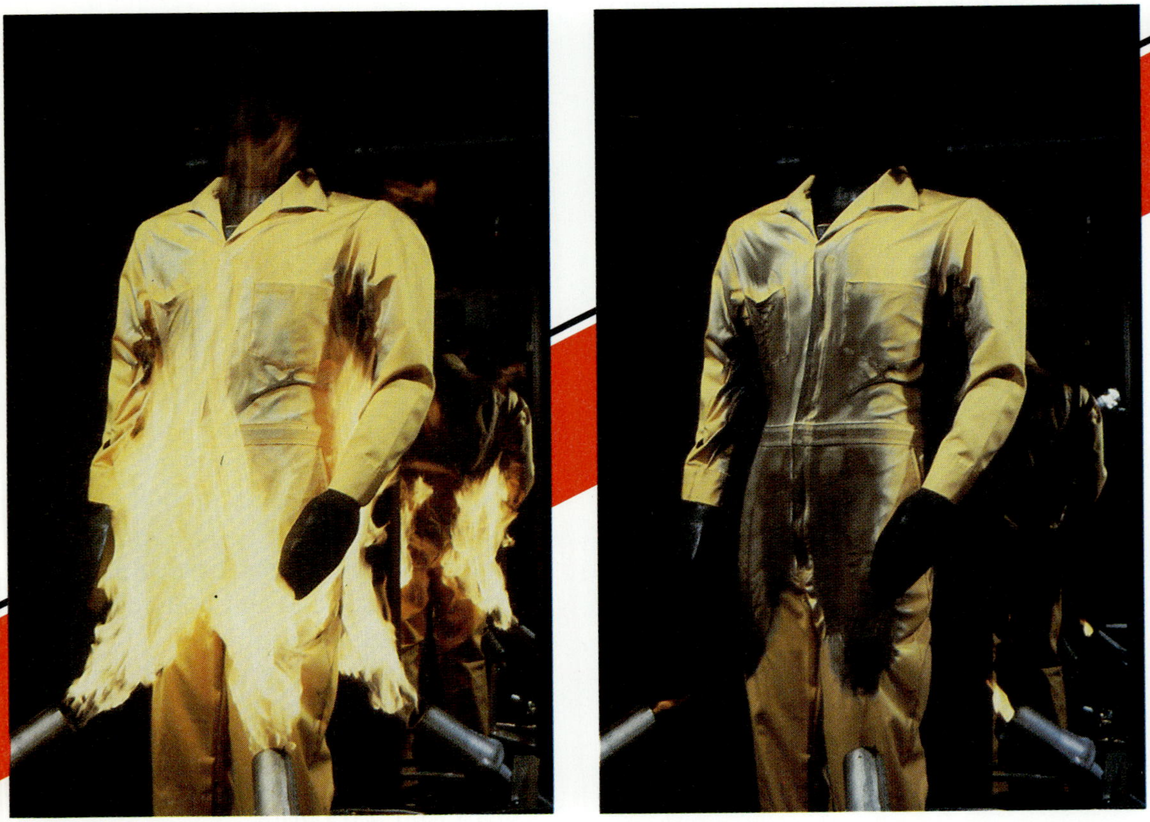

REVIEW-12

SUMMARY

Coloring improves the appearance of fabrics. Fabrics can be colored by printing or dyeing. Dyes and prints vary in their degree of colorfastness, so be sure to check care labels.

All fabrics are given some type of finish. A finish may improve appearance, improve performance, simplify care, or increase the fabric's safety.

CHECK YOUR KNOWLEDGE

1. What are greige goods?
2. How can printed fabrics be identified?
3. Name the three most common types of printing.
4. Describe rotary screen printing.
5. Describe the four methods of dyeing.
6. What is colorfastness?
7. *True or False:* All fabric finishes are permanent and cannot be washed out.
8. Name four benefits that finishes may provide.
9. What does mercerizing do for cotton?
10. Why are some fabrics deliberately singed?

EXTEND YOUR KNOWLEDGE

1. Bring to class examples of printed fabric and dyed fabric.
2. Design a print for a fabric that could be used for a child's sleeper. For a dress. For a shirt.
3. Write a research report on the methods used to dye fabrics in ancient times.
4. Find out what the following finishes mean: Sanforized®, Scotchgard®, Zepel®, Zelcon®, Bioguard®.
5. Do a report on the benefits and drawbacks of treating fabrics to make them flame-retardant.

BUYING CLOTHES

Remember the wardrobe planning you did in Chapter 9? First you identified your clothing needs. Then you looked at the clothes you have. Based on your activities, the season of the year, and what's "right" for you, you decided what your wardrobe lacked.

Now you're ready to shop. But wait! Where will you shop? How will you pay? What if you're not happy with your purchases? Buying clothes calls for decision making. In this unit, you'll learn how to make those decisions wisely.

Unit 4

CHAPTER 13

BEFORE YOU BUY: MAKING A PLAN

A clothing store is an exciting place. So many colorful, attractive things are on display! It makes you wish you could buy them all.

A store has one major goal in mind: to sell clothes. For that reason, the store displays clothing in a way that encourages you to buy. Will you be able to resist, or will you buy things you don't need? Will you perhaps pay too much for those you do need?

Before you shop, make a plan. Use what you have learned about decision-making to prepare for shopping. If necessary, review the decision-making steps on page 42. You'll save time, energy, and money, and you'll be happier with what you buy.

As you read this chapter, keep these questions in mind:

- How can you get the information you need to make wise buying decisions?
- Who or what influences your buying habits?
- What should you do to get ready for shopping?

Look for These Terms

information ads
comparison shopping

GATHERING INFORMATION

The first step in making any kind of decision is to gather information. You will probably need to know the following:

- where to find the type of clothing you want
- which stores carry your size and have the most variety in that size
- which stores carry designs suited to your lifestyle
- what price ranges are available
- when stores are open

Where can you find this information? The most common methods are by listening to and reading advertisements, by comparison shopping, and by asking friends and family members.

ADVERTISEMENTS

The object of a clothing ad is to make you want to buy. The ad may do so by appealing to your desire to look fashionable or to belong to a special group. Or the ad may give information about the product, such as sizes, uses, fabric, and price, in an attempt to persuade you to buy. Although there is nothing wrong with ads that show the latest fashions, **information ads** are usually more helpful for making a final buying decision.

Clothing ads usually appear on radio and TV and in newspapers and magazines.

Radio and TV Ads

Radio and television ads usually sell brand or store names rather than individual garments. As a rule, they do not give much information. However, by means of radio or TV you might learn:

- what stores carry the brand
- when a store is having a special sale
- a toll-free number to use for finding stores in your area

Magazine and Newspaper Ads

Magazine ads, like those on radio and TV, usually sell brand or store names. They also may give some product information. Once in a while they tell where you can find the item. In general, however, magazine ads give you the best idea of what's fashionable or how to wear certain garments.

What messages does this magazine ad send to the reader?

Most magazines are directed toward certain readers. *Seventeen,* for example, speaks to young women in their teens. Stores or manufacturers who feature clothing for that group usually advertise in *Seventeen.* Reading through magazines that most appeal to your lifestyle and age group can give you an idea of the stores and brand names you might want to look for.

Newspaper ads will give you the best information about what is available in your area. Since newspaper ads are usually in black and white, they do not focus as much on the looks of the product. Instead, they give more practical information, such as sizes, fabric content, prices, and store locations.

COMPARISON SHOPPING

When you go **comparison shopping,** you visit different stores or look at different catalogs to compare styles and values. You probably already have some idea of the styles and prices to be found in local stores. But have you ever really compared item for item?

Choose a common, simple item carried by most clothing stores, such as pantyhose or men's handkerchiefs. Then make a list of those stores you would like to compare. Go to each store on your list. Next to the store name, make a note of that store's price for the item. If you can, look for items with the same brand name or of similar quality. Then look for the same item in a different brand. How do the prices compare? Which stores carry the most variety or the widest price range? How do the stores compare as to quality?

Make the same comparison with catalogs. Then compare catalogs and stores. At first glance, catalog prices may seem cheaper, but you must usually pay postage and a handling charge as well. The total cost may therefore be the same or even higher than the store price.

You can do comparison shopping at home by looking at catalogs from various companies. Newspaper ads can also provide information about styles and prices.

FRIENDS AND FAMILY

The clothing needs of your friends and family are probably similar to your own. You do many of the same things together and go to the same places.

Your parents and other family members can probably give you an idea of the stores and type of clothing in your price range. They may also be able to advise you as to quality—whether a certain brand or the items from a certain store hold up well under use.

Your friends may be good sources of information about where to find fashionable or trendy clothes. But be doubly careful to comparison shop before you buy any trendy garments. Their quality may not be good, and they are often overpriced.

You learned many of your buying habits from your family.

WHY DO YOU BUY THE CLOTHES YOU DO?

Many things affect your buying habits. Your family, your friends, advertisements, and fashions and fads all influence your choices.

FAMILY

While you were growing up, your family made all your clothing choices for you. You probably had little to say about what you wore. In the process, you learned a certain style of dress. You also grew familiar with the kinds of stores in which your family shopped and the prices they paid.

Although now some of your clothing choices may differ from those of your parents, you may still have some of their buying habits. You may want to keep the same habits or change some, but you should be aware that they affect how you shop.

FRIENDS

Right now your friends may be the strongest influence on what you buy. People who go to school together or work in the same place want to feel as though they belong to the group. They feel more comfortable if they dress like everyone else.

During your teen years the pressure put on you to fit in with your friends may be very strong. Keep this in mind as you shop. Try not to make foolish purchases based on what your friends might be wearing. As long as your clothes in general fit in, you do not have to be a carbon copy of your friends. They must like you for what you are, not just for how you look.

Wearing the latest fad item makes us feel stylish, but fads never last long. Don't let fads use up the money you need for basic, longer-lasting clothing.

ADVERTISEMENTS

Advertising can be both a good and a bad influence. As you have already seen, ads carry important messages. They give us information about products and stores. They keep us informed about the latest fashions.

Advertising can be a bad influence if it causes you to pay too much or to buy something you don't really need. Keep in mind when you read ads that they are designed to make you think you can't live without the product. If you don't buy Brand X jeans you'll look lumpy, dumpy, and frumpy! But will you really? Brand X jeans may not be best for you at all. They may be cut wrong for your figure type. They may be overpriced. You may already own all the jeans you need.

HELPFUL HINT: Wise shoppers know advertising for what it really is—informative and fun, but not the last word on what they should buy.

FASHION AND FADS

Almost everyone buys clothing based on fashion. Even if you did not want to be fashionable, you would still have to buy what was available, and stores stock clothing based on fashion trends.

Fashion can be fun. New styles or "looks" make us feel attractive and on top of things. They make us feel good about ourselves.

Unfortunately, few people can afford to buy a completely new wardrobe every season. When you shop, remember that fashions, like advertisements, are created not just for our pleasure but to sell clothes. Manufacturers do not want you to wait until a garment is worn out before you replace it. They are hoping you like the current styles well enough to buy something new just to look up-to-date.

Fads inspire clothes worn just for fun. Their appeal usually does not last more than a few months. Obviously, they are not the sort of thing you would want to invest a lot of money in. The more extreme the style is, the more "out of it" it will look when its time is past. If you wish to follow clothing fads, choose those that do not cost a lot.

GETTING READY TO SHOP

Once you have gathered information, your shopping plan is almost finished. Only a few tasks remain: making lists, deciding whether to shop alone, and dressing for the job at hand.

MAKE LISTS

Don't waste time and energy going to stores that don't have the things you want. If necessary, call the store first to check their supply. Then make a list of the places you intend to go. Use the list as a sort of "travel" plan.

HELPFUL HINT: Group the stores by location so you won't be zigzagging back and forth across town.

Under the stores on your list, write the items you want to look for at each store. Don't try to make too many large purchases in one day. If you're tired or feel rushed, you may buy something you really don't want.

SHOULD YOU SHOP ALONE?

If you're uncertain about what looks best on you, you may want to take a friend or family member along. Pick a person whose taste is similar to yours and whose advice you can trust.

If you can get more done on your own, then you may want to shop alone. Even well-meaning friends can distract you from your goal and cause you to waste time.

DRESS FOR THE TASK

If you're shopping for jeans, then wear a shirt and shoes you'd wear with the jeans. If you're buying dress clothes, be sure you wear or take along dress shoes. Wear any special undergarments that might affect the looks of what you're buying. Men who are buying suits should wear a dress shirt and tie.

If you're trying to match an item you already own, wear the item or bring it along if possible. Clothes come in a huge variety of colors, and even shades that are similar may not be close enough.

If you have trouble making up your mind, shop with a family member or friend who can help you make decisions.

Getting Your Money's Worth

LOOK FOR THE LABEL

Consumer protection laws require that certain information be placed on labels or tags of clothing.

- *Fiber content.* The generic name and the percentage of each fiber making up a garment must be listed. The fiber making up the largest percentage is listed first. Other fibers are listed in descending order. Fibers that make up less than 5 percent of the fabric need not be listed unless they affect the garment's characteristics.
- *Care instructions.* These include basic information such as "Dry-clean only" or "Do not use chlorine bleach." Manufacturers must stand behind these instructions. If you follow the care instructions exactly and something goes wrong, you can return the garment.
  Makers are required to list only the best or tested care method. Others may also be safe. At the same time, harmful methods are not listed either. If washing will ruin a garment, the label does not have to say so.
- *Location of manufacture.* If the garment was imported, the name of the country where the garment was made must be listed.
- *Size.* The size must be stated. Often, it is on a separate label sewn into a seam.

The following kinds of information *may* appear on labels or tags. They are not required by law.

- *Trademark or brand name labels.* When you discover a brand that fits you well, you may wish to buy other garments by the same maker.
- *Store name.* Some stores buy directly from a factory and put their own label in a garment. But chances are good that, unlike brand name garments, clothing with a store name is not all produced by the same maker.
- *Certification labels.* These are like guarantees. They state that the garment will perform in a certain way under certain conditions.
- *Union labels.* These tell which union made the garment. They are found on garments made in the United States.
- *Logos.* These are symbols of a maker or an association. One example is the Wool Mark logo, which you may have seen on wool clothing.
- *Designer or signature labels.* These are like brand names. They are often placed on the outside of a garment as a status symbol. Garments with such labels are often more expensive.

Before you buy a garment, read the labels. You'll learn useful information that will help you make better buying decisions.

REVIEW-13

SUMMARY

Before you shop, make a plan. Gather as much information as possible about stores and the items you're looking for. Advertising, comparison shopping, and friends and family can all help you find what you're looking for. As you plan, be aware that your buying habits are affected by outside influences. Family, friends, advertising, and fashions and fads can all affect your clothing decisions. Your shopping plan should also include a list of things to buy and places to go. You should decide if you want to take a friend or family member along. You should also dress for the kind of clothing you intend to buy.

CHECK YOUR KNOWLEDGE

1. What is comparison shopping?
2. In what two ways does advertising persuade you to buy?
3. What information can be gathered from newspaper clothing ads?
4. What information might your family be able to give you about buying clothes?
5. During your teen years, what group probably has the strongest influence on your shopping habits?
6. When is advertising a bad influence?
7. Why shouldn't you spend a lot on a clothing fad?
8. Why should you make a "travel plan" before you shop?
9. What is the advantage of shopping with someone else?
10. How should you dress when you shop?

EXTEND YOUR KNOWLEDGE

1. Over the next week make a collection of newspaper and magazine clothing ads. Select five of each. Compare them as to information given and how they persuade people to buy.
2. Comparison shop for the following items: designer jeans, a pullover sweater, and a white shirt. Go to five stores. Report your findings to the class.
3. Pretend you want to buy a winter coat (or a raincoat). Write a brief description of what you'd like. Below it, list what you think your family and two close friends would say about the style. Which would have the most influence on you?
4. Design your own magazine or newspaper ad for a prom outfit.
5. Make a report to the class on clothing fads of the 1920s and 1930s. Who or what started the fads?

CHAPTER 14

WHEN YOU BUY: CARRYING OUT THE PLAN

Now that you've worked out your clothing needs and developed a plan of action, it's time for the fun part. It's time to shop!

But before you rush out the door, are you sure you know the best times and places to shop? There are also things to consider before you try on different garments.

As you study this chapter, you'll learn answers to these questions:

- When should you shop?
- Where should you shop?
- How can you get your money's worth?
- How will you pay?

When you have considered these things carefully, you're ready to go!

Look for These Terms

seasonal sale
personal shoppers
seconds
consignment
thirty-day charge account
revolving charge account
layaway plans

WHEN TO SHOP

Some times are better for shopping than others. How do you decide whether it's a good time to shop? Consider the amount of time you have, the time of the day, and whether there are any sales going on.

THE TIME YOU HAVE

If you can, shop when you're not rushed. You will be more likely to make a wise purchase if you can look in several stores and compare quality and prices. If you have only twenty minutes to buy a new shirt, you will probably have to get it at the first store you enter. Unless you are lucky, you may not be happy with your purchase later.

Some items may require more time to buy than others. For example, you may want to try on several pairs of shoes to be sure you choose the most comfortable. More expensive items also deserve more consideration.

THE TIME OF DAY

The time of day can also affect shopping. Do you know the best time for trying on shoes? Shoes should be tried on later in the day. If your feet are the type that swell, you will want to be sure the new shoes will still be comfortable after a long day.

Stores are often less busy at certain times. Your shopping can be more relaxed if you don't have to fight crowds. For most stores, the weekends are busy. During the hours right after school, however, there may be fewer shoppers.

SALE TIMES

A good time to buy something you need is when it's on sale. Most clothing stores advertise sales in the newspaper and on radio and television. Buying clothing on sale can save you money.

People buy most of their clothing for a certain season. You probably have two different wardrobes, one for winter and one for summer. Often the biggest savings a store offers are at a **seasonal sale**—all clothing for a certain season is marked down.

Before a season arrives, watch for "pre-seasonal" sales. These sales are designed to:

- sell items left over from the year before
- catch your attention and start you thinking about the new season

Before you buy a sale item, ask yourself: (1) Do I need it? (2) How does the sale price compare to regular prices elsewhere? (3) Is the garment well made?

The best bargains are at the "end-of-season" sales. New-season garments are on their way to the stores. The stores want to get rid of as many of the past season's items as possible. They reduce prices, sometimes a second and third time, to sell as much as they can.

The key to taking advantage of seasonal sales is planning. Plan what you need, then wait. Watch for the sales to be advertised. Or ask store clerks when sales are scheduled.

HELPFUL HINT: Shop as early as you can. If you wait until the last day, sale choices will be fewer.

WHERE TO SHOP

There are many types of places to buy clothing. Choices include department stores, discount or variety stores, clothing outlets, specialty shops, mail order, and used-clothing sources. Consider what you want to buy, how much you can spend, and how far you need to travel before deciding where to shop.

Shopping malls are popular. What are the advantages of shopping in a mall? What are the disadvantages?

DEPARTMENT STORES

There are two advantages to shopping in department stores. They generally have the largest, most fashionable selection of clothing. They also offer many services. Some offer free delivery, free alterations, charge accounts, and mail and telephone order services. Some even have **personal shoppers**—people who will help you shop or even do your shopping for you and send the items to your home. Most department stores have a complaint department to respond to consumer needs. Because of the selection and services they offer, these stores usually have higher prices.

DISCOUNT AND VARIETY STORES

These stores carry a wide variety of name brand items at reduced prices. They keep their costs down by offering few services and locating in low-rent areas. These savings are then passed on to the customer. The clothing selection is not always large and may be limited to more casual styles.

HELPFUL HINT: Learn the store's policy on repairs, exchanges, and refunds before you buy.

Outlet stores offer low prices on seasonal, discontinued, or flawed merchandise.

OUTLET STORES

Outlet stores buy clothes at a low cost from manufacturers or other stores at the end of a season. They then sell to customers at a lower price. Some outlet stores sell **seconds**—garments which are flawed or not of standard retail quality. Some outlets are operated by the manufacturers themselves near the factory or warehouse. They, too, carry returned, flawed, or discontinued merchandise.

Clothes sold in an outlet store may be without labels. If so, ask for care instructions before you buy. Always look the clothing over carefully. Also, check the store's return policy. Most outlet stores accept returns, but some may not.

SPECIALTY SHOPS

Specialty shops—also called boutiques—usually sell one kind of item. They can be compared to one department in a department store. Some shops may feature such things as all handmade items or garments in one size range. The salespeople often give more personal attention to each shopper. Usually they will special-order garments in a color or style that is not in the store. Prices compare with those in department stores.

MAIL ORDER

Shopping from catalogs was popular when people lived on farms or in small towns and had to travel long distances to shop. Today, catalog shopping is handy for those who wish to save time and gasoline. However, shipping or delivery charges must be added to the cost of the merchandise.

When you order from a catalog, you can't try the item on first. If it doesn't fit, it may have to be returned. Returning takes time. Sometimes the customer must pay the cost of shipping the garment back.

Helpful hint: Find out about the return policy before you order.

Some stores have a mail-order department. You can order, pick up, and return catalog merchandise there.

Getting Your Money's Worth

ORDERING FROM A CATALOG

Mail order shopping can be fun. Catalogs used to be called "wish books" because most of us wish we could order everything!

Before you decide to buy from a catalog, however, add up your total purchases. Include any tax, shipping, or handling charges. How do prices compare to store prices? Be sure you are not paying a lot extra for the fun of wish-book shopping.

When you have made up your mind what things you want to buy, gather the following information about each item:

- page of the catalog on which it appears
- name of the item
- how many of each item you want to buy
- price for each single item
- total price for each item
- size
- color
- any personalizing, such as initials

Be sure when you give details, such as size, that you do it exactly the way the instructions tell you to. If the size is given as "S," then don't write "small." Most catalog orders are fed into computers. If you state the information in a slightly different way, the computer may reject your order.

For most catalog shopping, you may order by mail or by phone. Include or have ready the following:

- your name
- your address
- your phone number, if needed
- total cost of your order, plus tax, shipping, and handling
- any payment or charge card information needed—DO NOT SEND CASH

Keep a list of what you ordered, and note when you placed the order. Also keep on hand the company's address or customer service number. If you don't receive your order when promised or within a reasonable time, write or call the company and ask about it.

Most catalog companies guarantee your money back if you're not happy with your purchase. If you picked up the item at a store's catalog department, then all you have to do is take it back. If the item was mailed, be sure you check the instructions on how to make returns. Some companies ask that you write to them first about the problem. Wrap the item as carefully as it was wrapped when you received it. Include labels or tags. Be sure you include your name and address, too. Some companies include a return form to fill out. For others you must enclose a letter.

Garage sales and yard sales are good places to look for used clothing, especially children's wear.

USED-CLOTHING SOURCES

Some stores specialize in used clothing. Often these stores sell on **consignment.** People bring clothes they no longer want to the store. If the store manager sells the clothes, he or she gives the original owner a percentage of the payment. If the clothes are not sold within a certain time, they are returned to the owner.

Other sources of used clothing include garage and yard sales, flea markets, bazaars, and estate sales. These usually last only a day or two. Watch newspaper ads and yard signs for information about such events.

You can find some real bargains in used clothing, if you have time to hunt for them. Always check the clothing carefully for stains, flaws, or needed repairs. There are no returns or refunds, so be sure the garment is something you want and need.

IS IT A GOOD BUY?

Most of us do not have unlimited funds to spend on clothing. If we make an unwise purchase, we may be wasting our hard-earned money. But even for those who do not have to watch their pennies, a bad bargain is still a bad bargain. Who wants a closet full of clothes that fall apart or are unattractive?

How do you know if you're getting your money's worth when you shop? The two most important things to consider are garment quality and fit.

JUDGING QUALITY

Quality means that a garment is well made with good fabric. Quality means it will wear well. See the table on pages 148 and 149 for features you can look for in a garment to help determine its quality.

Look for quality in clothes you plan to wear often or for a long time. For example, quality is probably more important in a pair of jeans than in a beach cover-up. You probably won't wear the beach cover-up nearly as often as the jeans.

Don't forget quality when you buy items on sale. Look for flaws or damage. Damaged merchandise may have a bargain price tag, but the needed repairs might cost more than the money saved.

Quality Features in Clothing

Things to Check	Good	Poor
General appearance	■ Clean, no tears or snags ■ All parts complete	■ Soiled, torn, or snagged ■ Missing belts, buttons, etc.
Fabric	■ Suitable weight and texture ■ Resists wrinkling ■ Durable ■ Stripes or plaids match	■ Unevenly woven or knitted, lacks body ■ Wrinkles easily ■ Stripes or plaids do not match
Seams	■ Close stitching ■ ½″ or more seam allowance ■ Edges finished and reinforced at places of strain ■ Seams lie flat; hang straight ■ Thread matches fabric	■ Loose, uneven stitching ■ Less than ½″ seam allowance ■ Edges raw, with no reinforcement ■ Seams pucker; hang crooked ■ Thread does not match
Collars and Lapels	■ Lie flat and smooth	■ Pucker and pull
Topstitching (stitching that shows on outside of garment)	■ Even, firm	■ Uneven and loose
Sleeves	■ Set into armholes evenly, without twist or pucker ■ Both sleeves the same	■ Twist or pucker at armhole ■ Uneven in length
Waist	■ Waistband straight and smooth ■ If garment designed for belt, waistband has at least 5 belt loops (one in center back) sewn securely	■ Waistband crooked or puckered ■ No belt loop in back
Fasteners	■ Firmly attached ■ Extra button included ■ Zippers lie flat ■ Thread matches fabric	■ Loosely attached ■ Zippers pucker ■ Thread does not match
Pockets	■ Lie smooth and flat; have reinforced stitching at corners	■ Bunch or pucker; no reinforced stitching at corners

(Continued on next page)

Quality Features in Clothing (Continued)

Things to Check	Good	Poor
Hem	■ Even; hangs straight ■ Deep enough to let down ■ Stitches invisible on outside	■ Uneven ■ Less than 2″ deep ■ Stitches visible on right side of garment
Care	■ Label included ■ Fabric is colorfast ■ All parts of garment can be cleaned the same way	■ No label ■ Difficult to clean or iron

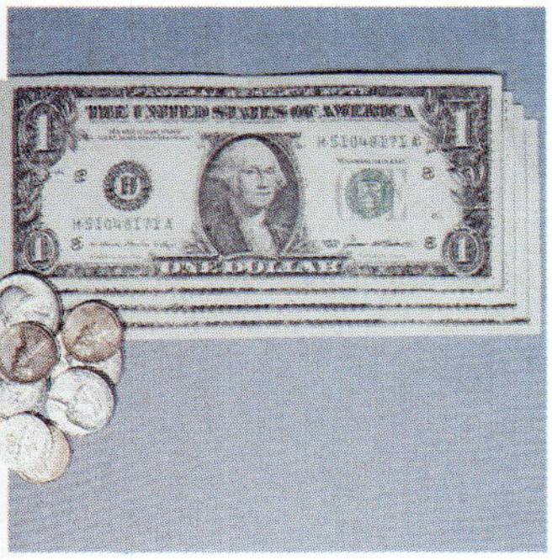

Getting Your Money's Worth

THE 29¢ JEANS

Cost-per-wearing is what getting your money's worth is all about. For example, let's say you have just bought a pair of jeans. If you wear them twice a week for the next year, that's 104 wearings. If you paid $30 for them, they will have cost you about 29¢ per wearing. The jeans are a bargain!

But what if you pay $30 for a beach cover-up? If you wear it twice a week for 10 weeks during the summer, it costs you $1.50 per wearing. That's a pretty expensive investment!

As a rule of thumb, it's best to put the most money into those garments you wear the most.

Basic size categories for women and girls. In addition, there are subcategories, such as petite and tall sizes.

GETTING A GOOD FIT

The fit of a garment is how it conforms to your body structure. The desired fit in clothing changes with fashion. At one time, the baggy look may be popular. A few years later, close-fitting garments may be in fashion. There are no definite rules for clothing styles. However, regardless of styles or personal preference, all garments should:

- allow for body movement
- be attractive for your body type

Clothes

Sizes are a guide to how clothes may fit. However, sizes vary with manufacturers. Some manufacturers allow more ease, or room for movement, in their clothes than others. Less expensive garments tend to run smaller. The cut or style of a garment may also affect the fit.

Sizes are based on a set of body measurements, such as the chest or bust, waist, and hips. For example, a size 10 dress is designed for a woman who measures about 34 inches at the bust, 26 inches at the waist, and 36 inches at the hips.

For females, there are six basic size groups. For most groups, there are also variations for petite and tall figures.

- *Girls'.* Designed for small, undeveloped figures.
- *Young Junior/Teen.* Also called preteen. For young, developing figures.
- *Junior.* Designed for teens and young women with a well-proportioned but slender figure. These sizes have less fullness and a shorter back waist length than misses' sizes.

Is It a Good Fit?

Here are some features to look for when trying on a garment.

Comfort

Can you bend, stretch, sit, and walk with ease? Does the waistline stay in place when you bend over? Can you lift your arms over your head with ease? Is the neck opening comfortable?

Construction

- Does the garment hang smoothly, without pulling or sagging?
- Are seams in the right places? Armhole seams should be at the edge of the shoulder, unless the garment is designed otherwise. Side seams should fall in a straight line. Folds or pleats should fall evenly. Darts should point to the fullest part of the body.
- Do buttonholes, zippers, and other closures lie smoothly?
- Do long sleeves cover your wrist bone?
- Is the hemline even around the bottom?

Style and Color

- Do the style and color hide features you don't want to call attention to?
- Do they accent features you wish to highlight?

If all answers are yes, then this garment is a good fit for you.

- *Misses'.* For a well-proportioned and well-developed figure.
- *Half-Size.* For full-figured but short-waisted women. Waist and hips are larger in proportion to bust than other figure types.
- *Women's.* Designed for a larger, more mature figure.

For males there are three basic size groups. Within each group are variations for shorter, taller, slimmer, or heavier figures.

- *Boys'.* Designed for small, undeveloped bodies. Chest and seat are about the same size.
- *Teen Boys'.* Also called student sizes. For slim teens and young men. Larger chest and thinner waist in proportion to seat.
- *Men's.* Designed for adult figures.

Basic size categories for boys and men.

Some types of clothing are labeled by the body measurement. Men's dress shirts, for example, are sized by neck and sleeve measurements. A 15/33 shirt is sized for a 14 ½ inch neck and 33 inch sleeve length. (The extra ½ inch at the neck is for wearing ease. The sleeve length is measured from the bone at the base of the back neck, across the shoulder, around a bent elbow, to the wrist bone.) Men's pants are sized by waist and inseam measurements. (The inseam is the inside leg measurement, from the crotch to the ankle bone.)

Loose-fitting garments, such as robes, may be sized simply as Small, Medium, Large, or Extra Large. For women, Small equals misses' size 8 to 10; Medium equals size 10 to 12; and Large equals size 12 to 14. For men, Small is for a chest measurement of 34 inches to 36 inches. Medium is for 38 inches to 40 inches. Large is for 42 inches to 44 inches, and Extra Large is for 46 inches to 48 inches.

Remember, the fit varies with the manufacturer and the style. You may need to try on several different sizes to find the best fit for you.

Shoes

Both feet should be measured when you are buying shoes. Some people have one foot that is larger than the other. They should buy shoes the size of the larger foot.

Shoes should be ½ inch longer than your longest toe when you're standing. Be sure to walk around in a pair of shoes before you buy them. Your toes should not be pinched. If the heels slip, the shoes are too large.

Remember when buying shoes:

- Leather softens with wear; plastic doesn't.
- Leather allows moisture to escape; plastic doesn't.
- Suede needs to be brushed frequently and can be damaged by water.
- You don't need much toe room in sandals, so try a half-size smaller.
- Padded insoles absorb shock and are therefore more comfortable.

When trying on shoes, walk around in them. If the shoes pinch or slip don't buy them.

If a garment needs only minor alterations in order to fit you, it may be worthwhile to buy it and have it altered.

Planning for Alterations

Sometimes a garment is just what you've been looking for, but it's a little too big or too small. A seam may need to be taken in or let out or a hemline adjusted. If you like the garment well enough, you may wish to buy it and make alterations.

Some stores make alterations as a part of their service. Other stores charge for alterations. Be sure to get an estimate of the alteration cost before you buy the garment. Or, if you can sew, you may wish to make your own alterations.

To tell if a garment can be altered, look closely at its fabric, design, and construction. A tightly woven fabric can withstand alterations much better than a loosely woven fabric. Check the label. If the fabric was treated with a wrinkle-resistant or wash-and-wear finish, holes made by stitching will not close up again. In this case, letting out a seam would not be a good idea.

Check the width of the seams. After being let out, a seam should still be at least 1/4 inch wide. Seams should not be taken in more than 3/4 inch. If more is taken in, the look of the garment may be affected.

If a garment is too short, check if there is enough fabric for the hem to be let down. If the garment is too long, the hem can be taken up.

HOW TO PAY

After you have selected a garment, there is still one more decision to make. How will you pay for it? There are two basic ways to pay for the clothes you want to buy: cash or credit.

Paying cash is the least expensive way to buy clothes. There is only one payment and no interest charge. The disadvantage is that your ready cash cannot be used for other things.

When you buy on credit, you promise to pay later. You don't have to have the money with you at the time you buy a garment. Instead, you can keep your money in a savings account, earning interest, until a payment is due. The disadvantage is that credit usually costs extra in interest charges. Some credit card companies also charge a yearly fee for the use of the credit card. There are several methods of buying on credit:

- A **thirty-day charge account** is an agreement to pay the total amount of the charge within thirty days. If you make full payment in thirty days, there is no interest charge. If you do not make full payment, interest is added. Your account may even be cancelled.
- With a **revolving charge account** you do not have to pay the entire amount at once. You are billed each month. Interest is charged on the amount you owe and is added to your bill.
- **Layaway plans** are a form of credit. You place a deposit on a garment and then make payments at regular intervals. The store holds the garment until no payments remain. There is no interest charged on a layaway account. However, a fee may be added to cover the store's costs of handling the layaway.

Credit is useful if handled wisely. Charge only an amount you are certain you can pay. Sometimes people use credit as though they weren't really spending money at all. It's too easy for them to charge something and worry about the money later on. Before long they are over their heads in debt. The fun of buying a garment is lost if you do not pay as wisely as you shop.

Helpful hint: Keep a record of your charges by saving the receipts. They will help you to keep track of your spending. They are also useful for checking the accuracy of the bill.

What are the advantages of paying cash?

REVIEW-14

SUMMARY

The time when you shop depends on how much time you have to spend, the best times for buying certain items, and the times a store has its sales. Places to shop include department stores, discount and variety stores, clothing outlets, specialty shops, mail order, and used-clothing sources.

To be sure you get your money's worth when you buy a garment, you must consider the garment's quality and fit. Sometimes alterations, if they are minor, can make a garment a good buy.

Your clothing purchases may be made with cash or credit. The different credit plans usually cost you money in the form of interest. As a result, your clothing costs are higher.

CHECK YOUR KNOWLEDGE

1. What is a seasonal sale?
2. How can the time of day affect your shopping?
3. What is the difference between a department store and a discount store?
4. What is an outlet store?
5. What are the two things to consider when judging whether a garment is a good bargain?
6. Name the six categories of females' sizes.
7. Name the three categories of males' sizes.
8. Even if you know your size, you should try on a garment before buying it. Why?
9. What is the advantage to paying cash for a garment?
10. What is a revolving charge account?

EXTEND YOUR KNOWLEDGE

1. Find out the hours; the return, check cashing, and layaway policies; type of clothing sold; and credit plans for five stores in your area. Make a chart showing your findings.
2. Visit a used-clothing store in your town. Look at what they have available in jeans. Tell the class what you learned.
3. Look through your closet for an item you haven't worn in a year or so. Why did you buy it? Why did you stop wearing it? If you were to shop for the same item again, what would you do differently?
4. Make a report to the class on the use of credit today. Find out how much the average person pays to use it.
5. Make a report to the class on shoe quality. If possible, interview a shoe repair person and find out what to look for when choosing shoes that hold up well.

CHAPTER 15

AFTER YOU BUY: EVALUATING THE RESULTS

How do you know if you've made the right clothing decisions? Some decisions are easier to evaluate than others. For example, if you lived during the Stone Age and needed a new outfit, you might select a tiger with a nice set of stripes. Then you'd walk up to him and bean him with a rock. But what if the rock wasn't heavy enough or the tiger had an especially hard head? You'd know right away if you had made the wrong decision. Your mistake would probably be hot on your heels.

If you buy the wrong items in a store, they will not get up and chase you. But other things may go wrong. A shirt may shrink even though you followed washing instructions. A pair of shoes may fall apart after one wearing.

In this chapter you will find answers to these questions:

- What are your responsibilities as a consumer?
- What are your rights?
- If something goes wrong, what should you do?

Look for These Terms

refunds
warranty
shoplifters

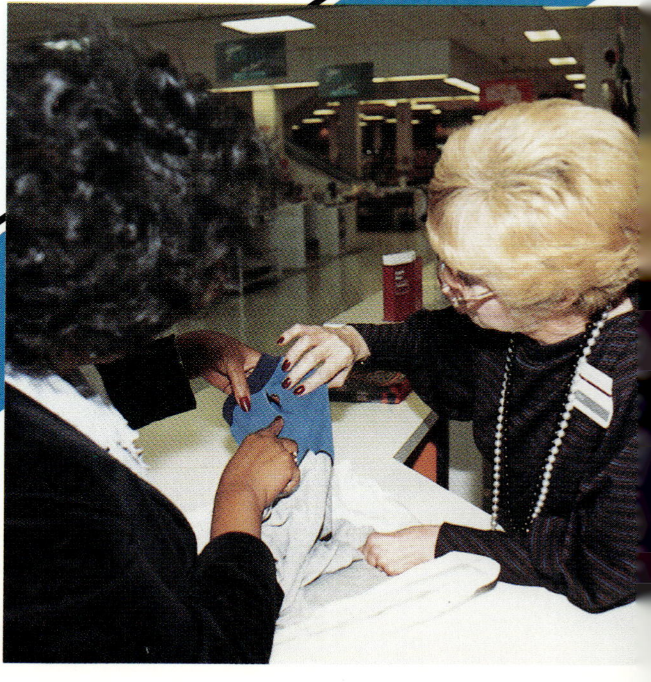

YOUR RESPONSIBILITIES

Most of us want a store to treat us right. We want helpful, courteous clerks and reasonable prices. We want to be able to exchange items when necessary. But if we expect fair treatment from stores, we have to be willing to be fair ourselves. We must be informed and thoughtful shoppers.

BE INFORMED

Before you make a purchase, learn a store's policies.

- Are returns accepted? Is there a time limit?
- Do they give **refunds** (give money back) or only credit?
- Are sale items returnable?
- Do they accept charge cards? Which ones?
- Do they accept personal checks?
- What is their layaway policy?

Know the store's hours. Don't go in at five minutes to closing and expect to try on ten different garments. Store employees have a right to go home at quitting time just as you do.

Don't expect salespeople to have all the facts on every garment. Read labels. If you don't recognize the name of a fabric but need care information, do some research. Fashion and consumer magazines often publish articles about such things as fasteners and fabrics.

Save all receipts, tags, or warranties that come with the item. (A **warranty** is a written promise that a product will perform as stated.) The store may not accept returns if you can't prove you bought the items there.

Be aware of current events. For example, did you know that certain designer clothes have been copied and sold for the real thing? Like counterfeit money, they look the same but aren't. Informed shoppers are less likely to be cheated.

HELPFUL HINT: Several consumer magazines and books are published regularly to help shoppers choose products. Check your local library for copies.

BE THOUGHTFUL

When you go through racks of clothing or try on garments, treat them gently. If you tear off labels or loosen buttons, you make extra work for store employees. If you rip a garment or soil it, the store may not be able to sell it. That would cause the store to lose money. To make up for the loss, the store owners may raise prices.

This garment fell off the rack. What might happen if the shopper left it on the floor?

When you've finished trying on garments, don't leave them in the fitting room. They'll be knocked on the floor or will get in the way of other shoppers. Put them on the rack outside the fitting rooms or return them to their original places.

If you must return an item you've bought, take it back as soon as possible and in the same condition in which you bought it. If something has gone wrong with it, explain to the clerk. Be patient and reasonable. After all, the clerk isn't the one who made the item. If you damaged the item yourself, don't expect the store to accept it back.

Keep in mind that costs for things like damaged merchandise are usually passed on to consumers. If you're a thoughtful shopper, you'll be doing yourself a favor in the long run.

Perspective

SHOPLIFTING: WHO REALLY GETS HURT?

In a recent year, the amount of money stores lost from theft reached almost $8 billion. About a third of such thefts are carried out by **shoplifters**—people who hide some item on their person and then walk out with it.

Many stores have installed protective devices to stop shoplifters. One device is a video camera mounted near the ceiling that keeps an eye on people as they shop. In a back room a guard watches on a TV screen what the camera sees. If anything suspicious happens, the guard contacts other guards on the floor of the store, and the shoplifter is caught.

Another device is a plastic tag attached to each garment. The tag must be removed with a special tool. If someone tries to leave the store with a garment and the tag is still attached, an alarm goes off.

Store owners are spending more than ever on ways to stop shoplifters. Who really pays for these devices and for the stolen merchandise? The consumer, of course. Store owners must raise prices on the things you buy to make up for their losses. Shoplifters do not really steal from what they think is a big company with an endless supply of money and goods. They steal from you.

The best way to help keep the costs of theft down is to be a concerned citizen. Report shoplifters to store personnel. If any of your friends suggest shoplifting for "fun," tell them who really gets hurt.

YOUR RIGHTS

Years ago shoppers had to be pretty careful. If they bought shoddy merchandise or were cheated in other ways, little could be done. Then in 1962, because many people had complaints about products, President John F. Kennedy urged Congress to do something about how consumers were treated. Laws were soon passed that gave all consumers these rights:

- *The Right to Safety.* What you buy should not be dangerous to your health or safety.
- *The Right to Be Informed.* What you learn about an item through advertising, labeling, or other means must be true. You have a right to enough facts to make a good choice.
- *The Right to Choose.* A variety of goods and services at reasonable prices should be available to you.
- *The Right to Be Heard.* The government must listen to what you have to say and must enforce consumer laws.
- *The Right to Redress.* Any wrong done to you must be corrected.
- *The Right to Consumer Education.* A means of learning how to be a better consumer must be available to you.

As you have already learned, the United States government has also made a number of laws having to do with fabrics, labels, and consumer credit. All these laws protect you as a consumer.

Many manufacturers have their own sets of standards which their products must meet. Some even put their products through independent testing laboratories to be sure the quality is good.

If a manufacturer or store does not respect your rights, there are government and private agencies that can help you. The Better Business Bureau is one of the private agencies. It can tell you if other people have complained about a firm. It can also help settle disputes.

HELPFUL HINT: The Better Business Bureau and other local agencies are listed in your phone book.

HOW TO COMPLAIN

If something is wrong with a purchase you have made, don't be afraid to do something about it. At the same time, no matter how disappointed you are, be reasonable and courteous. What happened is usually not the clerk's fault. Don't take your disappointment out on her or him.

When you have to complain, follow these steps:

1. Return the product to the store where you bought it. Be sure you have the sales slip and any tags that came with the garment. If the store has a customer service department, go there. Otherwise, try a salesperson or the manager. Most complaints can be taken care of at the store.

2. If store personnel can't help you, write a letter to the store president or owner. If necessary, call the store office and ask for the president's name and business address. Send along photocopies of the sales slip, any special tags, and any canceled checks. Never send originals.

No matter how you were treated in the store, be sure your letter is polite and businesslike. Include your name, address, and phone number. Give a simple but complete explanation of what happened. Include any special facts needed, such as style number and store location. Then tell what you would like done about the problem.

HELPFUL HINT: Keep a copy for your own records.

Below is a sample complaint letter.

3. If the store can't help, write to the manufacturer. Address your letter to either the customer relations department or the president. Your library can help you find the correct name and address. Enclose copies of any letters you sent to the store.

4. If still nothing has been done, contact the Better Business Bureau or a government consumer protection agency in your area. Look in the white pages under the name of your city, state, or county. The agency will tell you what further steps to take. If a local newspaper or radio station helps with consumer complaints, you may also want to contact them.

If all else fails, you may have to take legal action. If your area has a legal referral service, it can advise you of what to do next.

Phone: 555-6471
471 Hope St.
Weeping Willow, CO 00000
August 17, 19XX

Ms. Elizabeth Goleman, President
New Design Shops
2245 Stanley St.
Boston, MA 00000

Dear Ms. Goleman:

On July 25 I purchased a cotton sweater for $21.04 from your New Design Shop in Denver, Colorado. The manufacturer is Cuddly Sweaters, and the style number is 617. Copies of my sales receipt and the sweater care label are attached.

I wore the sweater twice and then washed it. The instructions on the care label said to use a cold water wash and to dry flat. That is what I did. When the sweater was dry, however, it had shrunk so much it did not fit me any longer.

On August 10 I tried to return the sweater to the New Design Shop in Denver. I spoke to the manager, Mr. Grundle. He told me I should have dry-cleaned the sweater instead of washing it. He refused to refund my money.

As I understand it, the care label is supposed to tell the approved cleaning method. If dry cleaning was the best method, wouldn't the label have said so?

Since I followed instructions and the sweater was ruined, I would appreciate your refunding my money. If you'd like me to send the sweater directly to you so you can see it for yourself, I'd be happy to do so.

Thank you for your help.

Yours truly,

Angela Mariko

Angela Mariko

REVIEW-15

SUMMARY

As a consumer you have both rights and responsibilities. Your responsibilities are to be informed about stores and products and to be a thoughtful shopper. Your rights entitle you to fair treatment from stores and manufacturers. If you must complain about a product, do so courteously. First contact the store, then the manufacturer, and then consumer agencies.

CHECK YOUR KNOWLEDGE

1. Name three ways you can be a thoughtful shopper.
2. When you finish trying on a garment and don't want to buy it, what should you do with it?
3. How does a store pay for the cost of goods damaged by shoppers?
4. Name the six rights you legally have as a consumer.
5. How do manufacturers help maintain product quality?
6. How can the Better Business Bureau help consumers?
7. What four steps should you take in making a complaint?
8. Why should you be courteous when complaining?
9. If you have to write a complaint letter, what information should be in it?
10. Why should you keep tags or receipts for items you buy?

EXTEND YOUR KNOWLEDGE

1. Make a report to the class on the history of the consumer movement.
2. Visit five clothing stores. Take a look at the fitting rooms for a person of your sex. Were clothes left there? Were racks available for them outside? Was there an attendant? Report your findings to the class.
3. Interview the owner of a small, local clothing store. Find out about the costs involved in merchandise damaged by customers.
4. Make a poster illustrating the six consumer rights.
5. Look through the back issues of consumer magazines at your local library. Find an article related to clothing. Read it and report on it to the class.

MAKING CLOTHES

Sewing is:

- fun
- relaxing
- creative
- a career opportunity
- a form of communication

and many more things to lots of people. By making clothes for yourself, you can save money and have exactly the look you want. Clothes you make for family or friends can be a special gift. Your interest in sewing may even lead to a career. (In Unit 7 you'll learn about jobs in the clothing industry.)

To be able to sew is a skill. Like playing basketball or the guitar, sewing is learned through training and practice. The more you do it, the better you will become. This unit covers the basics of making clothes. You'll find out how to select a pattern and fabric and how to lay out the pattern on the fabric. You'll learn how to cut out, sew, fit, and press garments. You'll also learn how to add finishing touches that will give your project a designer look.

Unit 5

CHAPTER 16

CHOOSING THE PATTERN, AND NOTIONS FABRIC,

The first step in making a garment is choosing a pattern, fabric, and notions. If you choose well, you'll be on your way to making a successful garment, one that is well made and looks good on you. A successful garment gives you a feeling of pride and a sense of accomplishment.

The information in this chapter will help you select patterns, fabrics, and notions. When you know the answers to the following questions, you can begin your sewing project.

- How can you select a pattern that will be right for your figure type and for the garment you are making?
- What should you look for when choosing fabric?
- How should you select notions?

Look for These Terms

pattern
fitting ease
nap
off-grain
remnants
drape
body
notions
interfacing

SELECTING A PATTERN

The **pattern** is the plan of the garment. It shows the shapes of the garment pieces and tells how to stitch them together. The shapes of the garment pieces are printed full size on thin tissue paper. Some of the directions are printed on these pattern pieces. Others are on a separate "guide sheet." The tissue paper and guide sheet are packaged in an envelope. The front of the envelope lists the garment's size and has a drawing or photograph of the garment. Usually, there are two or more variations shown. For example, "View A" of a dress pattern might have short sleeves, while "View B" has long sleeves. The back of the envelope lists useful information, such as the amount of fabric required.

To select a pattern, you need to know what kind of garment you will make and what size and style you want.

DECIDING WHAT TO SEW

Choosing a sewing project is like any other decision-making process. Start by determining what you need. Then consider your resources: time, money, and skill. If you are a beginning sewer, look for patterns with names like "easy," "super jiffy," or "beginner's choice." These patterns have fewer pieces and are less complicated to sew. They also take less time and often cost less than regular patterns.

Now you're ready to look at the alternatives. At the store, you'll find large, illustrated pattern books that show the finished garments. It's easier to make your selection from these than to look at all the pattern envelopes. As you look through the pattern book, think about the style of the garments and check what pattern sizes are available.

CHOOSING THE SIZE AND STYLE

All patterns are made from the same basic set of measurements. However, you may find that patterns from one company fit you better than patterns from another. Some patterns have more fitting ease. **Fitting ease** is the extra room built into a pattern to make the garment more comfortable. For example, the pattern will be wider across the shoulders than your body is. This is done so that you can move your arms and shoulders easily when wearing the garment. Some patterns are cut lower, higher, or fuller at the neckline, shoulder, or armhole. As you gain experience in sewing, you'll learn which company's patterns fit you best. For now, the most important thing is to select the right size.

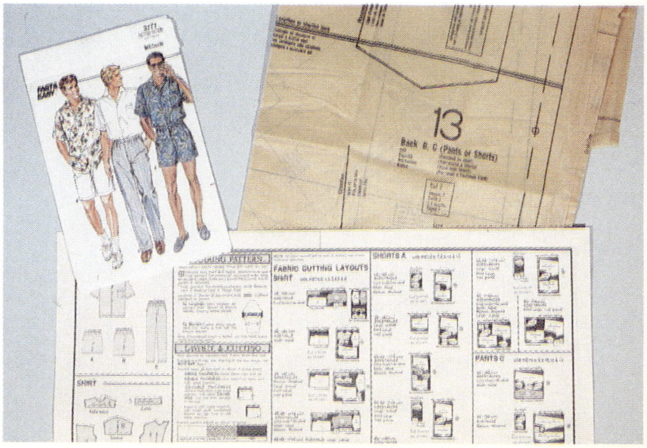

The pattern envelope contains the tissue paper pattern for the garment and a guide sheet of sewing instructions.

—Perspective

HOW TO MEASURE YOURSELF

Before you buy a pattern, take your measurements. Write them down and take the list to the store with you. Then compare your measurements to the charts in the pattern books to find the right pattern size for you.

Here's how to measure yourself. All measurements should be taken over the undergarments you will wear under the new garment.

- The *bust or chest measurement* is taken over the fullest part. Be sure the tape measure is straight across your back. The tape should be snug but not tight. You should be able to slip one finger between the tape and your side.
- The *waist measurement* is taken at the natural waistline. Again, pull the tape snug but not tight around your body.
- The *hip measurement* is taken across the fullest part of the hips. Measure in a straight line around the body.
- To measure your *back waist length,* ask a friend to help you. The measurement begins at the bone at the base of your neck. This bone is noticeable along the shoulder line when the head is bent forward. From this point, measure down the back to the natural waistline.
- Measure *crotch length* while seated. Measure from your natural waistline to the chair seat.
- *Inseam and side seam length* are measured while standing. Inseam length is the length from the crotch to the ankle on the inside of the leg. Side seam length is measured from the natural waistline down the outside of the leg to the ankle.

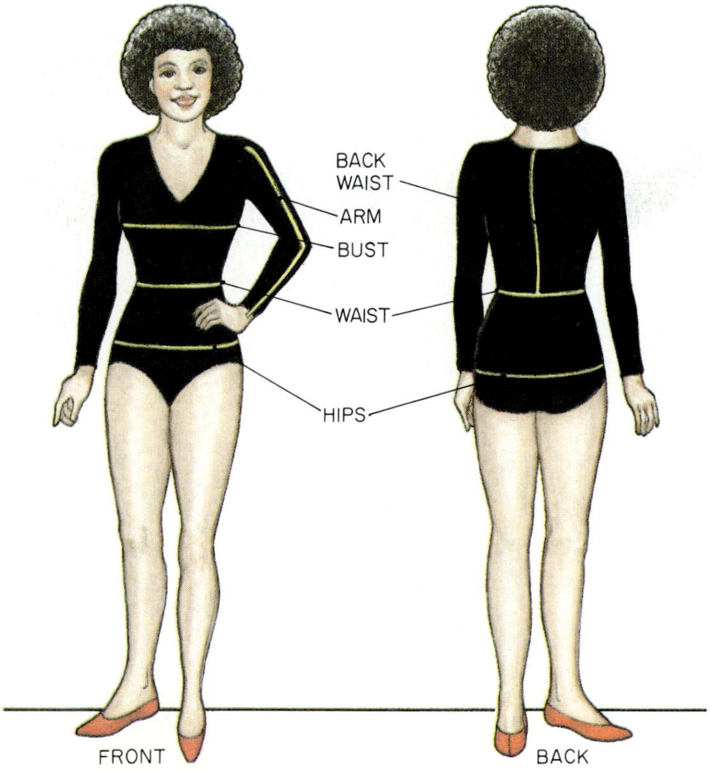

- For *height measurement,* take your shoes off and stand against a wall. Have a friend mark the wall where the top of your *head (*not your hair) reaches. Measure from this point to the floor.
- *Arm length* (sleeve length) is measured along a bent arm because a bent arm needs more fabric to cover it. For girls' and women's garments, arm length is measured from the shoulder, around the elbow, to the wrist bone. For boys' and men's garments, it is measured from the bone at the base of the neck, around the elbow, to the wrist bone.

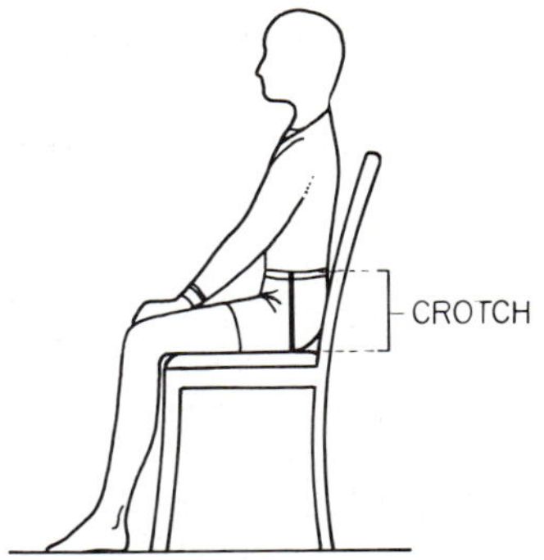

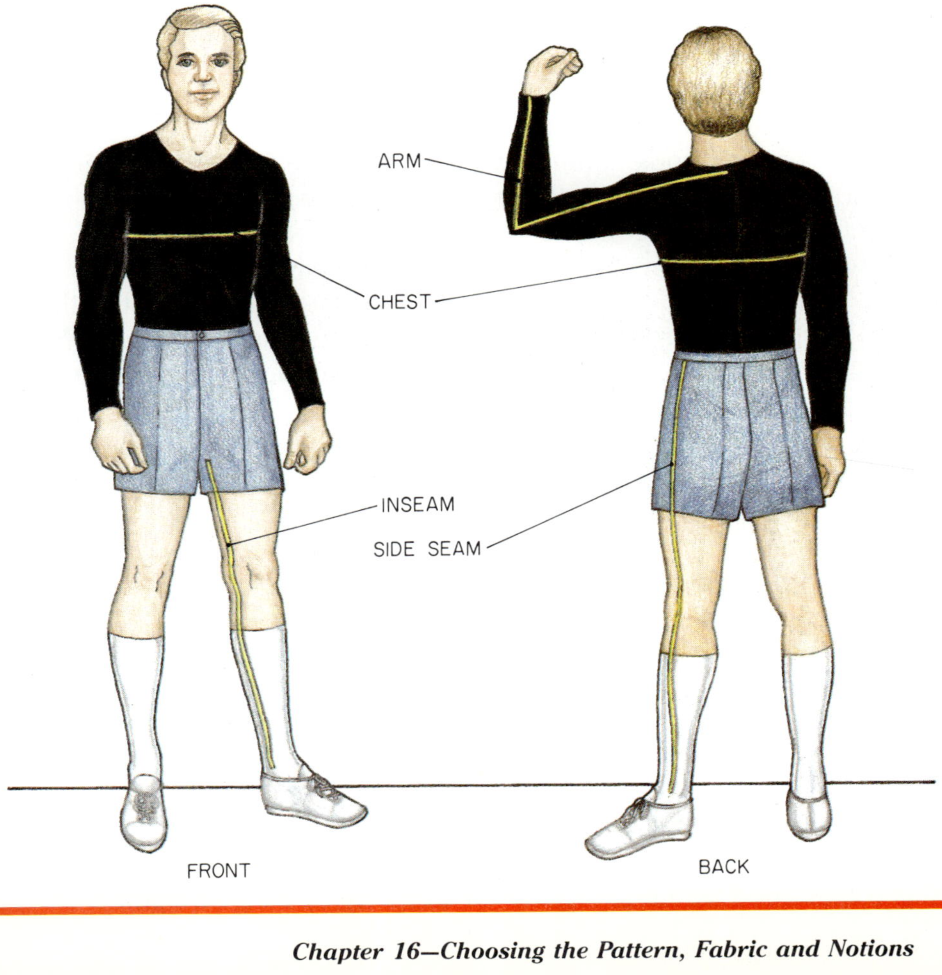

When you buy fabric, ask the salesclerk to include a care label. You can sew the label into the garment.

The pattern size you need may not be the same size you wear in ready-made clothes. To select the pattern size you need, turn to the measurement charts in the back of the pattern book. Compare your height and measurements with those given for each figure type. Select the figure type and size which best match your measurements.

Sometimes body measurements and pattern measurements do not match. When this happens, the pattern can be altered. Some alterations are easier to make than others. Use the following tips to select pattern size and make alterations easier.

- Blouses and shirts—fit the neck and shoulder; alter the chest or bust.
- Full skirts—fit the waist measurement.
- Pants and semi-fitted skirts—fit the hip and alter the waistline.

The style of pattern you select should help you look your best. Refer to your notes from Chapter 5. Will the garment being considered hide your figure faults and highlight your good features?

CHOOSING A FABRIC

In deciding which fabric to purchase, there are several things to consider. Some of them are:

- How often will I wear the garment?
- Can the fabric be washed?
- What color do I want?
- What is my sewing skill?
- How much can I spend?

Also consider the characteristics of the fabric. Some fabrics are easier to sew than others. Characteristics of fabrics that are easy to handle are:

- tight weave
- medium weight—not too thin or bulky
- smooth surface—no nap (**Nap** is a soft, fuzzy surface. For example, velvet has a nap.)
- solid color or a small, all-over design (Plaids, stripes, and large designs require more skill because they must be matched.)
- middle-range color—not too dark or light

When buying woven fabric, look closely to be sure the lengthwise and crosswise yarns run at right angles to each other. If they don't, the fabric is said to be **off-grain.** Some off-grain fabrics can be straightened, but many cannot. Garments made with off-grain fabrics may not fit properly or hang straight.

Fabric is priced by the yard. It is purchased from a bolt or as a remnant. **Remnants** are short lengths of fabric. They may be the remainder from a bolt, or they may have a flaw. Remnant pieces usually cost less per yard. If you wish to buy a remnant, be sure to check for flaws. If there is a flaw, decide whether you can work around it.

COORDINATING FABRIC AND PATTERN

When designers create garments, they have certain fabrics in mind. These fabrics are listed on the back of the pattern envelope under the heading "suggested fabrics" or just "fabrics."

Another place to find ideas for choosing a fabric is in the garment picture on the envelope front. Note whether the garment was made in a solid color, print, or plaid.

Garments with gathers or unstitched pleats need a fabric that has drape. A fabric with **drape** lies close to the body when gathered. To decide whether a fabric has drape, gather it in your hand. Do the gathers lie close together, or do they stand out stiffly?

Garments with straight seam lines and no gathers need fabrics that have body. A fabric has **body** if it has some stiffness to it.

The back of the pattern envelope includes useful information about fabric types, notions, and garment's appearance. It also tells how much fabric is needed (see photo in Appendix).

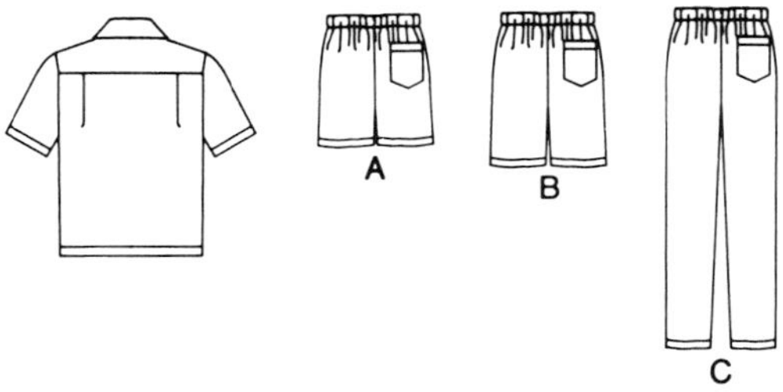

MEN'S SHIRT, SHORTS & PANTS Very loose-fitting, shirt has notched collar, extended shoulders, back pleated into yoke with forward shoulder seams, pocket and above elbow length sleeves. Shorts (two-lengths) or straight-legged pants have elastic waist with snap closing, mock fly zipper, back pocket and slanted front pockets. All hems are stitched in place.
NOTIONS: Shirt: Four ½" (13mm) Buttons. Pants, Shorts: 11" (28cm) Trouser Zipper, One Heavy Duty Hammer-on-Snap, Seam Binding and 1¼" (32mm) Elastic; 1 yd. (1.0m) for Sizes Extra Small thru Medium and 1¼ yds. (1.2m) for Sizes Large thru Extra Large.
FABRICS: Lt.wt. Broadcloth, Chambray, Oxford Cloth, Handkerchief Linen and Challis. Unsuitable for obvious diagonals. Allow extra fabric to match plaids or stripes. Use nap yardages/layouts for pile, shaded or one-way design fabrics. * with nap. ** w/o nap.

CHEMISE, SHORT & PANTALON (Homme) Chemise très ample, avec col tailleur, carrure élargie et manches au-dessus du coude; dos monté à plis dans empiècement à coutures d'épaules surbaissées et poche plaquée. Short (2 longueurs), ou pantalon à jambes droites, avec taille coulissée d'élastique et fermeture à pression, braguette simulée à glissière et poches: plaquée dos, cavalières devant. Ourlets piqués.
MERCERIE: Chemise: 4 boutons (13mm). Pantalon, short: Fermeture à glissière (28cm) - Gros boutons-pression à sertir - Extra-fort - Elastique (32mm): 1.0m pour tailles très petite à moyenne; 1.2m pour tailles grande et très grande.
TISSUS: Toile de coton légère - Chambray - Chambray-Oxford - Lin à mouchoir - Challis. Grandes diagonales ne conviennent pas. Compte non tenu des raccords de rayures/carreaux. * avec sens ** sans sens.

DECIDING HOW MUCH YOU NEED

Fabrics come in a variety of widths. The most common widths are 36 inches, 45 inches, and 60 inches. The wider the fabric, the less yardage you may need to purchase.

To find out how many yards of fabric to buy, look at the fabric yardage chart on the back of the pattern envelope. Yardage amounts are given for each fabric width, garment style ("view"), and size.

Locate the garment style you want on the chart. Move across the line to the column for your size. Note the amount of yardage needed. If more than one fabric is used in the garment, you will need to find the yardage amounts for each fabric.

SELECTING NOTIONS

Notions are items in addition to the pattern and fabric which are needed to sew a garment. They include such items as:

- thread
- zippers, buttons, and other fasteners
- elastic
- hem tape
- seam binding
- interfacing

The notions needed for a garment are listed on the back of the pattern envelope, usually near the bottom. Notions for a garment should be bought when you buy the fabric. This makes it easier to match colors and fibers.

If you cannot match thread color, select thread one shade darker than the fabric. Thread usually appears lighter when it is stitched into fabric.

If the color of the zipper, seam binding, or hem tape does not match, select items that are one shade darker or a neutral color. The darker shade or neutral color will stand out less. For example, if you cannot find a dark blue zipper for dark blue slacks, select a black zipper.

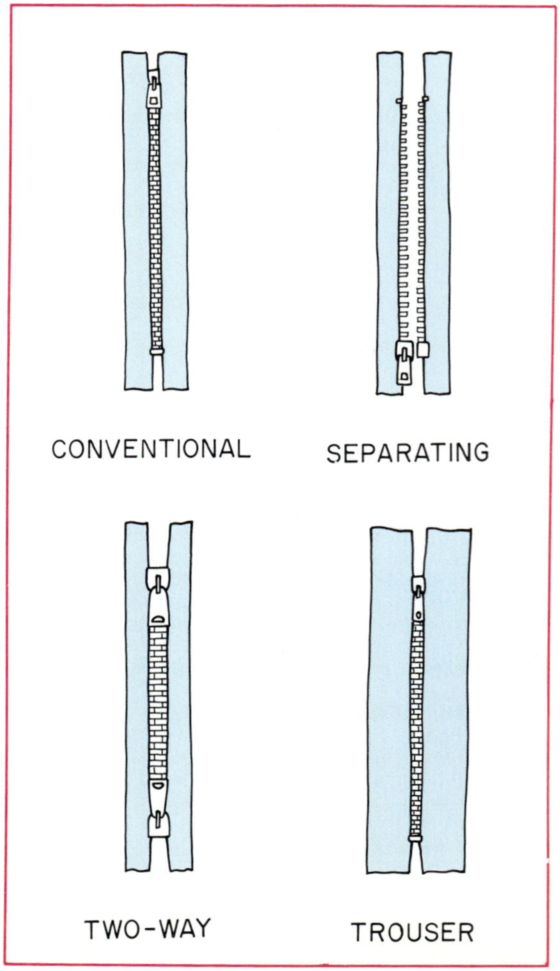

Zippers come in various colors, lengths, and types. Check the pattern envelope to find out the type and length your garment needs. Select a color that closely matches the fabric.

Buttons can be both decorative and functional in a garment. Choose buttons that harmonize with the garment. For example, for a simple cotton shirt, you could select plain white buttons. For a dressy satin blouse, pearl buttons would be a good choice. For some garments, you may want to buy buttons that can be covered with the same fabric used for the garment.

Hooks, eyes, and snaps come in many sizes and weights. Hooks and eyes used at the waistline in place of a button should be large and heavy duty. Hooks, eyes, and snaps used to hold a tab or facing in place should be lightweight and small. Use black hooks, eyes, and snaps on dark-colored fabrics. Use silver-colored ones on light-colored fabrics.

Many easy-to-sew patterns use elastic to adjust the fit of garments. Elastic comes in several widths and weights. A wider width and heavier weight are needed at the waistline. A narrower width and lighter weight are used at the wrist, neck, or ankle.

Interfacing is a layer of special fabric placed between layers of the garment fabric. It is used in garments to add strength to areas of strain and weight to areas that must lie flat or take a shape. Interfacing is placed in waistbands, cuffs, collars, and facings. Interfacing may be stitched into the garment or fused onto the garment by ironing.

Interfacing should be the same weight as the garment fabric, or slightly lighter. To check the weight, place some of the interfacing between two layers of garment fabric. Bend the layers. Are they very stiff? Then the interfacing is too heavy. Are they limp? Then the interfacing is too light.

Helpful hint: The fiber content and care of notions should be compatible with the garment fabric. Otherwise, shrinking or fading may occur in the fabric or the notion.

Interfacing fabric may be woven or nonwoven, fusible or sew-in. The different weights are marked as to what they are best used for.

Sew-in **Woven Fusible** **Nonwoven Fusible**

—The Way It Was

THE MAGIC TISSUE

Before 1850, garments were made by draping and cutting fabric or with the use of diagrams. To use a diagram, a person needed special skills in tracing the diagram, cutting garment pieces, and sewing.

In the early 1850s a Philadelphia couple, William and Ellen Demorest, began mass-producing paper patterns for dresses that Mrs. Demorest designed. By the late 1870s the Demorests' "magic tissues" were available in Europe as well as America.

However, it was another husband-wife team that really launched the modern pattern industry. Ellen and Ebenezer Butterick worked as tailors in New England. Mrs. Butterick felt that mothers would like a pattern to help them make clothes for their children. She and her husband drafted a pattern for a child's suit. Soon they also began making patterns for men's shirts. They patented their patterns in 1863. In 1867 Butterick patterns for women's clothes were introduced. The pattern industry was launched and growing.

Today patterns are more convenient than ever. Instructions are simpler and sizes have been standardized. Now even people with limited sewing skills can enjoy using patterns to make some of their clothes.

Butterick garments from the 1870s. Sewing clothes like these took a lot of skill, time—and fabric!

REVIEW-16

SUMMARY

Choosing a pattern, fabric, and notions involves important decisions. All these items should work together to make an attractive garment. The right choices also make the garment easier to sew. When the sewing is easy, you enjoy making your garment and are eager to wear it. You'll be pleased with the garment and wear it often.

CHECK YOUR KNOWLEDGE

1. What is the purpose of a sewing pattern?
2. Why might a beginning sewer want patterns labeled "easy," "super jiffy," or "beginner's choice?"
3. How do you determine which size pattern to select?
4. Which area of the pattern is easier to alter—the shoulder or the chest?
5. List the characteristics of a fabric that are easy to handle.
6. What is a fabric remnant?
7. Where on the pattern envelope do you find ideas for choosing a fabric?
8. What is the difference between a fabric with drape and a fabric with body? When is each used?
9. What are notions? Name four.
10. When buying notions, it is sometimes hard to match colors. When colors do not match, what color should you buy?

EXTEND YOUR KNOWLEDGE

1. Take your measurements. Then compare them to the charts in a pattern book. What size pattern would fit you best?
2. Visit two fabric stores. Compare variety of fabrics and notions and availability of patterns. Select some fabrics and notions and compare their prices. Which store do you prefer? Why?
3. From a pattern book, select two patterns each for someone who is tall, someone with rounded shoulders, a short-waisted person, and someone who is overweight. Describe the garment and give reasons for your choices.
4. Select four garments from a catalog of ready-to-wear clothes. Find four similar garments in a pattern book. Compare the cost of the ready-made garments to the cost of sewing the garments.
5. Bring ten buttons from home. Describe what style of garment and what type and color of fabric the buttons would be suitable for.

CHAPTER 17

GETTING READY TO SEW

When you buy your pattern and fabric, you'll probably be eager to start sewing. But there are several things you need to do before you sew the first seam. The fabric should be preshrunk, and its grain line should be checked. The pattern may need to be adjusted to fit your body. The pattern pieces must be placed on the fabric. After all the pattern pieces have been pinned to the fabric, you can cut out the garment pieces. Next, you will need to transfer markings from the pattern to the fabric.

Doing all these things carefully takes some time, but it's worth it. Good preparation makes sewing easier, and you'll have a better looking garment.

After you study this chapter and learn answers to the questions below, you will be ready to sew.

- Why should you pretreat fabric?
- What can you do to make a pattern fit you better?
- How should the pattern be placed on the fabric?
- What are the tools and techniques for cutting fabric?
- What are the tools and techniques for marking fabric?

Look for These Terms

selvage
raw edge
straight grain
crosswise grain
pattern layout
basting

PRETREATING THE FABRIC

Before the pattern is placed on the fabric, the fabric should be preshrunk and the grain line checked. This pretreatment will help prevent problems later.

PRESHRINKING

Sometimes garments will shrink when they are laundered or dry-cleaned. If a lot of shrinkage occurs, the garment will not fit. Many fabrics today are preshrunk at the factory. However, just to make sure, you should preshrink fabrics before you place the pattern on them. The method of preshrinking should be the same as the cleaning method used for the finished garment. Fabrics that are washed and dried may need to be pressed.

CHECKING THE GRAIN

When fabric is woven, yarns are placed on the loom in a lengthwise direction. Other yarns are threaded crosswise through them. The side where the crosswise yarns end is called the **selvage** (SELL-vij). The selvage has a finished appearance; no loose yarn ends are visible. The side where the lengthwise yarns end is called the **raw edge.** The ends of the lengthwise yarns are visible.

"Grain" is a term used to refer to the lengthwise and crosswise yarns. The lengthwise yarn is called the **straight grain.** The crosswise yarn is called the **crosswise grain.** Fabric is woven with the straight grain and crosswise grain at right angles to each other. When the straight grain and crosswise grain are not at right angles, the fabric is said to be off-grain.

To check the grain, you first need to make sure the fabric is cut straight. To do this, remove from the raw edge any crosswise yarns that do not run from selvage to selvage. Then locate the first yarn that runs from selvage to selvage and pull it. A line of puckers will form. Use this as a guide to cut off the uneven fabric.

This close-up shows the lengthwise and crosswise yarns. The selvage is at the right. Note the raw edge at the top, where the ends of the lengthwise yarns can be seen.

Clip one selvage. With a pin, pick out the crosswise thread. Pull it with your fingers. If it breaks, cut along the line until you can again pick up the thread. Continue pulling and cutting until you reach the other selvage.

To test the grain, lay your fabric flat on a long table. Fold the fabric along the lengthwise grain so that the selvages are on top of each other. Check the raw edges. Are they even? If so, the fabric is on-grain. If not, the fabric is off-grain.

Some off-grain fabrics can be straightened. Ask your teacher to show you how. Fabrics that were pulled off-grain during the finishing process cannot be straightened. However, if the fabric is only a little off-grain, you can still use it. You will have to be careful when laying out the pattern. Make sure the layers of fabric under the pattern are smooth and flat.

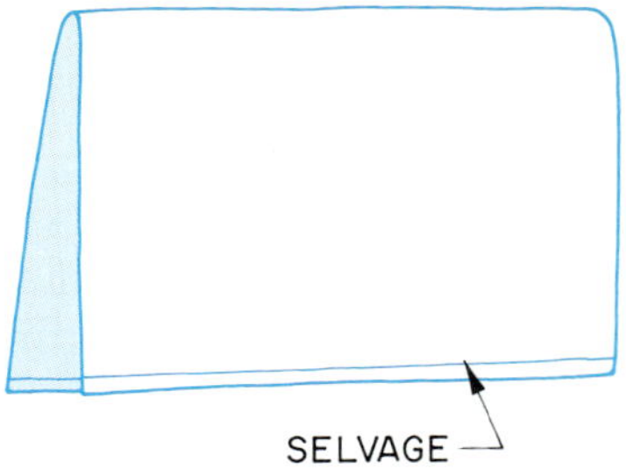

This fabric is off-grain. The selvages match, but the ends do not. If the ends are matched, wrinkles form.

PREPARING THE PATTERN

Pattern pieces are printed on large sheets of tissue. Cut apart those pattern pieces which are needed for your garment. Put the extra pieces back into the pattern envelope. If the pieces you will use are wrinkled, iron them with a barely warm iron. If you are making the garment in class, it's a good idea to write your name on the pattern pieces, envelope, and guide sheet.

ALTERING THE PATTERN

Sometimes the pattern you have selected does not quite fit your body. When this happens, you need to alter the pattern before it is placed on the fabric.

To decide where alterations are needed, compare your measurements with those on the pattern envelope. Note areas where the pattern is too big, too little, too long, or too short. Figure the amount of change needed in each area. Keep in mind that you'll usually need to alter both the back and the front pattern pieces.

Two types of alterations occur most often. They are changes in length and in width.

LENGTHENING OR SHORTENING THE PATTERN

When pattern pieces are too long or too short, the extra amount needs to be taken away or added. This is usually done in a special place on the pattern. It has two parallel lines labeled "lengthen or shorten."

If the pattern needs to be shortened, fold a tuck along the parallel lines. Tape the tuck in place. The width of the tuck should be *one-half* of the total amount needed to shorten the piece. Why one-half? Think about it. Take a piece of paper. Draw two parallel lines 2 inches apart across the paper. Bring the two lines together and crease the paper. Now measure from each line to the fold. Each distance will be 1 inch.

If the pattern needs to be lengthened, cut the pattern apart along the parallel lines. Place a piece of tissue paper under the cut area of the pattern. Spread the two pattern pieces apart by the *whole* amount needed to lengthen the pattern. Tape the pattern pieces in their new positions to the tissue paper.

Some patterns say to lengthen or shorten the garment at the bottom. Simply add or subtract the whole amount needed.

After an alteration has been made, the cutting lines may need to be redrawn. Use a pencil to draw the cutting lines. Draw gently. The tissue paper tears easily.

Pattern Symbols

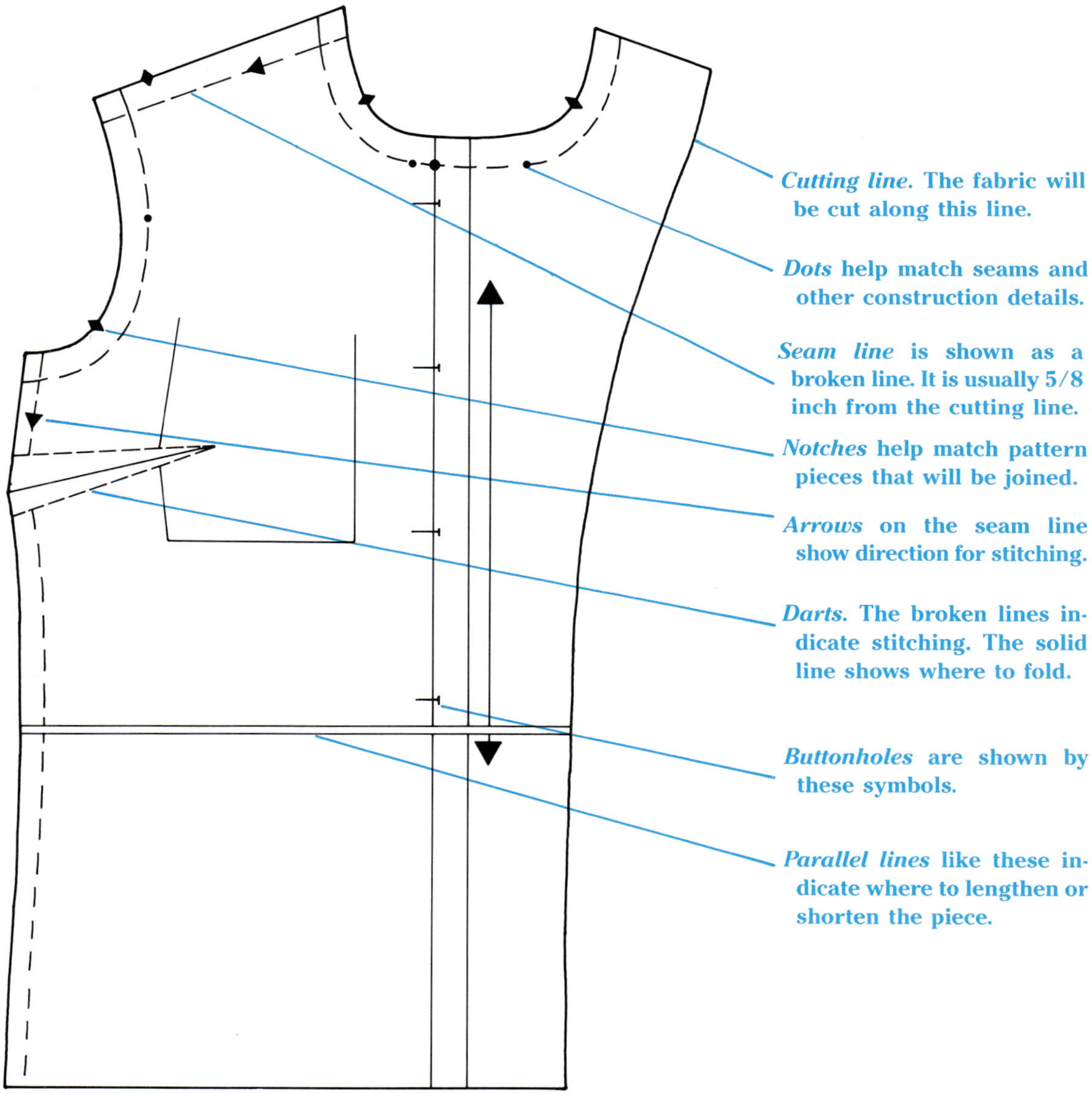

INCREASING OR DECREASING PATTERN WIDTH

When the pattern is too wide or too narrow, the width of the pattern must be altered. To change the pattern width, use both the front and back pattern pieces.

Using a ruler and pencil, draw a line parallel with the grain line on the pattern. The line should run the length of the pattern piece. You will make alterations along this line. Keep the line away from darts or other construction details, if possible.

How much should each pattern piece be increased or decreased? Look at the illustration on this page. The pattern piece is for *one* side of the skirt front—or one-fourth of the whole skirt. You want to distribute the alteration evenly among the four sides.

To increase pattern width, cut the front pattern apart on your pencil line. Place a piece of tissue paper under the pattern pieces. Spread the pattern apart *one-fourth* of the total amount of increase needed. Tape the pattern pieces in their new positions. Repeat with the back pattern piece.

To decrease pattern width, divide the total amount of decrease into *fourths.* Fold a tuck along your pencil line. The width of the tuck should be *one-half* of the amount to be removed from each pattern piece. For example, if the total amount of decrease is 2 inches, you will decrease each pattern piece by ½ inch. The width of each tuck should be ¼ inch.

If your increase or decrease line crosses darts or pleats, the stitching lines will need to be redrawn. Using a ruler and pencil, draw the new stitching lines.

Before you place your pattern on the fabric, have your teacher check your pattern alterations. If you've made a mistake, you can correct it before pinning the pattern in place.

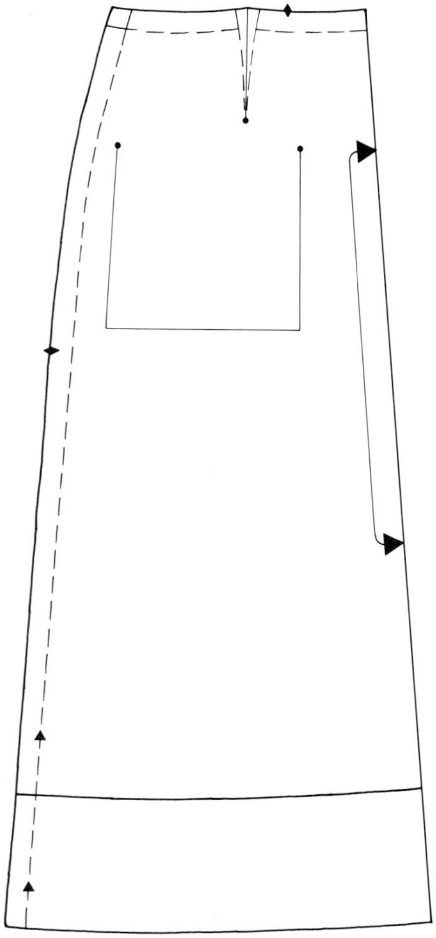

This is one-half of a skirt front. If you wanted to widen the whole skirt by 2 inches, how much would you add to this piece?

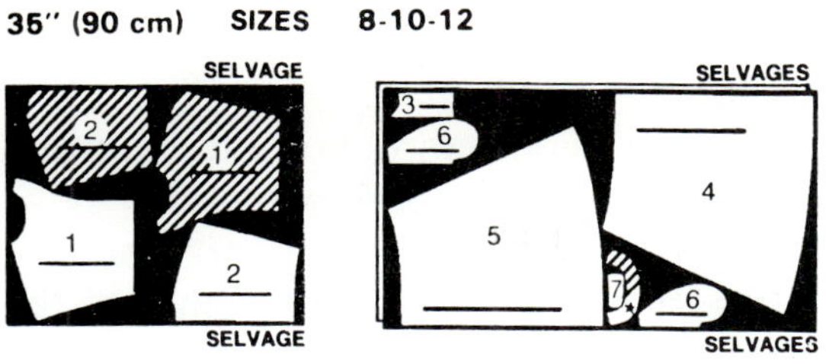

Cut pieces as shown.

What pattern sizes and fabric widths would require a layout like this?

PATTERN LAYOUT

The **pattern layout** is the arrangement of pattern pieces on the fabric. The guide sheet will suggest a layout for your pattern size, garment view, and fabric width. Draw a circle around that layout so you can find it easily as you work.

On a large, flat surface, fold your fabric as shown in the layout. If you must work on a short table, lay the extra fabric on a chair. This will keep the fabric from sliding off the table.

Place pattern pieces on the fabric as shown in the layout. That way you can be sure all the pieces will fit on the fabric. Place pattern pieces as close together as possible.

Most pattern pieces are placed on a double thickness of fabric. Some, however, are put on a single layer. Check the guide sheet to be sure you are placing the pieces correctly.

Safety Tip

Don't carry pins or needles in your mouth. Use a pincushion.

Use straight pins to fasten the pattern pieces to the fabric. Begin by pinning the pieces that are placed on the fabric fold. These pieces have a double arrow that points to a straight edge of the pattern. (See drawing below.) Place the pattern piece so this edge exactly matches the fold in the fabric. Pin the pattern piece in place.

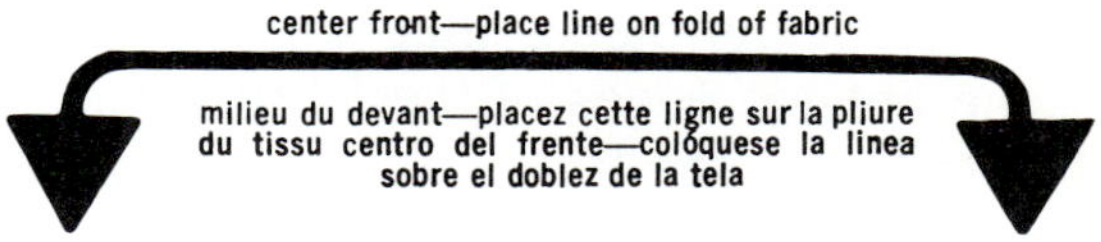

Pattern pieces that are placed on the straight grain have a long straight arrow on them, as shown below. Beside the arrow are the words "place on straight grain." Pin one end of the arrow to the fabric. Measure the distance from this pinned end to the selvage. Move the pattern until the other end of the arrow is the same distance from the selvage. Pin the second end of the arrow to the fabric.

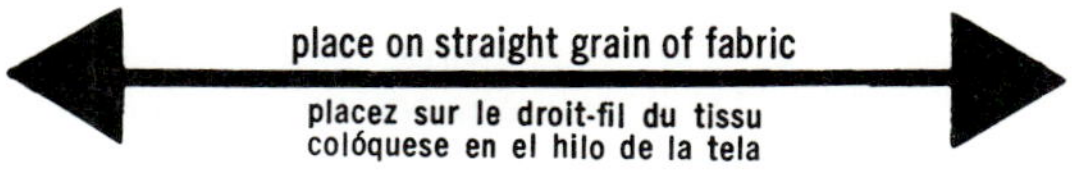

As you pin, keep the pattern pieces and fabric smooth. Pin about every 4 inches. Keep the ends of the pins about ¼ inch from the cutting line.

In this book, garment pieces are shown as follows:

Right side of fabric

Wrong side of fabric

Interfacing

CUTTING

When you have finished pinning, cut out the garment. Use sharp, bent-handled shears. Cut with long, even strokes. Here are some tips:

- The fabric and pattern should be smooth and wrinkle-free before cutting.
- For better control of the shears, stand up while you cut.
- First cut the pieces that are pinned to the outside edges of the fabric. (These are usually the larger pieces.) Then cut the pieces in the center.
- As you cut, hold the shears with one hand and rest the other hand gently on the fabric to keep it from slipping. Do not lift the fabric.
- Follow exactly the cutting lines on the pattern.
- Cut notches outward, not into the seam allowances of the garment.
- When cutting corners or short places, it is easier to cut with the points of the shears.
- To identify center front, center back, shoulder seams, and darts at seam edges, make a ⅛-inch cut into the seam allowance.
- Do *not* cut places marked "clip." The clips will be made later.

Fold the pattern pieces as they are cut, leaving the pattern pinned to the fabric. Save small scraps of the fabric for test-marking and test-stitching.

Perspective

TOOLS FOR CUTTING

Did you know shears were once a luxury item? Shears were invented in the 1300s. They were a long piece of metal, sharp on both ends and folded in half. Because they were expensive to make, only the rich could afford them.

Today we have many tools for cutting fabric and thread. Knowing which tools to use and when to use them will help you make a better garment.

Dressmaker shears (1) are about seven inches long. They have a small ring handle for the thumb and a larger, oblong ring handle for two or three fingers. The back of the shears is made straight to rest flat on the table during cutting. The bent handle makes it easier to keep the fabric flat on the table as you cut.

Scissors (2) range from three to six inches in length. They have ring handles of equal size and sharp points. Scissors are used for clipping threads, ripping seams, opening buttonholes, and cutting ribbons.

Pinking (3) and scalloping shears are used for seam finishing and decorative trim. Pinking shears make a pointed, zigzag edge. Scalloping shears make a rounded edge. Neither should be used to cut out a pattern. With the uneven edge they make, it would be hard to sew the correct seam allowance.

Seam rippers (4) are made to cut and remove machine stitching. The point slips under a stitch as the cutting edge lifts and cuts it.

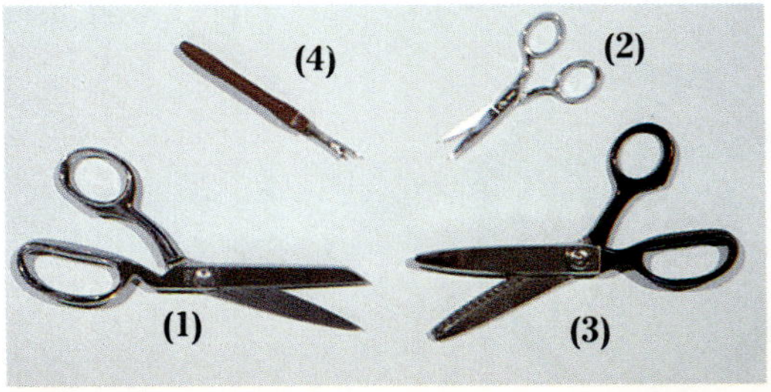

MARKING

Before removing pattern pieces from the fabric, transfer all pattern markings to the wrong side of the fabric. Mark darts, tucks, center front and center back lines, buttonholes, large and small dots, squares, and triangles. Do not mark seam lines unless they are small, curved areas or sharp corners which might be hard to follow with the seam guide on the sewing machine.

There are several ways to transfer pattern markings. You could mark the fabric by using a tracing wheel and paper, or pins and tailor's chalk. You could also do basting or make tailor's tacks.

USING A TRACING WHEEL AND PAPER

Test the tracing wheel and tracing paper on a scrap of fabric to find out which color and amount of pressure to use. Use a color dark enough to see on your fabric but light enough so it does not show through to the right side.

Remove a few of the pins from the pattern and slip the tracing paper under the pattern. The waxy side of the tracing paper should be against the wrong side of the fabric. Roll the tracing wheel over all the symbols and lines to be marked. Use enough pressure to leave marks. Use a ruler to guide straight-line markings. Place an X on circle markings. Mark the end of darts with a straight line.

HELPFUL HINT: Since the tracing wheel might dig through the fabric into the table surface, place an old magazine or heavy cardboard between the fabric and the table.

HELPFUL HINT: Since both sleeves look very similar, mark the right sleeve with an "R" on the wrong side with chalk. This will help you sew the correct sleeve in the right armhole.

By placing the tracing paper like this, you can mark both pieces of fabric at the same time. Be sure to press firmly on the tracing wheel.

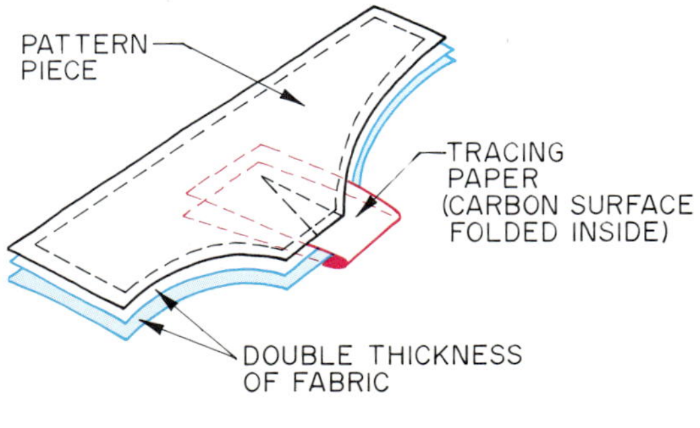

USING PINS AND TAILOR'S CHALK

Stick pins straight down through pattern symbols and all fabric layers. Gently separate the fabric layers, being careful to keep the pins through both layers. With tailor's chalk, mark the location of the nearest pins. (Be sure to mark on the fabric's wrong side.) Remove those pins and separate the fabric to the next pins. Mark their location. Repeat this process until all pattern symbols have been marked.

BASTING

Sometimes the right side of the fabric must be marked. For example, you may need to mark where a pocket is to be placed or a buttonhole sewn. You can do this by basting. **Basting** is sewing long, loose stitches to hold fabric together temporarily. Use a hand-sewing needle and a long piece of unknotted thread.

—Perspective

TOOLS FOR MARKING AND MEASURING

A tracing wheel (1) and tracing paper (2) can be used to mark all smooth-surface fabrics. The tracing paper has a waxy surface and comes in a variety of colors.

Pins (3) and tailor's chalk (4) are helpful in marking heavier fabrics. These marks rub off easily or disappear when pressed. The chalk comes in squares or in pencil form.

Marking pencils (5) leave a light blue or red line that can be removed with water. Do not use them on sheer or light-colored fabrics because the mark will show on the right side of the fabric. Test the marking pencil on a scrap of fabric before using it.

A tape measure (6) is used for taking body measurements.

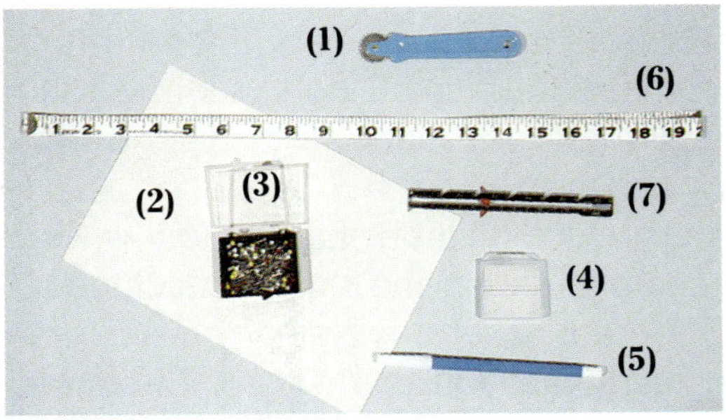

A sewing gauge (7) is a 6-inch ruler with a movable indicator. It's handy for transferring measurements, as when you're laying a pattern on the straight grain.

MAKING TAILOR'S TACKS

To make tailor's tacks, use thread of a contrasting color so it will be easy to see against the fabric. A long, unknotted, double thread works best. At each point to be marked, make a stitch about ¼ inch long through the pattern and all the layers of fabric. Leave the thread ends at least 1 inch long. Make a second stitch in the same place as the first, leaving the threads in a loop about 1 inch long. Repeat at each point to be marked, using a continuous thread.

When all points have been marked, clip the threads between each marking. Remove the pattern very carefully. Then gently separate the fabric layers, cutting the stitches between the layers. The small thread ends remain as markings.

HELPFUL HINT: After transferring markings, leave pattern pieces on top of the fabric until you are ready to sew.

Tailor's tacks show on the right and wrong sides of fabric and are easily removed after machine stitching.

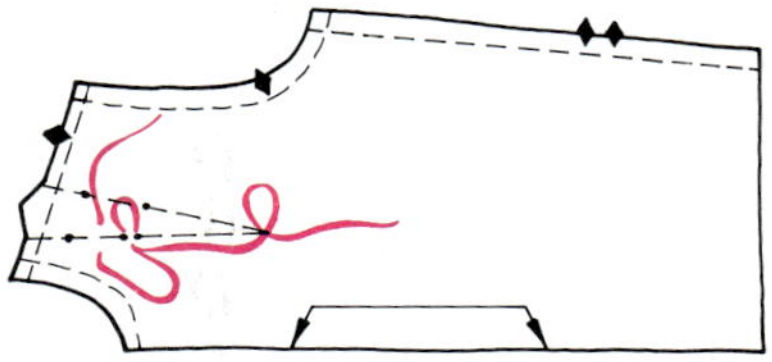

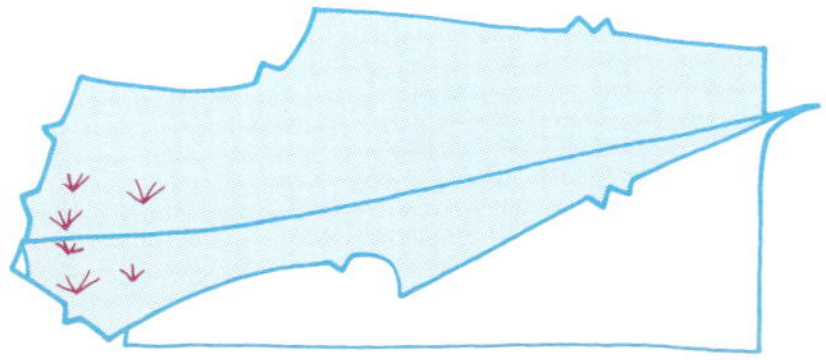

REVIEW-17

SUMMARY

Fabric pretreatment and pattern alteration are important first steps when making a garment. The pattern guide sheet gives you directions for making the garment. The layout pictures on the guide sheet show you how to place your pattern on the fabric. Accuracy in cutting out the pattern pieces helps you sew straight seams. Pattern markings need to be moved to the fabric. These markings help you match seams and garment pieces.

CHECK YOUR KNOWLEDGE

1. Why is it important to preshrink a fabric?
2. How do you preshrink fabric?
3. Describe how to check whether a fabric is on-grain.
4. How can you determine where pattern alterations are needed?
5. When shortening a pattern piece, how wide a tuck should you make?
6. When increasing pattern width, how much wider should you make each piece?
7. Where can you find a suggested layout for your pattern pieces?
8. Why should you place pattern pieces as shown on the layout?
9. Why should you stand up when you cut out a garment?
10. What pattern symbols should you transfer to the fabric?

EXTEND YOUR KNOWLEDGE

1. Demonstrate how to check whether a piece of fabric is on-grain.
2. From newspaper or magazine articles or from experienced sewers, gather tips on how to make fabric pretreatment, pattern alterations, layout, etc., easier. Combine these into a booklet of "Helpful Hints."
3. Find out how to work with plaids and stripes. How do the techniques for layout and cutting differ from those for plain fabrics?
4. Obtain a pattern that will no longer be used. Experiment with lengthening or shortening the pattern and increasing or decreasing its width. Show the results to your teacher.
5. Compare methods of marking fabric. Which do you think is best? Why?

CHAPTER 18

SEWING

A sewing machine is an extension of your hands, just like a car is an extension of your feet. It doesn't really do anything you can't do, but it does it faster and more precisely.

To use a sewing machine successfully takes practice. First learn about the machine and what it can do. Practice on scraps of fabric, or buy inexpensive fabric on sale. When you're ready to make a garment, start with something simple.

This chapter gives you a general overview of what is needed for different sewing tasks. To make a particular garment, you'll need to read and follow the instructions that come with the pattern. Your teacher will guide you through the steps.

In the following pages you'll find answers to these questions:

- What are the correct ways to use and care for a sewing machine?
- What are the basic sewing techniques?

Look for These Terms

facing	casing
upper collar	patch pockets
under collar	pleats
bodice	pressing

THE SEWING MACHINE

How well you sew depends largely on your skill in using a sewing machine. A sewing machine is easy to understand and use even though there are many different kinds. Once you learn the basics of one machine, you can easily apply what you have learned to other makes and models.

Before you use a sewing machine for the first time, learn the names of the parts and what they do. Otherwise, it will be hard for you to follow directions. See the drawing on page 186 for the basic parts of a sewing machine. Read the operator's manual for your machine to make sure you know all of its parts and how they work.

WINDING THE BOBBIN

There are two kinds of sewing machine bobbins. One is called the *self-winding bobbin.* After the machine is threaded, place this kind of bobbin in the bobbin case and push a button to start the bobbin winder. Then press on the foot or knee pedal to wind.

Self-winding bobbin. The bobbin winder is built into the bobbin case in the bed of the machine.

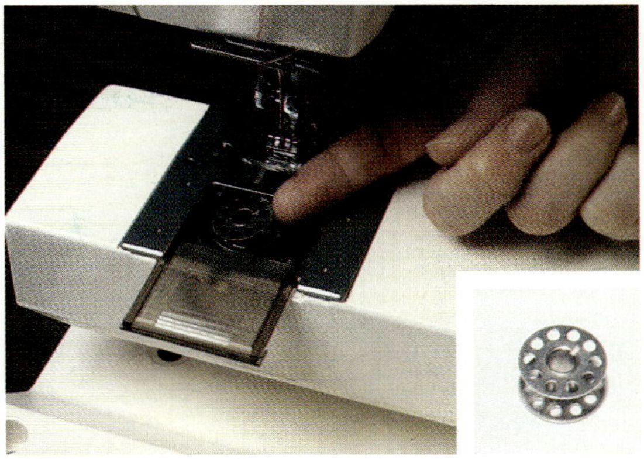

Conventional bobbin. It must be removed from its case and placed on the bobbin winder on the head of the machine.

The second type is the *conventional bobbin.* At one time, all sewing machines had this type of bobbin. These bobbins are filled on a special spindle on the head of the machine. To wind a conventional bobbin, follow these steps:

1. Partly unscrew the smaller knob in the center of the handwheel. This frees the wheel so your needle won't go up and down.
2. Place the bobbin on the bobbin winder.
3. Place the spool of thread on the spool pin and pull the thread through the metal thread guide on the top left side of the head. This holds it firm. Then thread it through one of the bobbin's small holes, starting from the inside.
4. Snap the bobbin into the winding position. Hold the end of the thread. Press the foot or knee pedal and let the bobbin wind slowly so it fills evenly.
5. When the bobbin is full, it will snap out of the winding position.
6. Retighten the handwheel knob.

The Sewing Machine

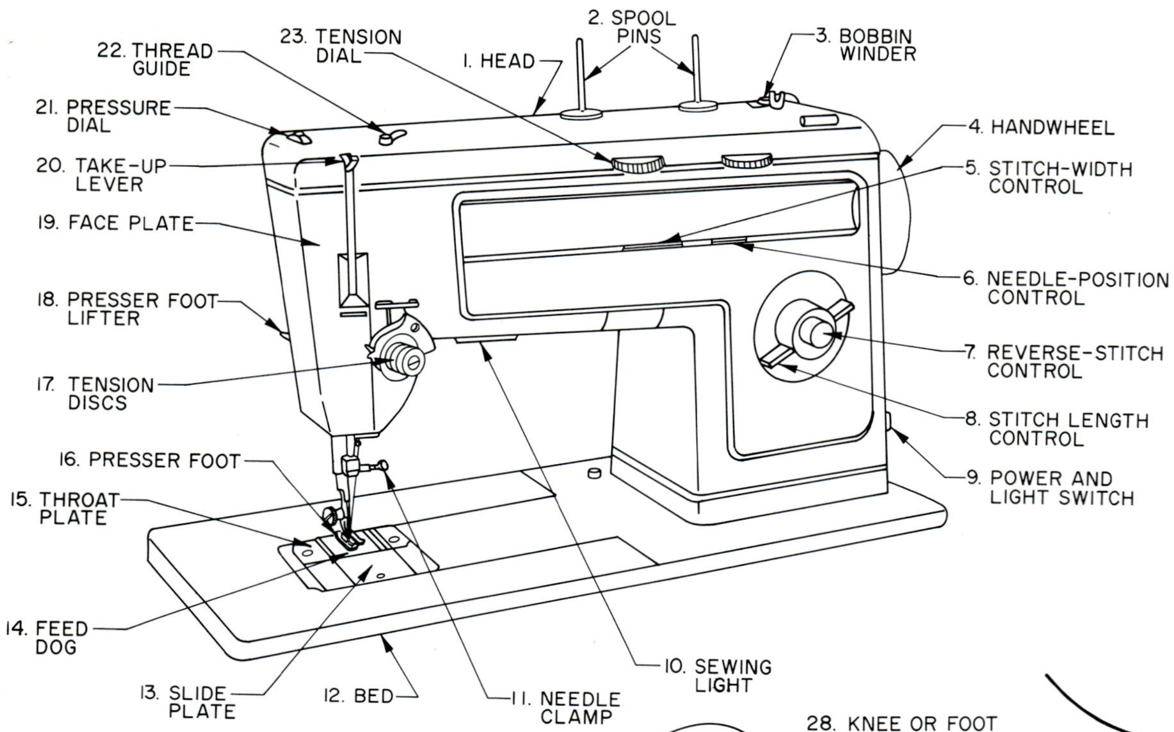

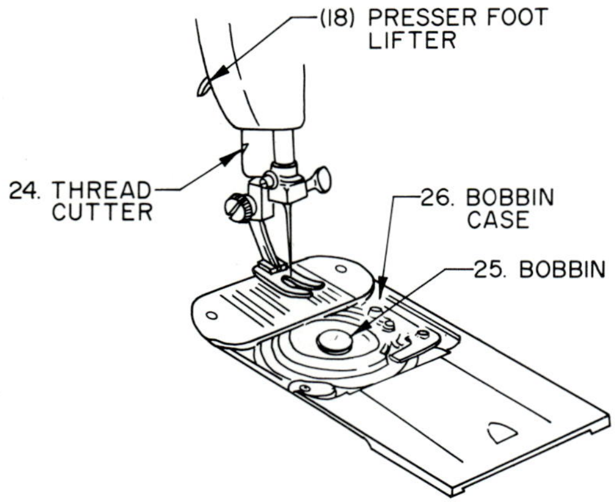

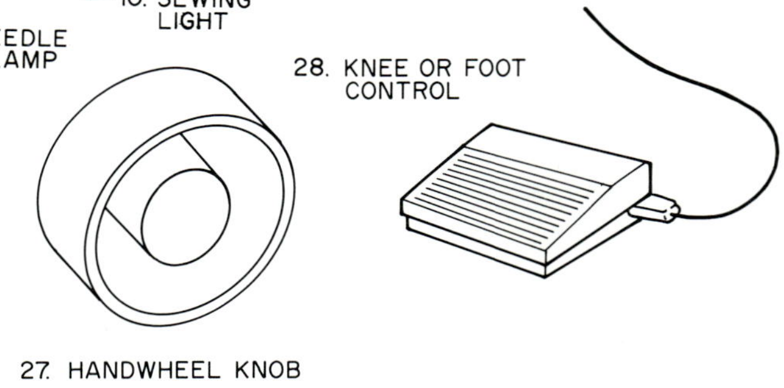

1. *head:* The upper part of the machine, not including the bed (base).
2. *spool pins:* Hold spools of thread.
3. *bobbin winder:* Holds bobbin for winding.
4. *handwheel:* Controls the up-and-down movement of the needle and the take-up lever.
5. *stitch-width control:* Found on zigzag machines. Controls width of zigzag stitches.
6. *needle-position control:* Positions needle at left, center, or right.
7. *reverse-stitch control:* Makes it possible to stitch backward.
8. *stitch length control:* A numbered dial for regulating the length of stitches.
9. *power and light switch:* Turns on machine and built-in sewing light.
10. *sewing light:* Lights up the sewing area.
11. *needle clamp:* Holds the needle in place.
12. *bed:* The flat base of the machine.
13. *slide plate:* Covers the bobbin and bobbin case.

14. *feed dog:* Moves fabric under the presser foot.
15. *throat plate:* Metal plate directly under needle. Has guidelines that help you keep the stitching straight as you sew.
16. *presser foot:* Holds fabric against the feed dog.
17. *tension discs:* Regulate looseness or tightness of upper thread (the thread that goes through the needle).
18. *presser foot lifter:* Lets you raise and lower presser foot.
19. *face plate:* Opens for access to some of the machine's inner parts.
20. *take-up lever:* Moves up and down, pulling thread from the spool for each stitch.
21. *pressure dial:* Controls pressure of the presser foot on the fabric.
22. *thread guide:* Holds and guides the upper thread when stitching.
23. *tension dial:* Regulates the tension (tightness) of the upper thread. Usually, the lower the number, the lower the tension.
24. *thread cutter:* Convenient for cutting threads.
25. *bobbin:* Metal or plastic spool that holds lower thread.
26. *bobbin case:* Holds bobbin and regulates tension of bobbin thread. Some cases are removable; some are not.
27. *handwheel knob:* Can be loosened to stop needle from moving when bobbin is winding.
28. *knee or foot control:* Used to start and stop the machine and to regulate the speed.

A modern electronic sewing machine.

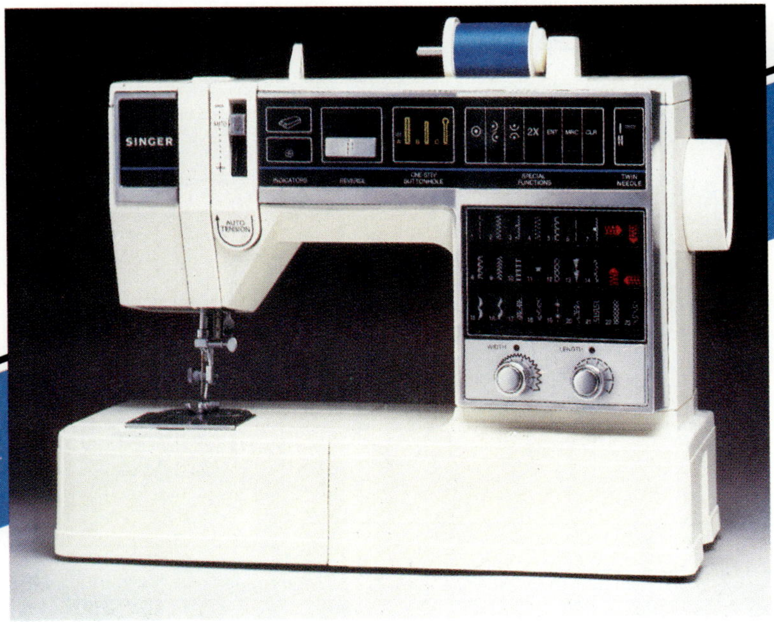

THREADING THE MACHINE

Every kind of sewing machine is threaded a little differently. Always be sure to follow the instructions for each machine. However, here are some general steps you can follow:

1. Raise the presser foot with the presser foot lifter.
2. Using the handwheel, raise the needle to its highest position.
3. Put the thread on the spool pin.
4. Pull the thread through the top thread guide or guides.
5. Loop the thread through the tension discs. Allow the thread to catch in the hook behind the discs.
6. If there is another thread guide, pull the thread through it.
7. Pull the thread through the take-up lever.
8. Pull the thread through any remaining thread guides.
9. Thread the needle from the same side as the last thread guide. There will be a long groove running past the eye of the needle on this side. Pull four or five inches of thread through the needle.

If you use a conventional bobbin, place it in the bobbin case under the slide plate. (A self-winding bobbin will already be in place.) Close the slide plate, leaving several inches of the bobbin thread lying on the bed.

Hold the *needle* thread loosely with your hand. Turn the handwheel toward you so the needle goes down and picks up the bobbin thread. Pull the loop out until the end of the bobbin thread appears.

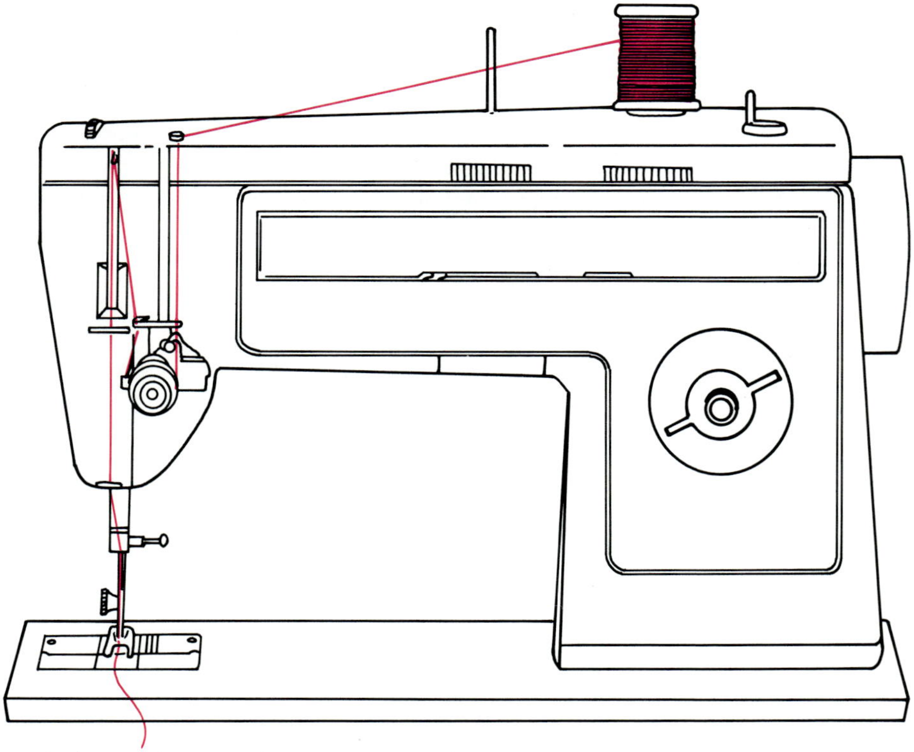

Threading a sewing machine. Not all machines are threaded the same way, so be sure to follow your teacher's instructions.

CONTROLLING STITCHES

Needles should be matched to your fabric. (See the needle in the drawing.) Replace needles as they become bent, blunt, or broken.

Sharp point. Use for woven fabrics.

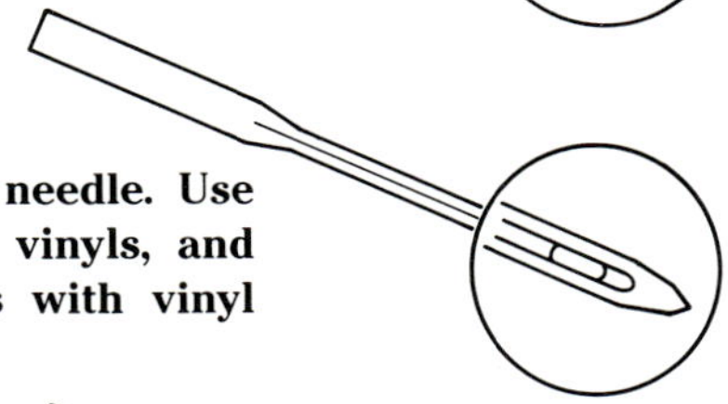

Wedge-point needle. Use for leathers, vinyls, and furry fabrics with vinyl backings.

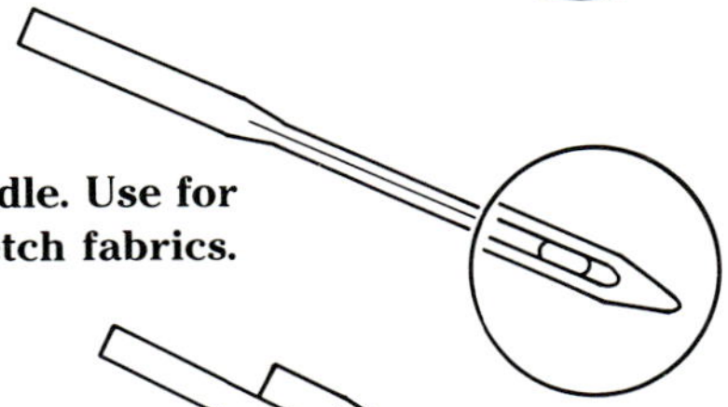

Ball-point needle. Use for knits and stretch fabrics.

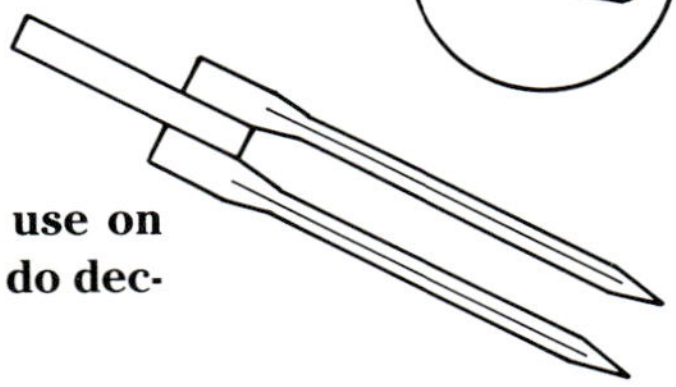

Twin needles. For use on machines that can do decorative stitches.

Sewing machine needles are numbered for size. The lower the number, the finer the needle. Lightweight or sheer fabrics need fine needles. Heavier fabrics need coarse needles.

The tension, or pull, on the needle and bobbin threads should be adjusted so that the two threads meet and interlock evenly between the two layers of fabric being sewn. Test the stitch on a scrap of fabric to be sure the tension is right. If the needle thread lies straight along the top of the fabric, the needle tension is probably too tight. Loosen it by adjusting the tension dial. If the bobbin thread lies straight along the bottom of the fabric, the needle tension is probably too loose. Move the tension dial to a higher number. The bobbin tension rarely needs to be adjusted. If it does, ask a repair person to do it.

The length of the stitches can be changed for different sewing jobs:

- 6 stitches per inch—use for basting or for sewing bulky, heavy fabrics
- 8 stitches per inch—topstitching
- 10 stitches per inch—regular seam stitching and staystitching
- 15 stitches per inch—reinforcement stitching; used for permanent stitching in areas where fabric will be trimmed or clipped close to stitching.

The width of zigzag stitches can be controlled by a lever. Narrow width zigzag stitches can be used to make stretchable seams. Wider stitches are used for edge finishing, mending, and decoration.

CARE OF THE SEWING MACHINE

Sewing machines will run smoothly and trouble-free if cared for properly. All machines must be kept clean and oiled.

Every time you use a sewing machine, check the bobbin case, feed dog, and tension controls for lint. Follow instructions for your machine to remove lint and dust.

Many machines need to be oiled regularly. The instruction book will tell you where and how often. After oiling, be sure you wipe up drips. Then place a piece of scrap fabric in the unthreaded machine, lower the presser foot, and stitch back and forth over the fabric.

HELPFUL HINT: Leave the needle in the fabric for two or three minutes to soak up excess oil.

Read the operator's manual for any cautions about use. For example, will the machine sew over pins, or must you remove them as you sew a seam?

Types of Machine Stitching

- **Directional stitching:** Also called "stitching with the grain." This is stitching done in the direction of the fabric grain. Rub your finger along a curved or bias edge of the fabric. In one direction, the threads will be roughed up. Rubbing in the other direction will smooth them down. Stitch in the direction that smooths the threads.

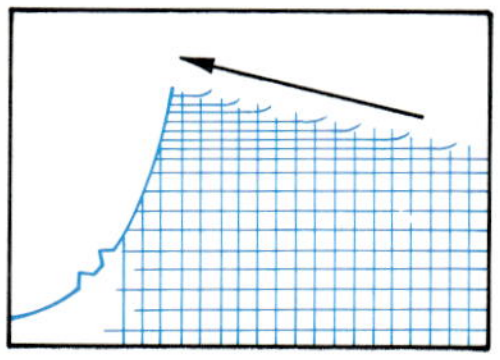
AGAINST THE GRAIN

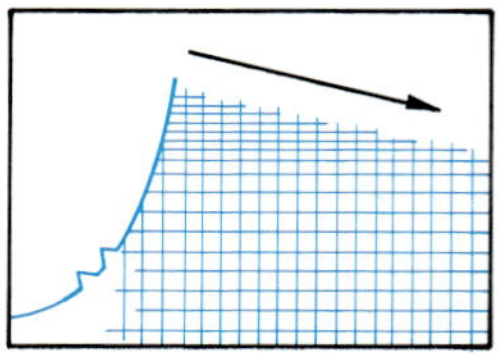
WITH THE GRAIN

- **Staystitching:** Keeps curved and bias edges from stretching. Staystitching should be done with the grain. Use 10 to 12 stitches per inch. Stitch ⅛ inch from the seam line, in the seam allowance.

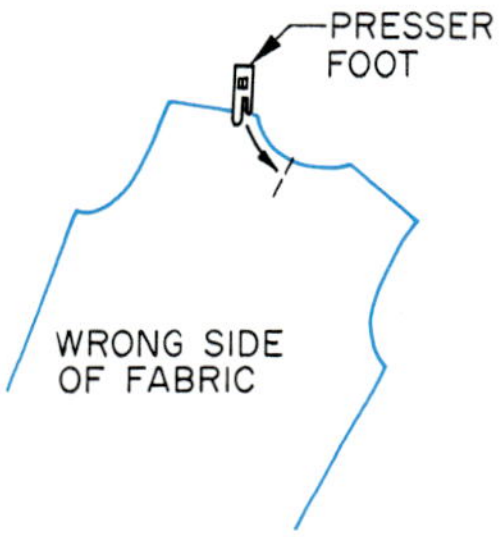

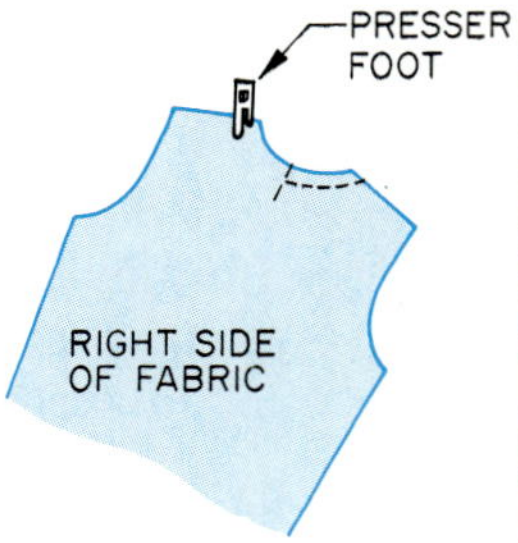

- **Backstitching:** Helps keep seams from pulling apart. Place needle ½ inch up the seam line. Set stitch control for reverse and sew backwards to the edge of the fabric.

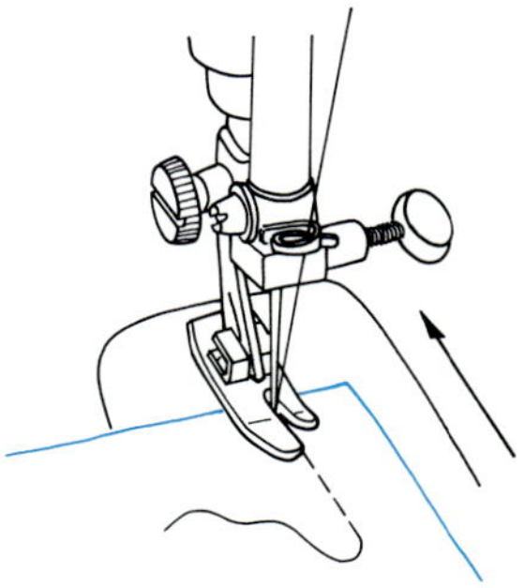

- **Topstitching:** Stitching done on the outside of a garment. Stitch on the right side of the fabric, using 8 stitches per inch.

(Continued on next page)

Types of Machine Stitching (continued)

- **Understitching:** Prevents edges of facing from rolling to the right side of a garment. Press seam allowances in the direction of the facing. Use regular length stitches and stitch on the right side of the facing, through the facing and seam allowances, about ⅛ inch from the seam line.

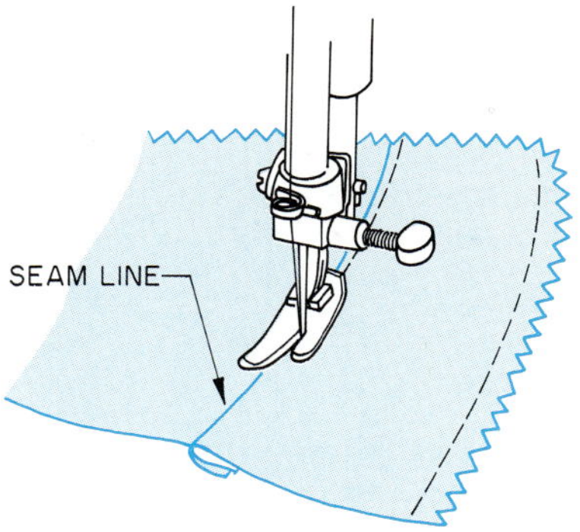

- **Stitching in the ditch:** Used to hold down facings and finish collars, cuffs, and waistbands. Stitch on the outside of the garment, in the groove formed by a seam, using regular length stitches.

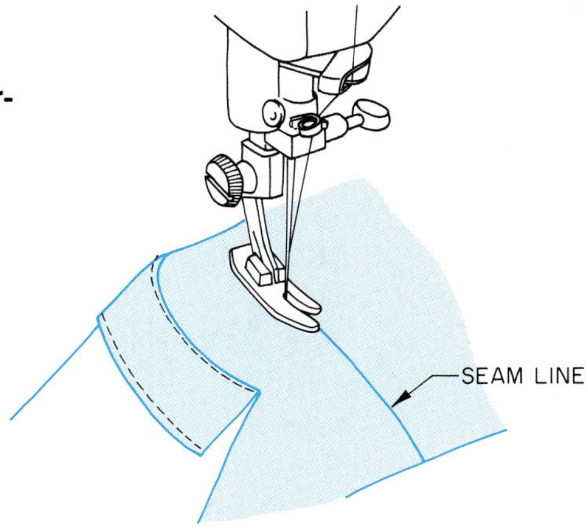

Safety Tips

- **Don't use the sewing machine before you have received complete instructions from your teacher.**
- **Occasionally a sewing machine needle may break during use. Be prepared; don't lean too close.**
- **Don't place a sewing machine cord where someone may trip on it.**
- **As you guide fabric through a sewing machine, keep your fingers away from the needle.**
- **Be sure your machine is one that can handle sewing over pins. If it can't, bent pins may jam in the feed dog and needles may break.**
- **Unplug the cord when you are finished with the sewing machine.**

TECHNIQUES FOR SEWING

This section covers the basic sewing techniques. Once you understand these, you can read your pattern guide sheet for specific directions. *If you are unsure about how to do something, ask your teacher to show you.*

DARTS

Darts are used to give shape to clothes so that they fit body curves. Sometimes darts are used for decoration. Some double-pointed darts (called fisheye darts) occur in the middle of a dress or blouse. They make the garment taper in at the waistline and out again over the hips.

Darts should first be carefully transferred from the pattern, as described in Chapter 17. To stitch darts:

1. Fold the fabric, right sides together. Pin along the stitching line.

2. Stitch from the wide end toward the pointed end, backstitching as you begin.

3. Do not backstitch at the pointed end. Instead, cut the threads a few inches beyond the fabric. Tie the threads in a double knot. Cut, leaving about 1 inch of thread beyond the knots.

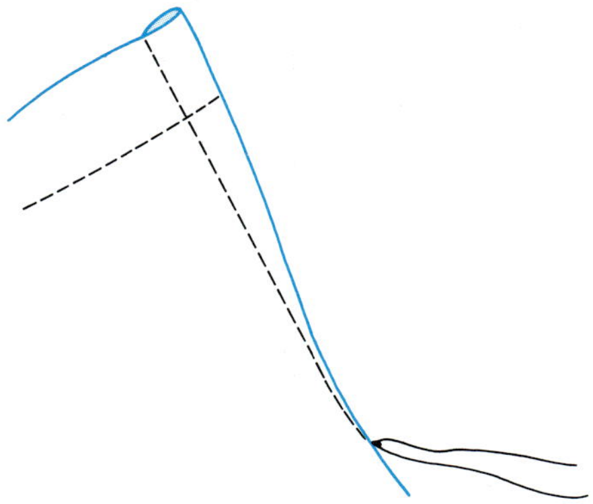

4. When stitching a double-pointed dart, begin in the middle and stitch to one end. Then return to the middle, lap 5 or 6 stitches, and stitch to the other end. Clip the dart at the widest part for "give."

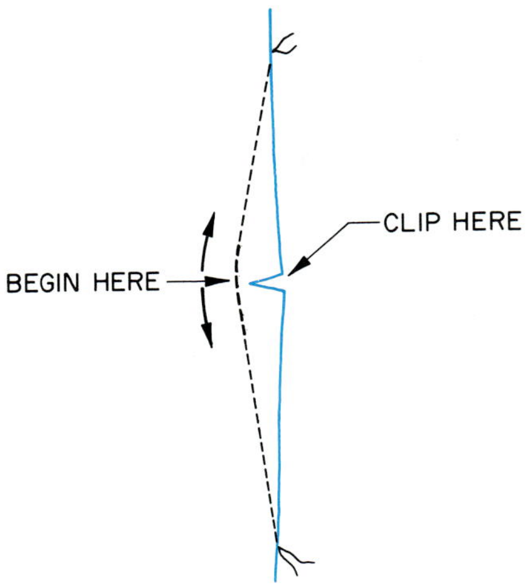

In wools and heavier fabrics, some darts may need to be slashed at least part of the way and pressed open. This reduces bulkiness.

SEAMS

Straight seams are the easiest of all to sew. Make them as follows:

1. Pin the seam, being sure to place right sides of fabric together, matching edges. Also match any notches or dots. Place the first pin at the start of the seam. Place the second pin at the end. Then pin in between as needed.

2. Set the guide on the machine for the recommended seam allowance. Usually this is ⅝ inch.

3. Backstitch to begin the seam. This will help keep the seam from pulling apart.

4. Now stitch forward to make the seam.

5. Backstitch also at the end of the seam.

6. Press seam open. (See page 210.)

Seam Treatments

Reducing Bulk—creates a crisper appearance; makes garment more comfortable

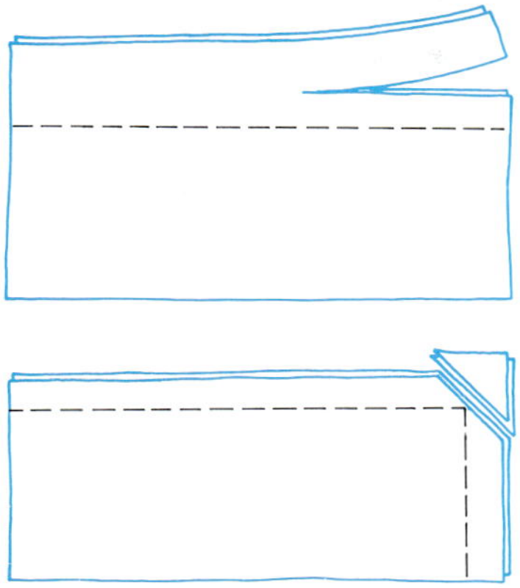

■ **Trimming** seams is simply cutting away half the seam allowance. Seams are also trimmed at corners to eliminate bulk when the corner is to be turned right side out. Trim corners by cutting diagonally about ⅛ inch from the stitching.

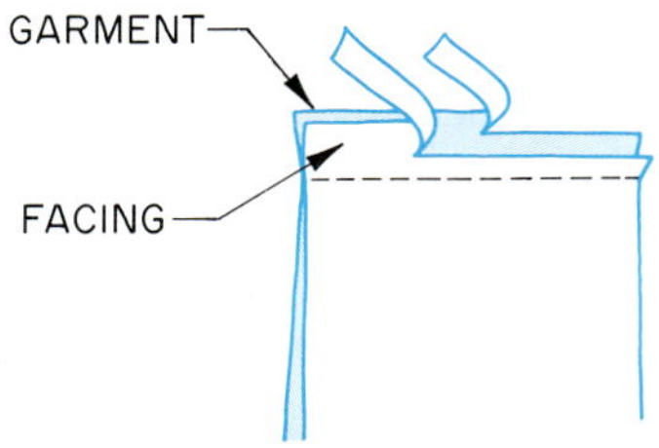

■ **Layering or grading** is done on seams with two or more thicknesses. Each thickness is trimmed to a different width. For example, at facings, cut away half the garment seam allowance. Then trim the facing seam allowance to a narrower width (about ¼ inch). This method prevents a ridge from showing on the right side of the garment.

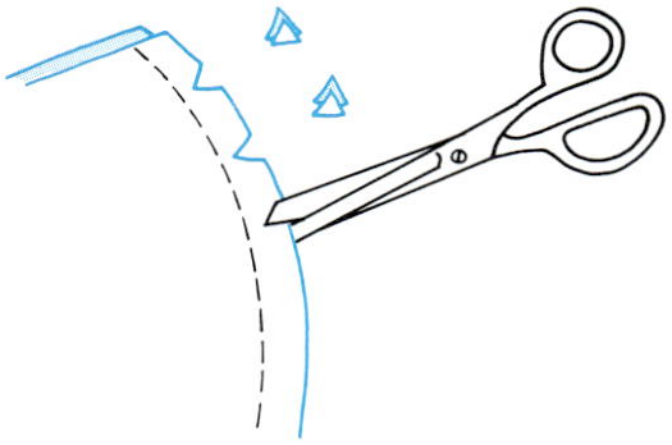

■ **Notching** is cutting small triangles out of the seam allowance. Do this on an outside curve to prevent bunching along the seam allowance when the fabric is turned to the right side.

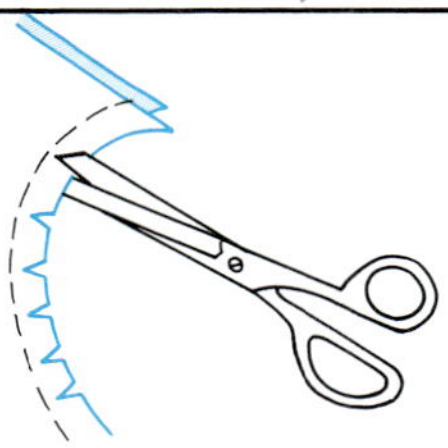

■ **Clipping** is slashing into the seam allowance on inside curves. The seam allowance will spread and lie flat when you press it. Be careful to slash no closer than ⅛ inch to the seam line.

(Continued on next page)

Seam Treatments (continued)

Finishing Seams—helps keep seam edges from fraying

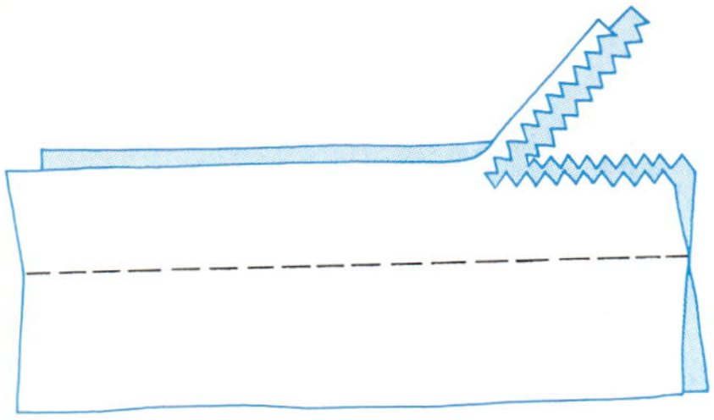

- **Pinking.** Before pressing it open, trim a plain seam with pinking shears along the outside edge of the seam allowance. This gives visible seams in unlined jackets an attractive look.

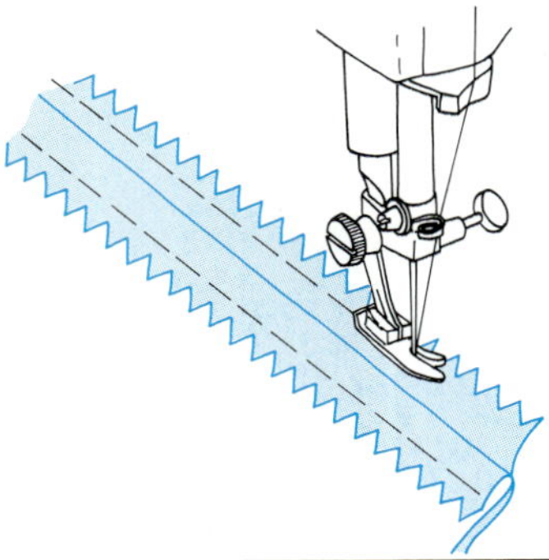

- **Pinking and stitching.** For fabrics that will ravel more easily, trim the outside edge of the seam allowance with pinking shears before you press the seam open. Then stitch each seam allowance separately, close to the pinked edge. Press open.

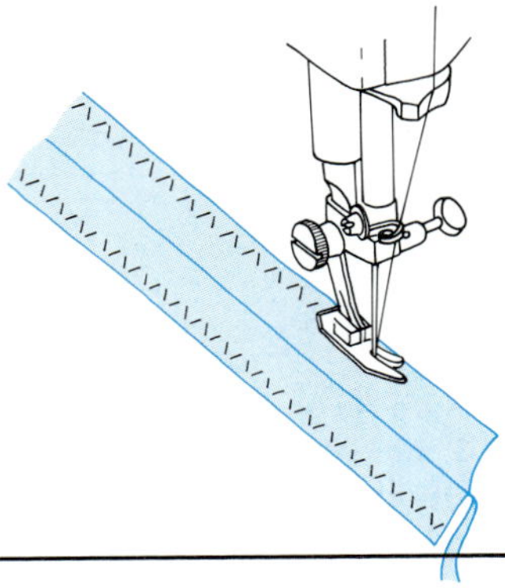

- **Zigzagging.** Use this seam finish on fabrics that ravel easily. Zigzag-stitch close to the seam edge or over the edge of a seam. It is best to press the seam before you zigzag each seam allowance.

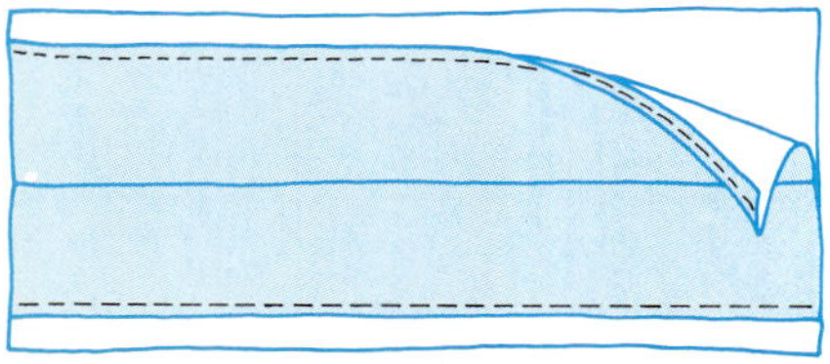

- **Clean-edge finish.** Turn under each edge of the seam allowance ¼ inch and stitch close to the folded edge. This hemming of the seam allowance gives a finished appearance to the inside of an unlined jacket.

FACINGS

A **facing** is a piece of fabric used to finish a garment edge. For example, facings are used at the armholes of most sleeveless blouses.

A facing may be an extended facing, a fitted facing, or a bias facing. An *extended facing* is part of the garment piece that is turned back or under. Shirts or blouses may have this type of facing at the front edges, where they button. A *fitted facing* is a separate piece of fabric sewn on. Fitted facings are found at necklines, waistlines, and armhole edges. *Bias facings* are made from a narrow strip of fabric cut "on the bias." This means the pattern piece was laid diagonally on the fabric. The facing is sewn on and then hemmed. The stretchiness of the bias-cut facing makes it easy to fit the bias strip to the gently-curved edges of a neckline.

Fitted facings are the most common. Usually they are made from two or more pieces of fabric. To make a fitted facing:

1. Staystitch the inside curves of the facing pieces just inside the seam line.

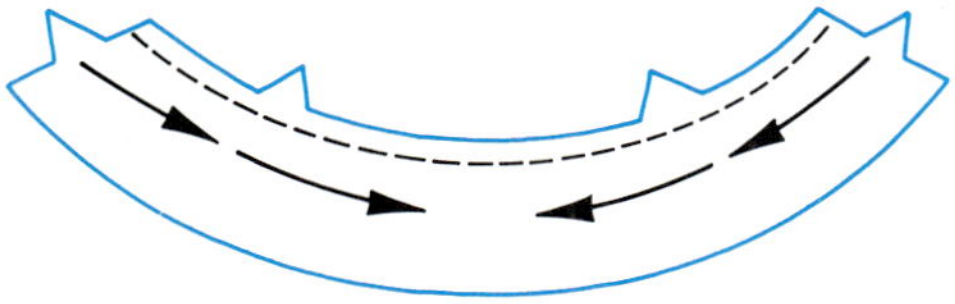

STITCH IN DIRECTION OF ARROWS

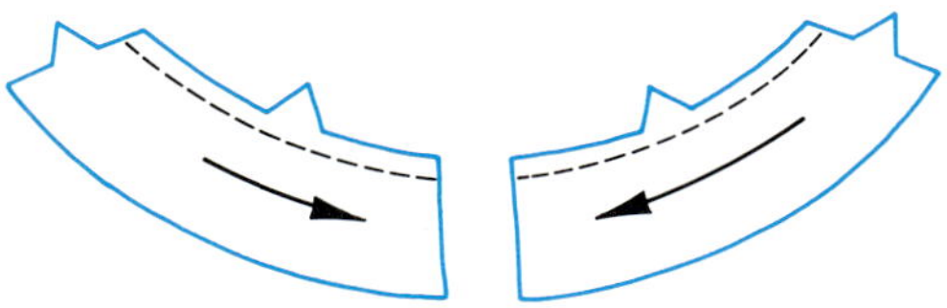

2. Place the facing pieces right sides together, matching notches, and stitch. Press seams open.

3. To prevent raveling, finish the outside edge of the facing. Staystitch ¼ inch from the edge and either pink the edge or turn it under at the staystitching and stitch on the fold. Or finish the outside edge by zigzag stitching all around it.

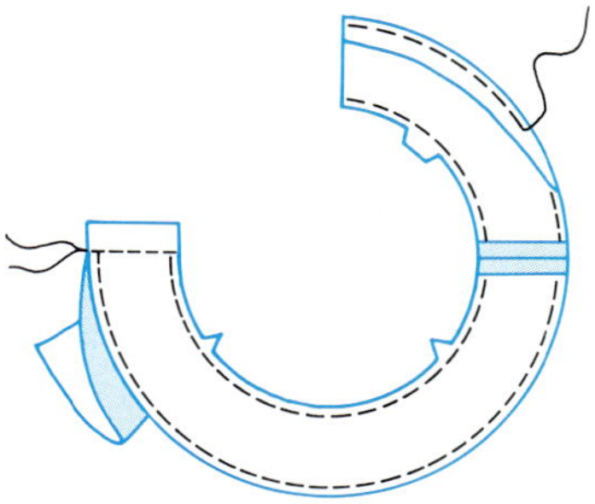

4. Place the facing on the garment piece, right sides together. Match seams and notches. Pin. Stitch on the seam line.

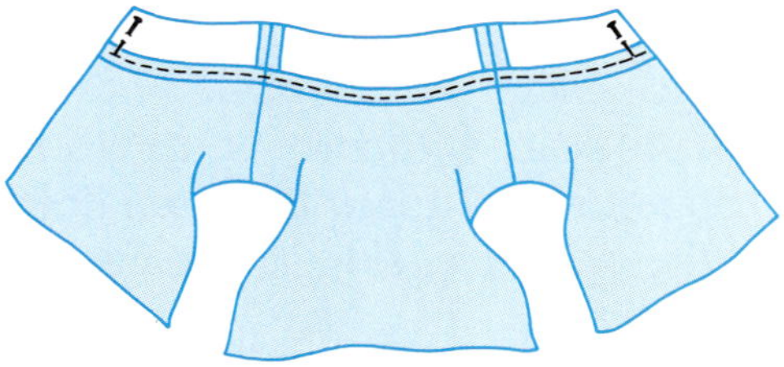

5. Facings will lie flat if you press all layers of seam allowance toward the facing and then understitch through the seam allowance and facing about ⅛ inch from the seam line. This also helps keep the facing in place so it does not show on the outside.

6. Turn facing to wrong side of garment. Press. Tack in place at seams with small hand stitches. Or, "stitch in the ditch."

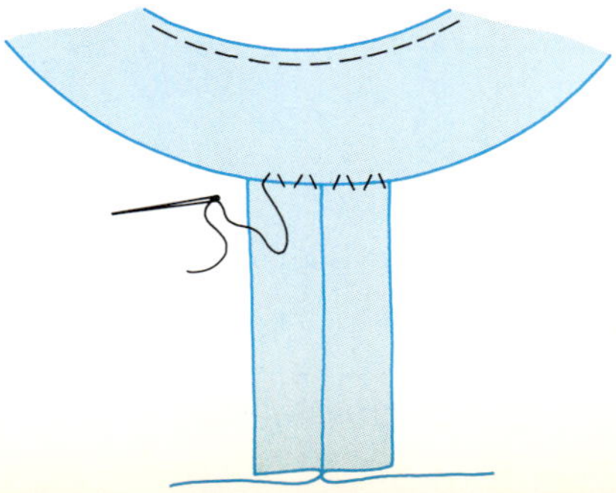

INTERFACING

An interfacing is sewn between the facing and the garment. Its purpose is to add strength and weight and to keep the garment from stretching. For example, it is used in collars and cuffs so they don't droop and in waistbands so they don't roll.

When *sewing* in interfacing, pin it to the wrong side of the fabric. Stitch ½ inch from the fabric edge. Trim interfacing close to the stitching line and cut corners diagonally to remove bulk.

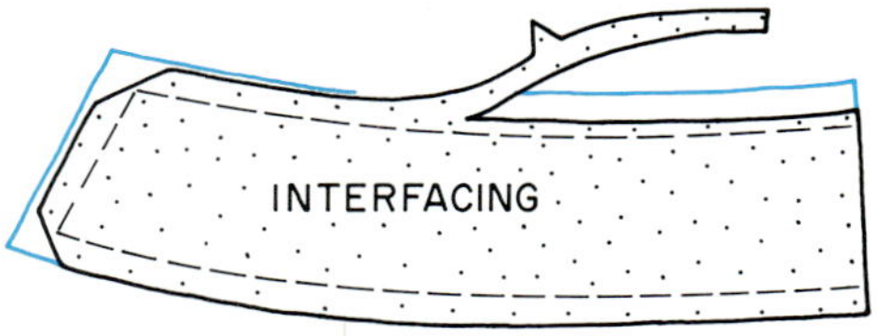

When *fusing* interfacing, trim off its seam allowance. Place the interfacing up to but not on the seam allowance of the fabric so you do not stitch it into the seam line. Be sure the adhesive side is facing down. Press in place.

Helpful hint: Do not slide the iron back and forth or the interfacing will wrinkle.

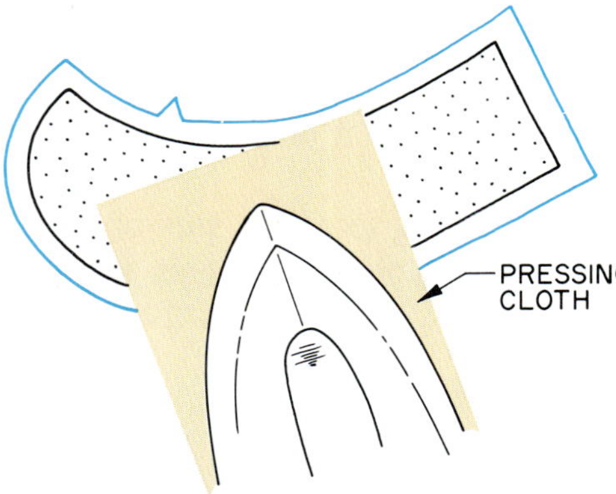

COLLARS

Collars vary in shape and size. Some are rounded on the edge; some are pointed. Some stand up; others lie flat. Some collars are finished with a facing, while others are finished with a band to hide the seam allowances. Three basic types include:

- *Flat collar.* This type lies flat against the garment. An example is the Peter Pan collar. Flat collars are used in untailored garments such as dresses and in children's wear.
- *Partial rolled collar.* This type first stands up from the neck edge in the center back. Then it curves down to rest on the garment at the center front. The line at which the collar folds is called the "roll line."

- *Full rolled collar.* This type remains above the neckline. It may be a narrow, single-width band, such as a mandarin collar, or a two-piece collar, such as the one on a man-tailored shirt.

Collars look better if they are interfaced for shape and body. The interfacing is attached to the upper collar. The **upper collar** is the part that is seen when the garment is worn. The **under collar** is like a facing. It finishes the edges of the collar and is hidden.

To *make* a flat collar, follow the instructions on your pattern. In general, you should:

1. Stitch or fuse the interfacing to the wrong side of the upper collar.

2. With right sides together, pin upper and under collars together along the unnotched edges and stitch along these edges. (The under collar is sometimes called the collar facing.)

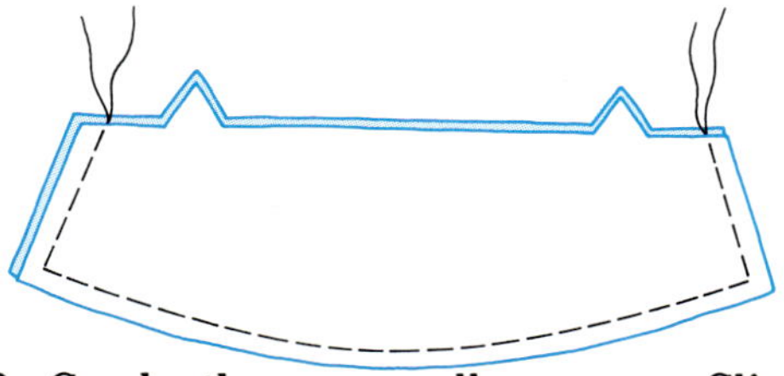

3. Grade the seam allowances. Clip or notch curves.

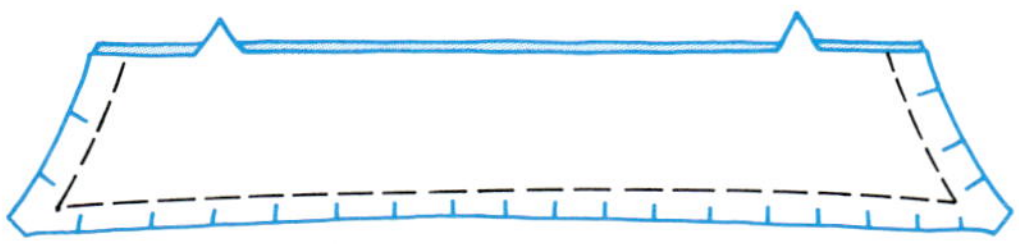

CLIP INSIDE CURVES

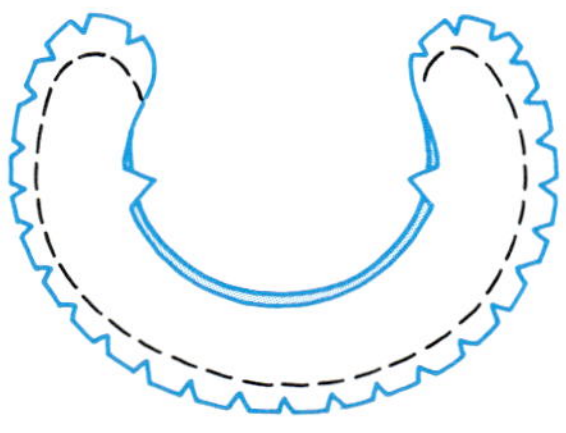

NOTCH OUTSIDE CURVES

4. Understitch the under collar to the seam allowance.

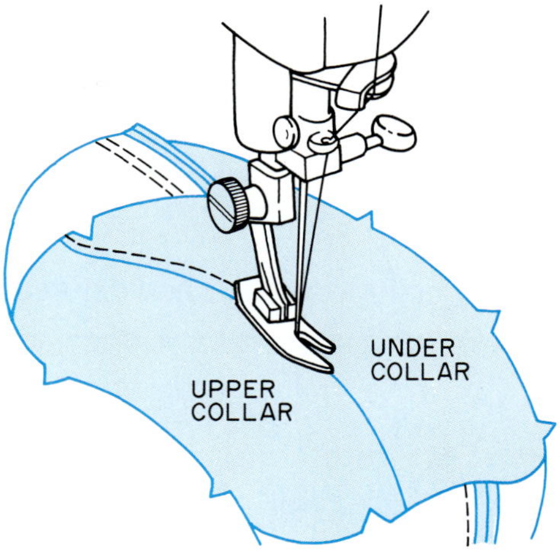

5. Turn the collar right side out. Gently pull out the points. (Pushing them out with scissors or other pointed objects could make a hole in the fabric.)

6. Press, rolling seam toward the under collar.

To *apply* the collar to the garment, follow these steps:

1. Prepare the neck facing: stitch pieces together, press seams open, finish outside edge.

2. Staystitch and clip the garment neckline.

3. Baste the neckline edges of the collar together.

4. Pin the collar to the neckline, with under collar against right side of garment. Match notches. Be sure the collar is centered. Baste.

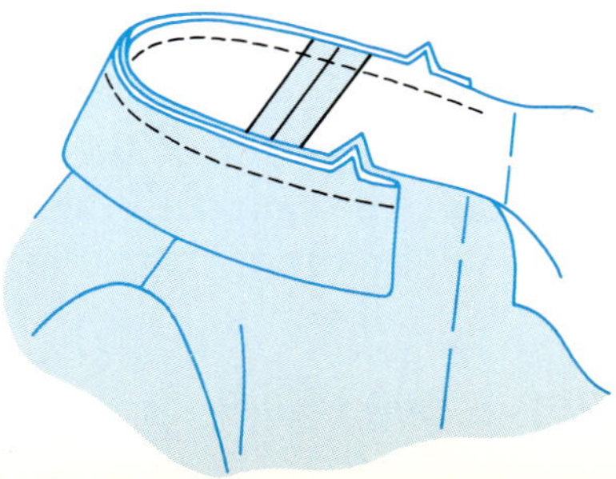

5. Pin and stitch the neckline facing to the neck edge, right sides together. (The collar should be between the facing and the garment as you sew.)
6. Grade seams and clip curves.
7. Turn facing to inside of garment and press.
8. Understitch facing to neckline seam allowance.
9. Tack facing edges to shoulder seams.

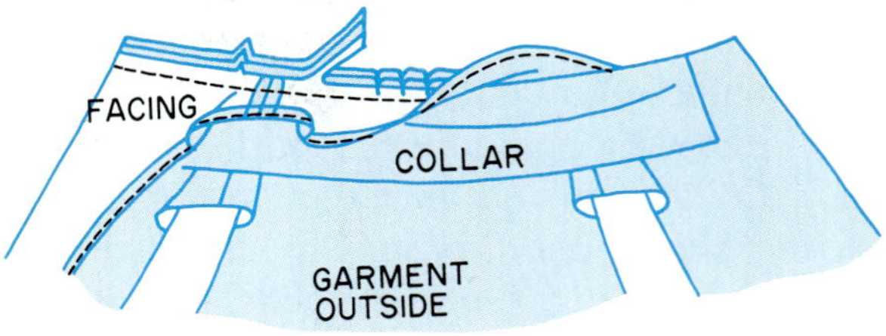

SLEEVES

There are three basic sleeve styles: the *set-in* sleeve, the *raglan* sleeve, and the *kimono* sleeve.

Set-in Sleeves

The set-in sleeve is attached to the garment with a seam running around the arm at the armhole. It is the most difficult to make but the most common. Usually the sleeve and bodice are made separately and then joined. (The **bodice**—BAHD-us—is the part of the garment above the waistline.) Sometimes, set-in sleeves are attached before the side seam of the garment and the underarm seam of the sleeve are sewn. Follow your pattern instructions. In general they will tell you to:

1. Make two rows of basting stitches around the sleeve top between notches.

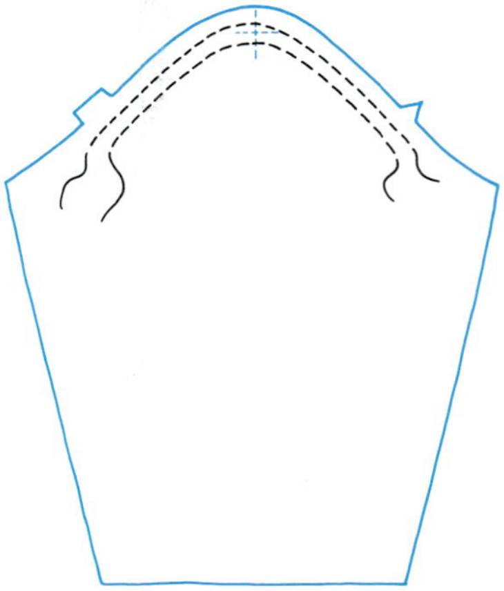

2. Stitch the garment shoulder seam and press open.

3. With right sides together, pin the sleeve to the armhole, matching all markings. Pull the machine basting until the sleeve fits the armhole. Evenly distribute the ease. Pin the sleeve in place.

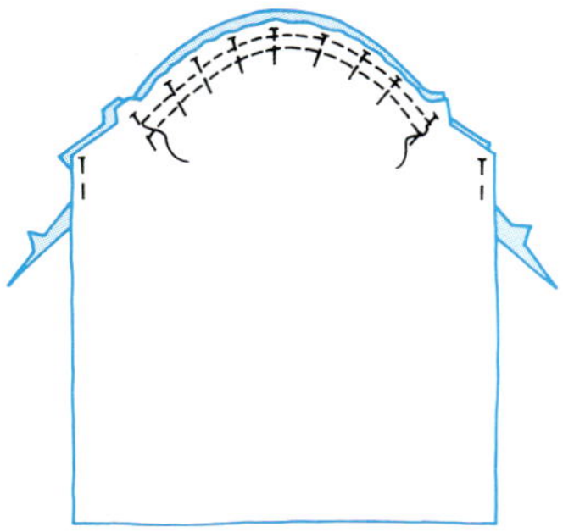

4. Stitch the armhole seam. Make a second row of stitching 1/8 inch from the first, inside the seam allowance.

5. Trim the entire seam if the fabric is bulky. Clip the curves.

6. With right sides together, pin the garment side seam and underarm sleeve seam.

7. Stitch the seam, going from the bottom of the garment to the end of the sleeve. Press seams open.

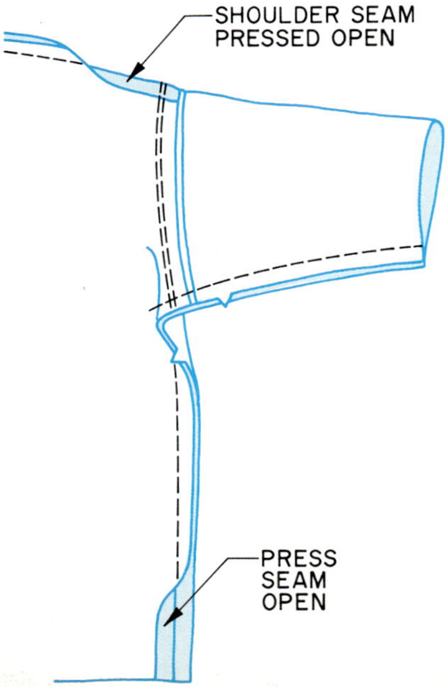

Raglan Sleeves

The raglan sleeve is attached to the garment by a diagonal seam from the underarm to the neckline. A raglan sleeve is usually attached this way:

1. Stitch the dart at the shoulder. Slash and press open.

2. With right sides together, pin and stitch the underarm seam on each sleeve.

3. Press the seams open flat.

4. Stitch the garment side seams. Press them open.

5. Pin the right side of the sleeve to the right side of the garment, matching notches and underarm seams.

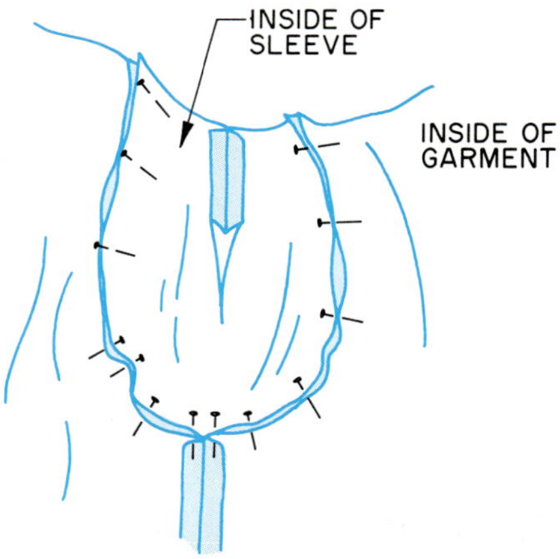

6. Stitch the seam. Reinforce seam between the notches by stitching again close to first stitching.

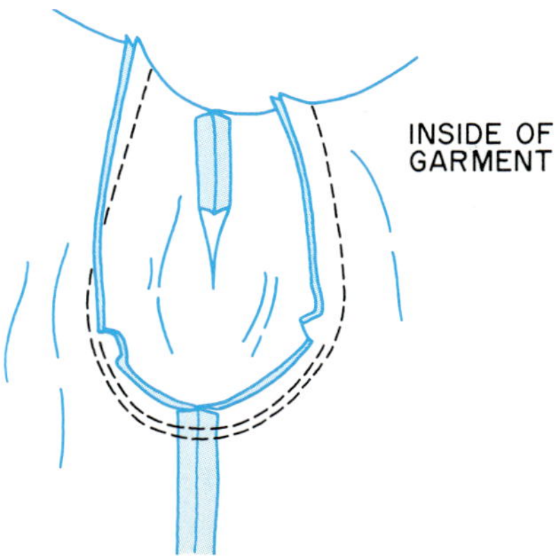

7. Clip and press the seam open above the notches. Press the seam at the underarm between the notches toward the sleeve.

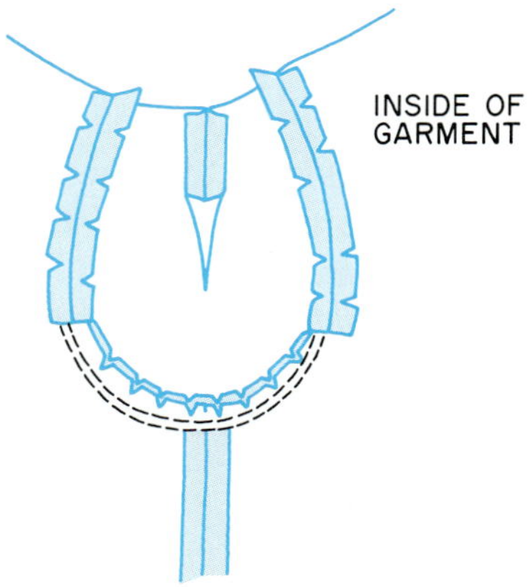

Kimono Sleeves

The kimono sleeve is cut in one piece with the garment.

1. With right sides together, pin and stitch the side seam of the garment and the underarm seam of the sleeve.
2. Pin and stitch the shoulder seam and upper-arm seam.
3. Clip the sharp curve at the underarm. Press the seams open over the curve of a pressing ham. (See page 210.)

WAISTBANDS

A waistband is stitched to the waistline seam of pants, jeans, shorts, and skirts to finish the seam edge and give a snug fit. Waistbands should be interfaced so they will not roll or stretch.

The most common method of sewing on waistbands is as follows:

1. On the *unnotched* edge of the waistband, press the seam allowance to the inside.

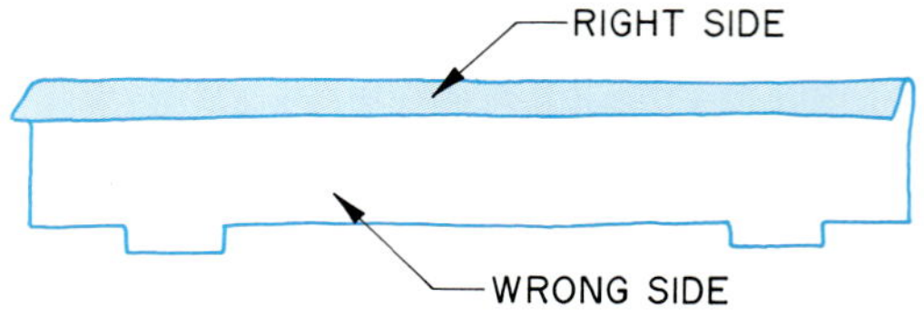

2. On the *notched* edge of the waistband, apply interfacing to the wrong side of the fabric.

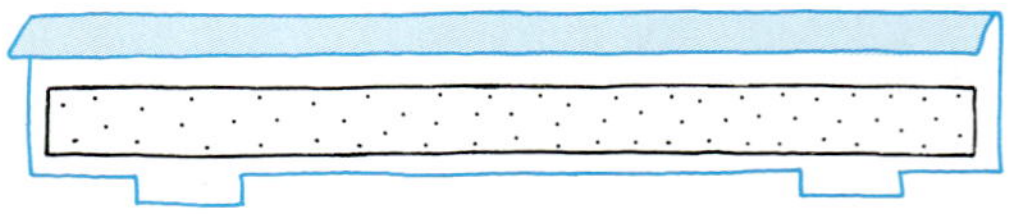

3. With right sides together, pin the band to the garment edge, matching all markings carefully. The band should be long enough to overlap and to make finished edges at both ends. The garment may have to be eased to fit. Stitch the seam.

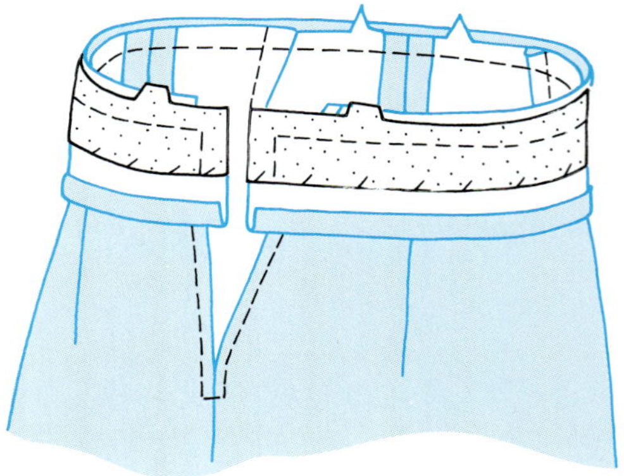

4. Grade seam allowances. Press toward waistband.

5. Fold the band in half with right sides together. Pin and stitch the ends. One end should come out even with the garment and the other end should extend 1 to 1 ½ inches beyond the garment.

6. Trim the seam allowances and grade if the fabric is bulky.

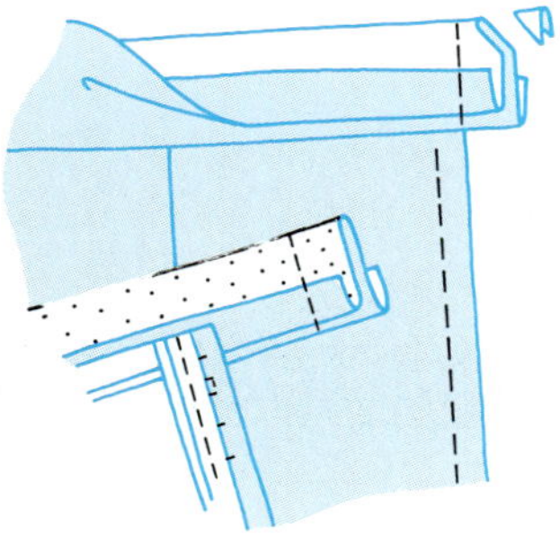

7. Turn the band right side out, being sure that the corners are pointed and curves lie flat. Press.

8. Turn the unfinished edge under along the seam line. Pin and hand stitch or machine topstitch it in place. Press again.

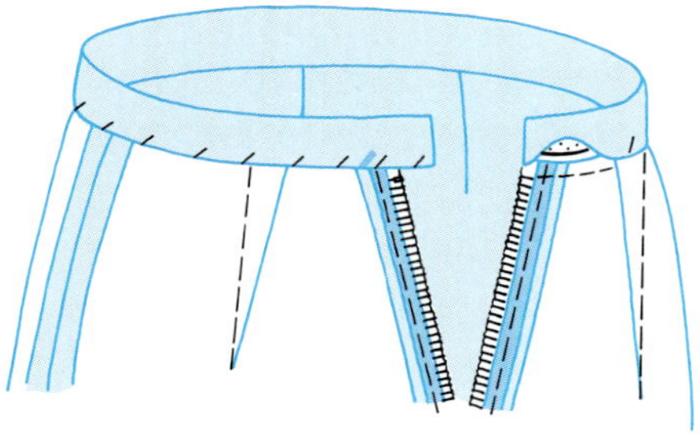

CASINGS

A **casing** is a fabric tube that holds a drawstring or elastic in place. Casings are often used at waistlines. *Applied casings* are made by sewing a piece of fabric to the garment. *Self-casings* are made by folding back the edge of the garment.

To make a self-casing for elastic at the waistline of a garment:

1. Turn the raw edge of the waistline seam in about ½ inch and press.

2. Fold the garment edge to the inside along the fold line. (The fold line will be marked on the pattern.) Press and pin.

3. Stitch the casing about ¼ inch from the edge, leaving a small opening so you can insert the elastic.

4. Insert the elastic.

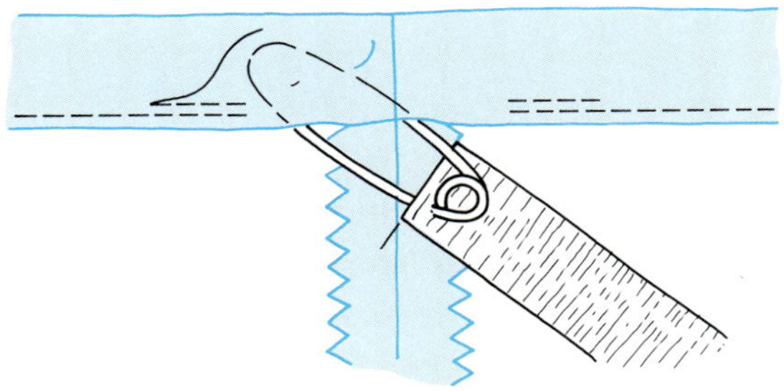

USE A SAFETY PIN TO PULL THE ELASTIC THROUGH

5. Pin the ends of the elastic together. Put on the garment and adjust to fit. With the ends of the elastic overlapped at least ½ inch and pinned, take off the garment.

6. Stitch the elastic together.

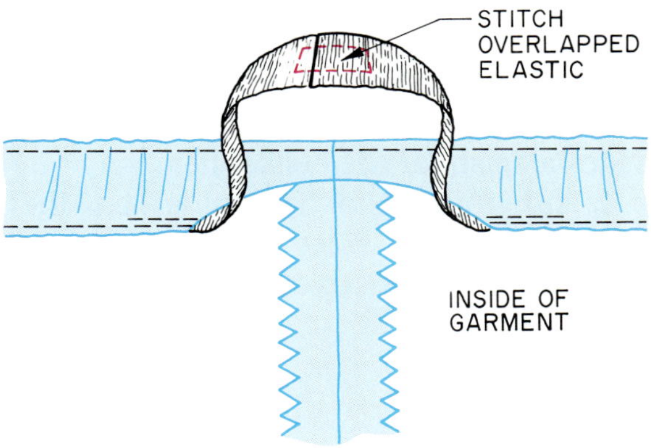

7. Stitch the casing closed.

CUFFS

The two most common types of cuffs are French cuffs and single, or barrel, cuffs. *Single cuffs* are buttoned. *French cuffs* are folded back and fastened with a cuff link.

Sleeve cuffs are made and sewn to the garment in the same manner as a waistband. They may be made from one piece of fabric folded in half or two pieces seamed together. Cuffs should be interfaced to add body and crispness and to prevent stretching.

POCKETS

Some pockets are hidden in seams. An example is a pocket set into the side seam of a dress. The pattern guide sheet will tell you how to sew these pockets.

Pockets that are sewn on the outside of the garment are called **patch pockets.** Patch pockets must be carefully made because they show on the outside of the garment. You should mark the pocket position clearly on the garment. Your pattern guide sheet will give you step-by-step instructions for sewing the pockets. In general, for patch pockets, you should:

1. At the top edge, turn ¼ inch to the inside. Stitch on the fold edge. This provides a finish for the pocket hem.

2. Turn the hem to the outside along the fold line; right sides together. Stitch around the three sides of the pocket on the seam line.

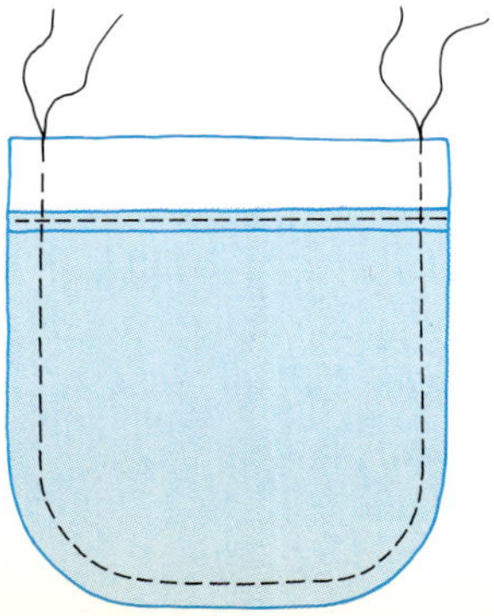

3. Trim hem corners; notch outside curves.

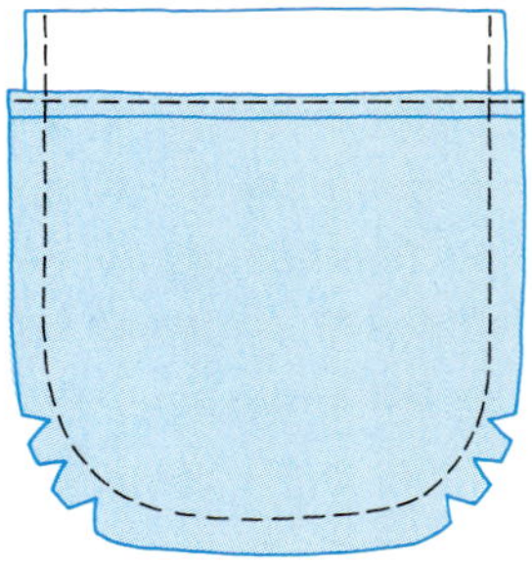

4. Turn the hem right side out. Press the seam allowances to the inside.

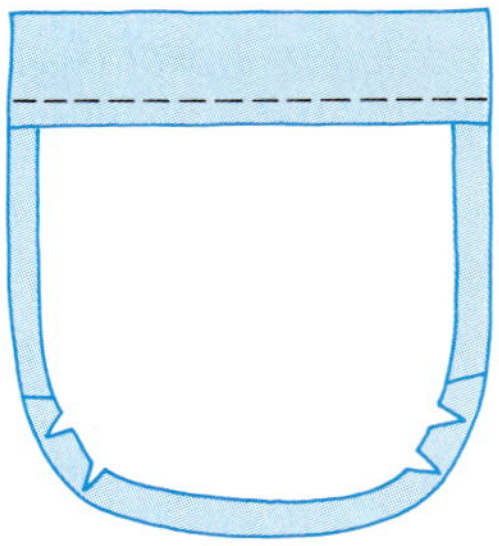

5. Pin the pocket to the right side of the garment.

6. Topstitch the pocket to the garment, backstitching at the two upper corners, where pockets receive a lot of pull.

PLEATS

Pleats are straight folds of fabric stitched in place. They are used to control fullness and to shape fabric to the body. Some pleats are stitched only where they join the rest of the garment. Others are stitched all along the pleat.

- *Knife pleats* all run in the same direction.
- A *box pleat* is two pleats turned away from each other.
- An *inverted pleat* is two pleats turned toward each other.

Make pleats with the right side of the fabric up. Follow the pattern markings to position them. Place pins at right angles to the pleat edges and baste the pleats in place.

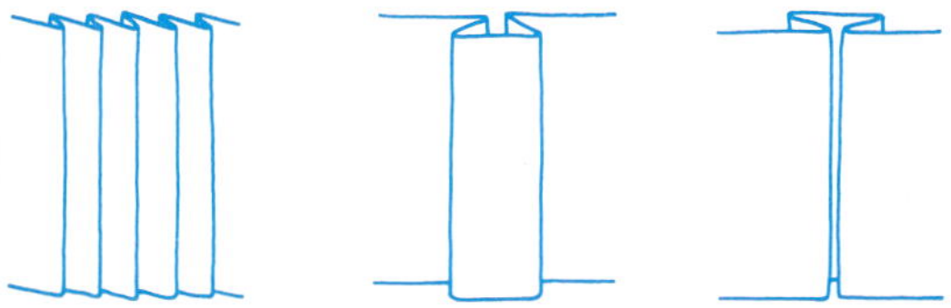

ELASTIC

Elastic may be inserted in a casing or sewn directly on the fabric. To attach it directly, stitch the elastic ends together flat. Divide the garment edge and the elastic each into four parts. Mark with pins. Now pin the elastic to the garment, lining up the two sets of marking pins. Divide the garment fullness evenly. As you sew, stretch the elastic to fit.

CLOSURES

Some fasteners are designed to add trim. Others are supposed to be "invisible." Fasteners should hold the garment together without pulling or allowing gaps. Be sure to follow pattern instructions for best results. Buttons, snaps, and hooks and eyes are sewn on by hand. Always use a double thread or even four strands for durability.

Buttonholes

There are two types of buttonholes: worked and bound. *Worked buttonholes* can be made by hand or by machine. *Bound buttonholes* are made with both hand and machine sewing. They are usually used in tailored, heavier garments, such as coats and suit jackets. Most buttonholes are the worked type.

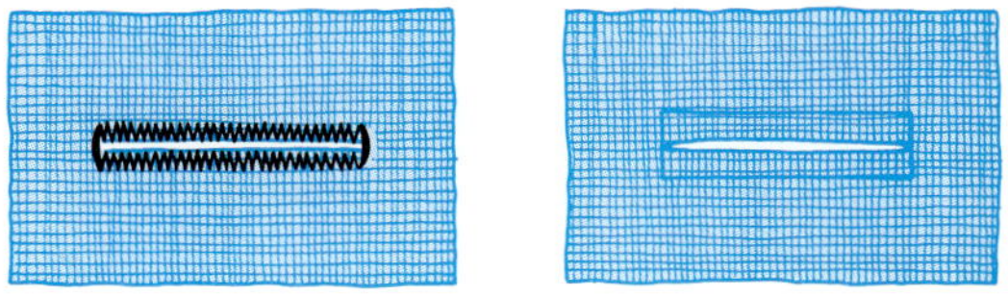

The length of the buttonhole depends on the size of the button you are using. Measure the diameter and thickness of the button and add together. The total should be the length of the buttonhole. Buttonholes should be evenly spaced.

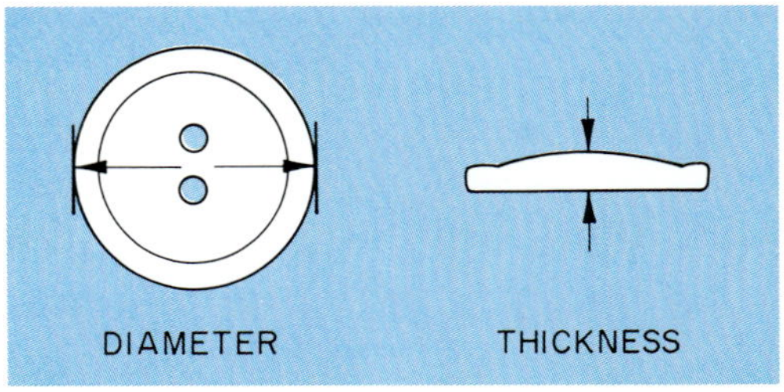

Most machines have attachments for making worked buttonholes. Check the operator's manual for specific instructions. To make worked buttonholes by hand, cut the buttonhole the desired length. Use a blanket stitch to cover the raw edges of the opening. This method is best suited for soft or delicate fabrics.

Buttons

Buttons are sewn on after buttonholes are made. To place the buttons, pin the garment closed, matching center lines. Put a pin through the opening of the buttonhole at the end nearest the garment's edge. Make sure the buttons are evenly spaced and in a straight line. Attach the buttons at the points you have marked with pins.

There are two types of buttons. Sew-through, or *flat buttons,* are those with holes going through them. *Shank buttons* have a little stemlike loop on the back.

To sew on flat buttons:

1. Secure the thread to the wrong side of the garment with a couple of small stitches.
2. Bring the thread up to the right side through one of the holes in the button.
3. Go back down to the wrong side through another hole.
4. On top of the button, slip a straight pin or toothpick under the thread between the button's holes. This creates room for the layers of fabric between the button and garment.

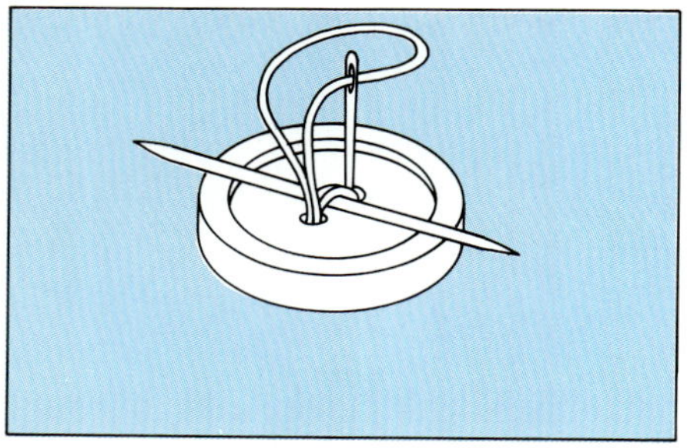

5. Repeat the stitching through the button's holes four or five times, ending on the inside of the garment.
6. Remove the pin or toothpick and lift the button so that the extra thread is between the button and the fabric.
7. Bring the needle back up to the right side, but do not go through the button. Wind the thread under the button, around the stitches, pulling it tight.

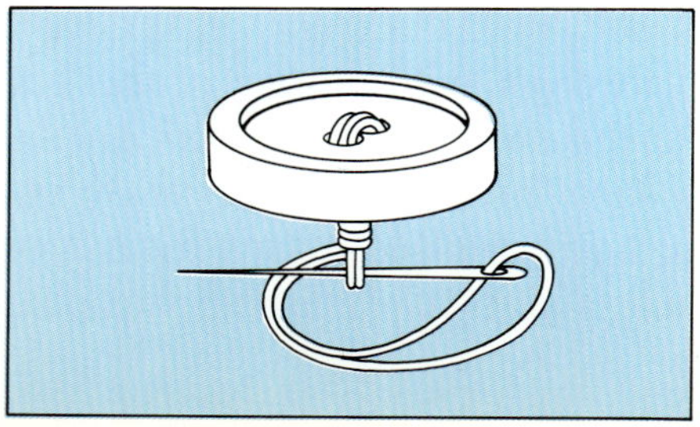

8. Take needle to wrong side again; secure thread with two or three stitches under the button.

If the button has four holes, sew in the same pattern each time you pass through the holes.

If your button has a shank, sew with small stitches through the shank and into the fabric. Repeat this four or five times. Fasten securely, keeping the stitches parallel with the edge of the fabric.

Snaps

Snaps are best for fastening edges that receive little strain. They come in a variety of sizes for different weights of fabric. Heavy fabrics require large snaps. Thin, lightweight fabrics need small ones.

A snap consists of two parts. One part is the ball (top) and the other part is the socket (bottom). The socket half of the snap is always sewn on the *right* side of the garment section closest to the body. The ball half is sewn to the *wrong* side of the overlapping section.

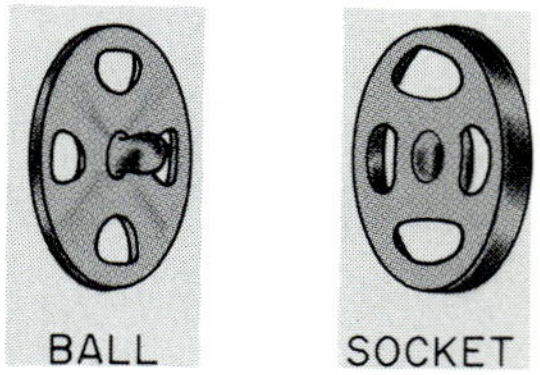

Make small stitches, picking up one or two threads of fabric, as you go through the holes of the snap. The stitches should not be seen on the right side of the garment. When going from one hole to another, slip the thread under the snap.

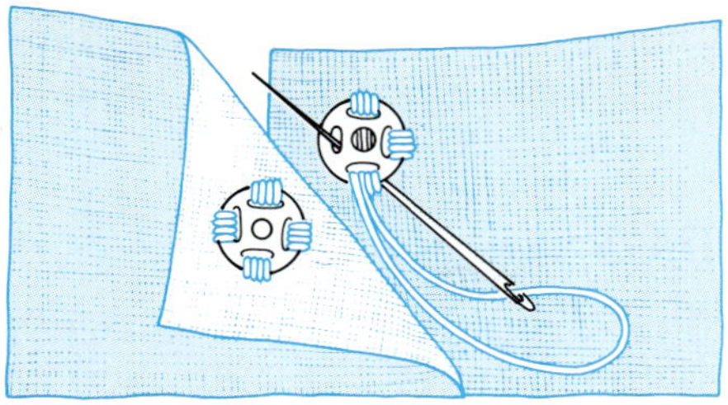

Some snaps are held in place with tiny teeth rather than with stitches. These snaps are called grippers. They are used on children's clothing and sportswear because they are stronger and larger. They do show on the outside and many times are made decorative. These should be applied following the manufacturer's instructions.

Hooks and Eyes

Hooks and eyes are more secure than sewn-on snaps and are used where there is more strain, such as at waistbands and neck edges. Like snaps, they come in many sizes. The shape of the hook is standard, but the eyes are available round or straight. When two edges overlap, such as on a waistband, a straight eye is used. If two edges just meet, a round eye works better.

The hook is sewn to the side that overlaps or to the right-hand side if there is no overlap. It is placed about ⅛ inch from the edge of the opening so that it cannot be seen. Small stitches or blanket stitches are worked around each of the loops to hold it securely in place. The stitches should not show on the right side of the garment.

Straight eyes are sewn to the top side of the underlap. Round eyes are sewn to the bottom side, sticking out slightly beyond the edge. Sew the eyes in the same manner as the hooks.

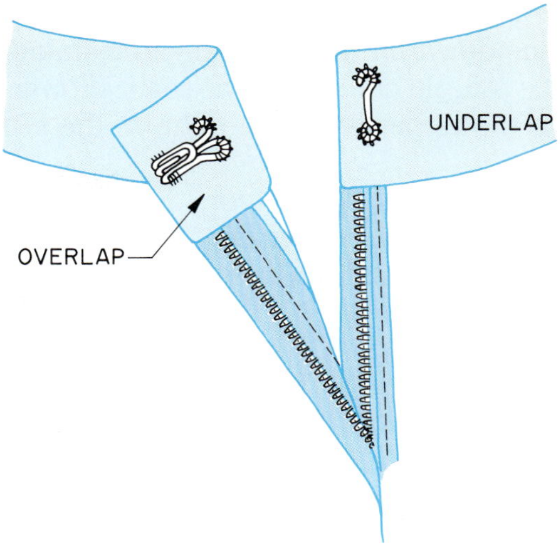

Zippers

On the pattern envelope under "notions" you can find what kind and length zipper you need for your garment. Try to match the color of the zipper to your garment as best you can. Most zippers are hidden in a seam or under a lap, but some are also decorative.

The most popular zipper closures are:

- lapped with one flap, as used on fly-front pants and sides of skirts
- centered with two narrow flaps, as used in the backs of garments

To insert a *lapped* zipper, follow pattern instructions. The zipper package may also tell how to insert the zipper.

The *centered* zipper is usually placed in the center back seam of a garment. The zipper is centered in the seam and is evenly stitched on each side of the seam. Both rows of stitching can be seen on the outside, and the laps formed on each side cover the teeth of the zipper.

To insert a centered zipper:

1. Baste the seam opening closed. Press seams open.

2. Open the zipper. Center the zipper face down on the seam line. Beginning at the top, pin one side to the seam allowance so the zipper teeth are right on the seam line.

3. Using a zipper foot, machine baste along the zipper guideline through the zipper tape and the one seam allowance.

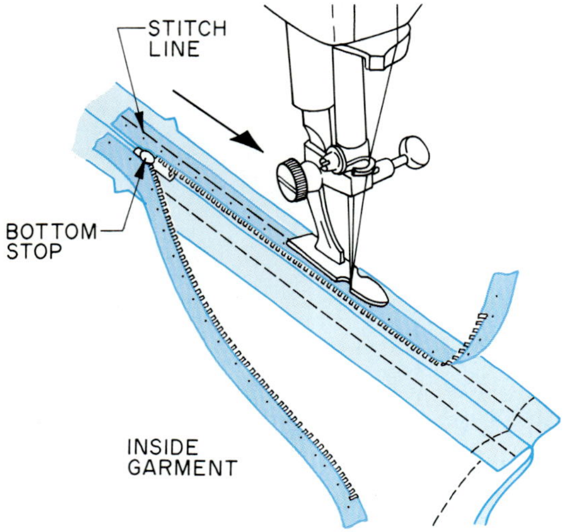

4. Close the zipper and place it flat against the fabric.

5. Stitch down the length of the zipper, across the bottom, and up the other side.

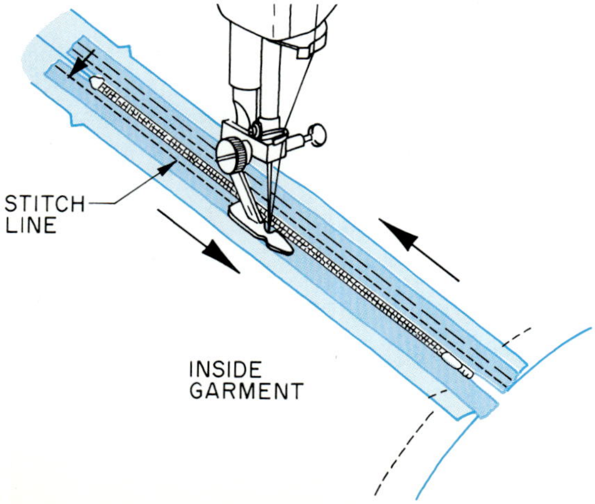

6. Remove the basting from the seam line.

LININGS

Linings help garments hang better and last longer. Linings give a finished look to garments on the inside and make them easier to slip on and off. Linings can also protect your skin from scratchy fabrics. When choosing fabrics for linings, remember that they should wear well and add body but not stiffness.

Linings for skirts and pants are made like the main garment but without closures or waistbands. Most are then attached at the waistband and hemmed.

HEMS

Let a garment hang overnight before you mark the hem. Sometimes garments stretch slightly, especially if they are cut on the bias.

To mark pants hems, turn up the fabric until the front of the pants just touches the top of your shoe and the back is about ½ inch longer. Place a pin at front and back on the folded crease.

To hem a skirt:

1. The most flattering skirt length for most women is one to two inches below the knee. However, the current style has a lot to say about hem lengths. Try on the dress or skirt with the shoes you will wear with it. Use a hem marker or a yardstick to mark off the best length for you. You can mark with pins or chalk.

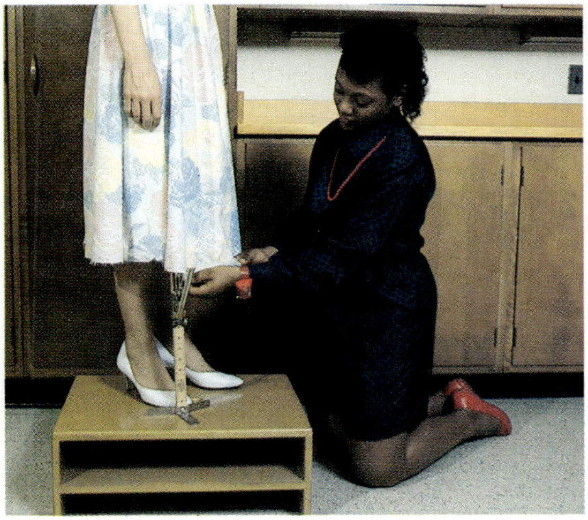

2. Turn the hem to the inside and place pins parallel to the edge of the hem about every 2 to 3 inches. Be careful not to pull the fabric as you are pinning; allow it to hang naturally.

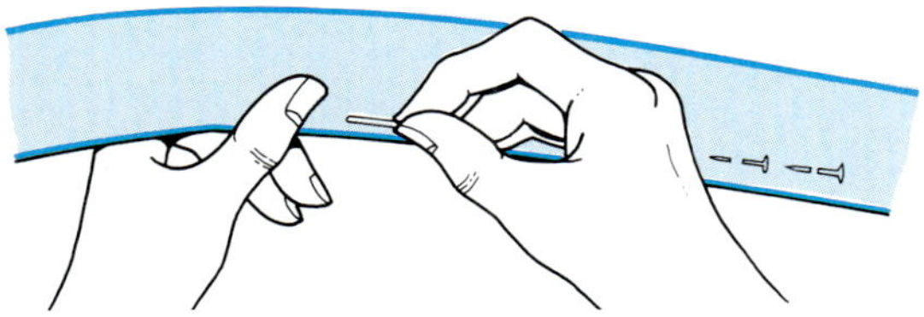

3. Press lightly, creasing the fabric at the point where the bottom of the hem will be.

4. On the inside of the fabric, measure the depth of the hem. The fuller the skirt, the shallower the hem should be. Mark the hem depth with chalk evenly all the way around. Trim away extra fabric, following the chalk markings.

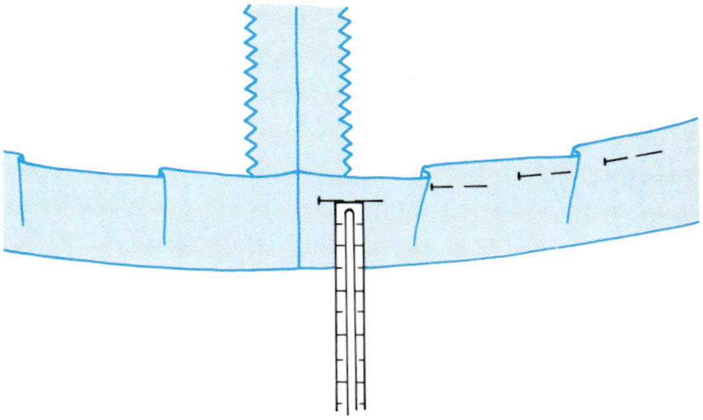

5. Finish the top edge of the hem with hem tape. Then stitch the hem in place by hand. Hem edges may also be zigzagged, pinked, or turned under and stitched.

—Perspective—

STITCHING BY HAND

Before the invention of the sewing machine, all clothing was sewn by hand. Can you imagine the time and effort it must have taken to make a man's suit or a floor-length ball gown? Often, more than one person worked on a single garment.

Today sewing is much faster and easier with a machine. But hand stitching is still needed for things like tacking facings and sewing hems. Here are some tips for hand sewing:

- Unless you're sewing on buttons or other fasteners, use a single strand of thread. Don't make the thread longer than 20 inches. Too long a thread tangles easily.
- To secure the thread in the fabric when you begin and end, make a few small stitches in one spot. This locks the thread so it doesn't pull out.

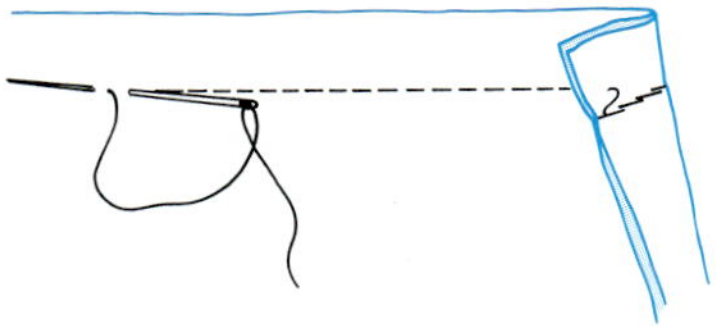

backstitch: A strong stitch, good for mending. Bring needle up, then insert needle 1/8 inch to the *right* of that point. Bring needle up again 1/8 inch to the *left* of the first point. Repeat, working back into same hole as previous stitch.

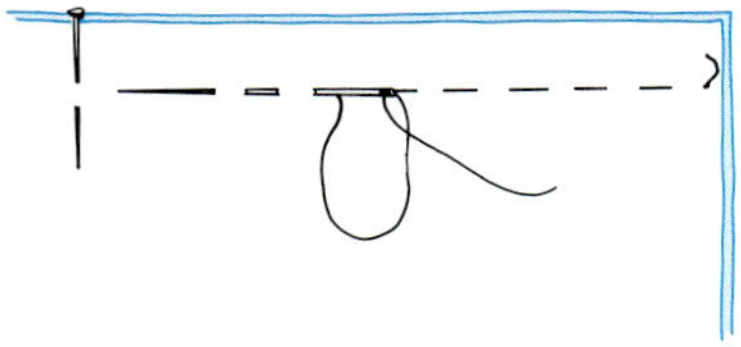

basting: Long, loose stitches for marking or holding fabric temporarily. Make stitches about 1/4 inch apart.

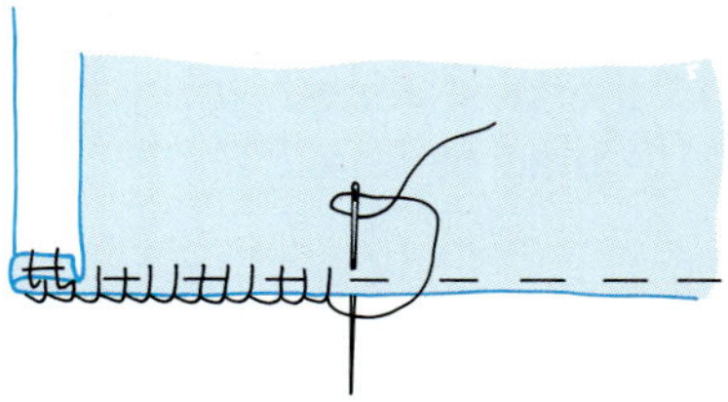

blanket stitch: Used for buttonholes and for hooks and eyes. Edge of fabric and point of needle should be facing you. Working from left to right, insert needle down through fabric and then through the loop formed by the thread.

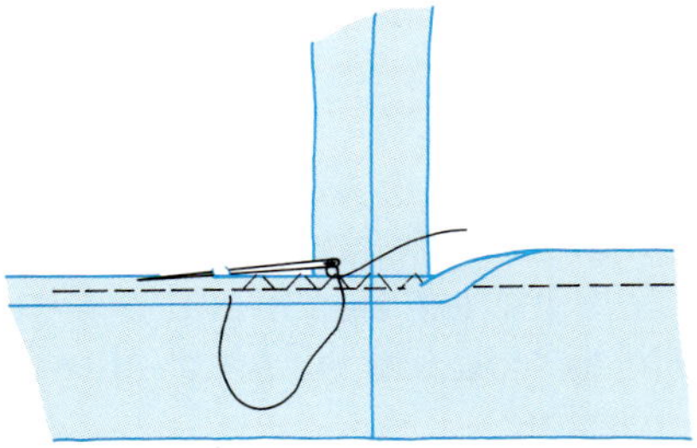

blindstitch: Makes hem stitches invisible on both sides of garment. Fold back the hem edge about 1/4 inch. At the fold line, pick up one or two garment yarns with your needle. Move needle to left about 1/4 inch and make a tiny stitch in the hem edge. Continue making alternate stitches in garment and hem.

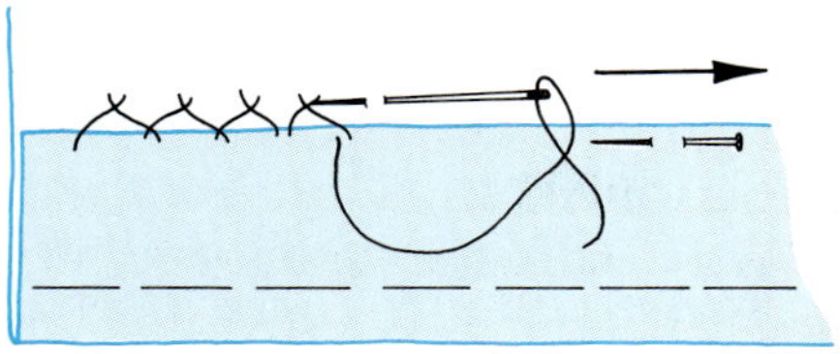

CATCHSTITCH

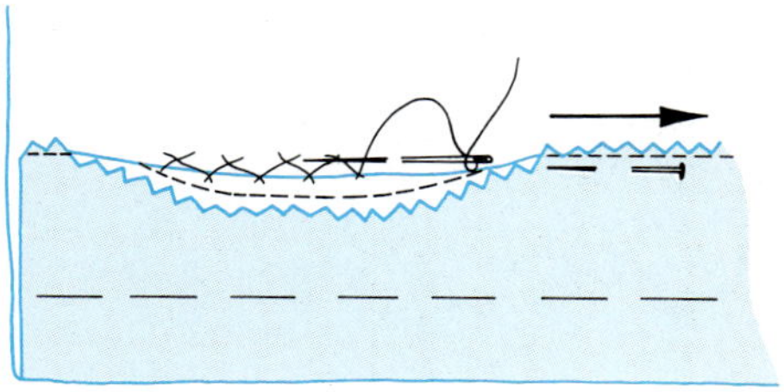

INVISIBLE CATCHSTITCH

catchstitch: A hem stitch ideal for knits because it has some "give." Make a horizontal stitch ¼ inch below hem edge. Move a little to the right and make a tiny horizontal stitch in the garment. Repeat. The **invisible catchstitch** is one that won't show on either side. Turn back the hem edge about ¼ inch. Make the catch stitches between the hem and the garment.

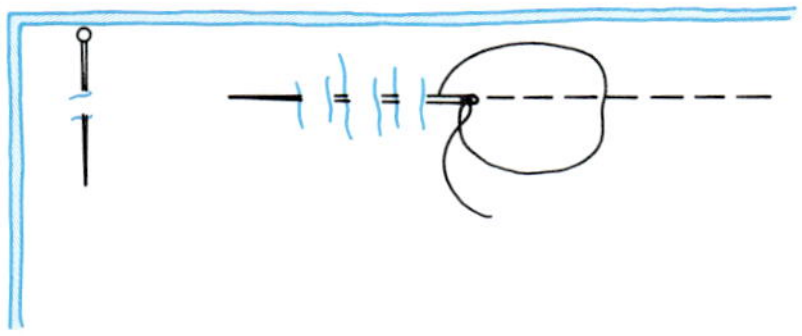

RUNNING STITCH

running stitch: Used for easing, gathering, and general sewing. Weave the needle in and out of the fabric, taking several stitches at a time. Make stitches about ⅛ inch long.

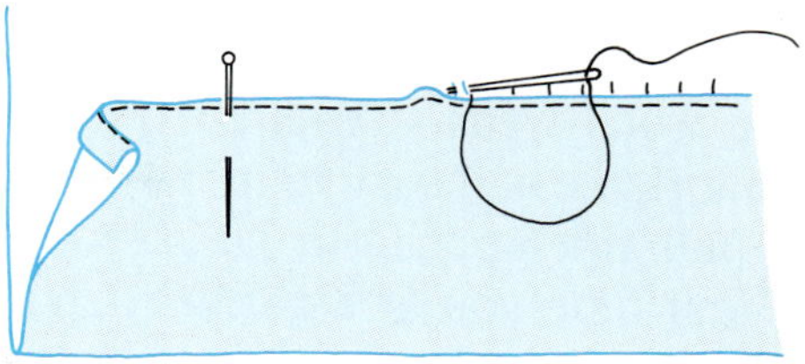

SLIPSTITCH

slipstitch: An invisible stitch for attaching a folded edge to a garment or for joining two folded edges. Pick up a single thread above the folded edge. Insert needle into folded edge, sliding it along for about ¼ inch. Bring out needle and again pick up a single thread above the folded edge. If joining two folded edges, slide needle ¼ inch in each edge.

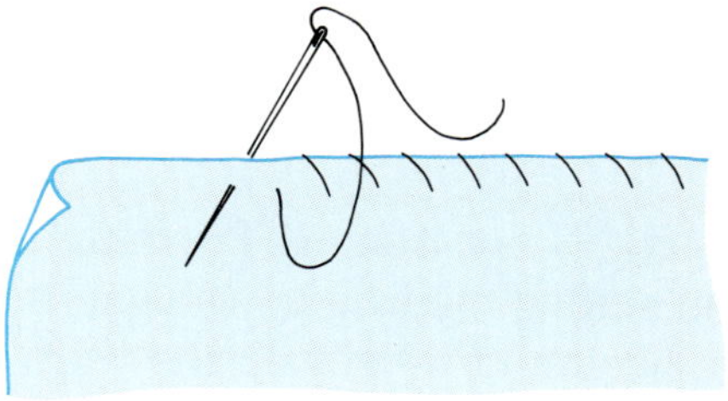

WHIPSTITCH

whipstitch: Also called **overcast stitch.** Used on raw edges to prevent raveling. Work stitches over fabric edge, holding the needle at right angles to fabric edge. Move from right to left, making slanted stitches about ⅛ inch deep and ¼ inch apart.

FITTING

No matter how good your sewing is, if the garment doesn't fit, it won't look good and you won't wear it. Well-fitted clothes are comfortable and easy to move in. They do not pull, ride up, bag, or hang crooked.

The first time you fit a garment should be before the side seams are stitched. Pin or baste the seams together and try the garment on. A full-length mirror will give you the best idea of how well it fits. Take in or let out seams or darts as needed.

How often you will need to check the fit as you sew depends on the style of the garment and your sewing experience. Make a final fitting before doing any top-stitching or hemming.

When you are finished, vertical seams should be straight, not wavy. Shoulder seams should be smooth and rest on top of the shoulder. Sleeves should hang straight to the elbow and then bend forward. Hems should be even and parallel to the floor.

PRESSING

Pressing is not ironing! **Pressing** is lifting and setting the iron down again so the steam, heat, and weight do the work. The iron is not moved back and forth, as it is for ironing.

Always press as you sew. All darts and seams should be pressed before going on to the next step. Use a steam iron to ease, to flatten seams, and to mold curves. See the illustrations on pages 211 and 212 for pressing equipment for special jobs.

"Finger press" seams open first with your fingers. Place paper under the seam allowance to avoid leaving marks of seam edges on the outer garment. Press with steam.

Guard your fabric. Test the effects of steam, pressure, and temperature on scrap pieces before you begin. When pressing garments on the right side, use a pressing cloth. This prevents fabric from getting shiny. Press with the grain and in the direction of stitching. As a rule, don't press over pins. Never press sharp creases until you have thoroughly checked the fit of the garment. When you are finished sewing a garment, give it an all-over touch-up pressing.

Try the garment on while you're making it. It's easier to make alterations before a garment is finished than after.

Safety Tips

- Check the iron's cord and plug for worn spots or other damage. A bad cord or plug can start a fire.
- When pressing or ironing, place the iron cord where it won't be tripped over.
- Rest a hot iron on its heel when you're not using it.
- Unplug the iron after use. Let it cool before putting it away.

(See page 230 for more safety tips.)

Pressing Equipment

- *steam iron:* makes steam when water is put into iron and temperature is set at wool or steam level.

- *sleeve board:* miniature ironing boards for pressing narrow garment sections.

- *seam roll:* allows you to flatten seams so the seam allowance doesn't make a "dent" on the outside; especially helpful for pressing seams in sleeves.

- *pressing ham:* used for curved seams, darts, and eased areas.

(Continued on next page)

- *pressing mitt:* **padded mitt which fits over your hand or the end of a sleeve board and is used for small curves.**

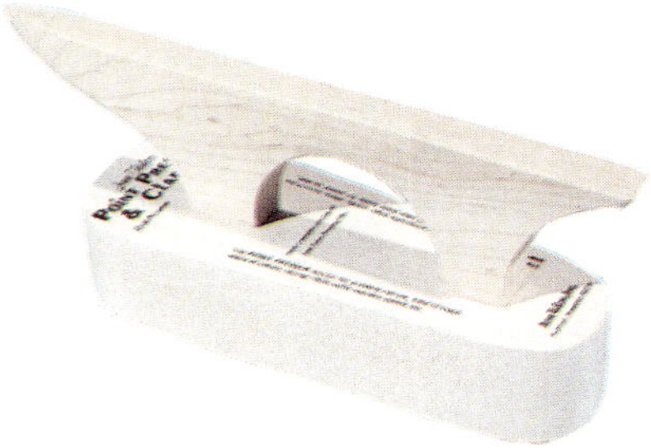

- *point presser:* **wooden block supporting a pointed wood strip; used to press corners and points.**

- *pounding block or tailor's clapper:* **rectangular wooden block used for making creases.**

- *needleboard:* **rectangular strip with hundreds of tiny needles; used under napped or fuzzy fabrics to prevent crushing the pile while you press.**

- *pressing cloth:* **protects fabrics from becoming shiny when coming into contact with hot iron; made of cheesecloth, drill cloth, or wool; placed between iron and fabric.**

REVIEW-18

SUMMARY

Learn the parts of a sewing machine and how to care for it before you begin. Practice winding the bobbin, threading the machine, and controlling stitches.

Basic sewing techniques you should learn include making darts and seams and attaching interfacings. Then you are ready to make the pieces of a garment. Basic pieces you should try include facings, collars, sleeves, waistbands, cuffs, casings, jackets, pleats, elastic, closures, linings, and hems.

Fitting and pressing the garment as you sew assures a successful and more professional-looking job.

CHECK YOUR KNOWLEDGE

1. What do the tension controls on a sewing machine regulate?
2. After oiling a sewing machine, why should you try it out on a scrap piece of fabric?
3. What is the purpose of darts?
4. Why should seams be backstitched?
5. What is interfacing used for?
6. Name the three types of collars.
7. What is a casing?
8. Name and describe the three kinds of pleats.
9. What is the difference between a flat button and a shank button?
10. What purposes do linings serve?

EXTEND YOUR KNOWLEDGE

1. Make a report to the class on the first sewing machines.
2. Interview someone in your town who repairs sewing machines. Find out what kinds of repairs are needed most often. How can they be prevented? Make a report to the class on your findings.
3. Get together with two other friends from class and put on a "fitting" style show. Model garments having straight or crooked seams, uneven and even hems, and so on. How can the poorly-fitting clothes be fixed?
4. Interview someone who sews. What are the advantages and disadvantages of home sewing? Write your findings in a report.
5. Give the class a demonstration of how to attach both sew-in and fusible interfacing.

CHAPTER 19

FINISHING TOUCHES

The next time you look through a fashion magazine, look for what makes a certain garment special. It may be the general style or fabric. Or it may be a finishing touch, such as a special belt or trim.

A simple style must be beautifully designed in order to "stand alone." Most garments look better with a bit of trim.

Do you know . . .

- What kinds of belts can be sewn?
- What easy embroidery stitches could be added to a garment?
- What stitches are best for appliqués?
- What trims can add design touches?

The answers to these questions can be found in the following pages.

Look for These Terms

embroidery
embroidery floss
appliqué
quilting

MAKING BELTS

Making belts saves money and allows you to choose the style of buckle you'd like. Good looking but inexpensive beltings come in leather, suede, imitation reptile skin, and webbing.

Belt widths change with fashion. When selecting belt width, consider both the fashion and the style that looks best on you.

For a leather or sturdy fabric belt, select a good pattern and follow those instructions. However, you can make a simple tie belt without a pattern.

1. Tie a string around your waist and cut it the length of the belt you want to make. Use the string to measure your fabric *length.* The *width* should be twice as wide as the finished belt plus 5/8 inch on all sides. Cut interfacing the same length but only the finished belt width.

2. Attach the interfacing to the back half.

3. Fold the fabric in half lengthwise, right sides together.

4. Stitch, leaving an opening about 4 inches long in the middle. You'll need this opening later for turning the belt right side out. Trim and grade seams.

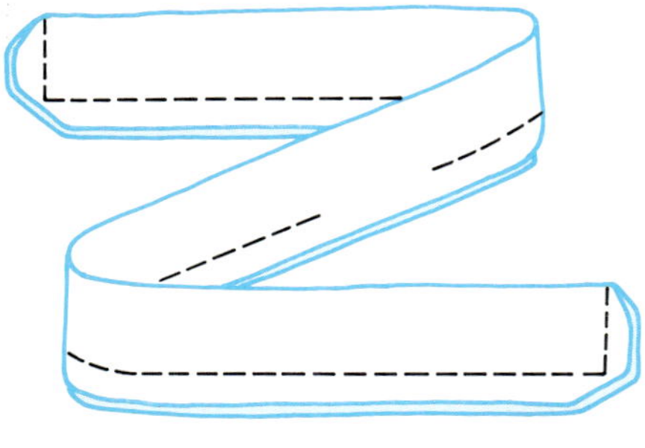

5. Turn the belt right side out. Press. Slipstitch the opening closed.

Remember the elements and principles of design? Embroidery adds color and emphasis to clothing.

EMBROIDERY

Embroidery is the art of decorating a fabric with colorful threads in interesting designs.

Embroidery is often done by hand. However, some sewing machines can make embroidery stitches.

Embroidery is done with strands of **embroidery floss,** a special cotton thread. Make sure that it can be cared for in the same way as the garment on which it is used. For example, if the garment is to be washed, the decorative stitches should also be washable.

Special needles are available for embroidery. These are sold either in a package or individually.

Before you embroider a garment, decide on a design. You can buy transfer designs at a craft store or make up your own. Page 216 shows how to do some popular embroidery stitches.

Embroidery Stitches

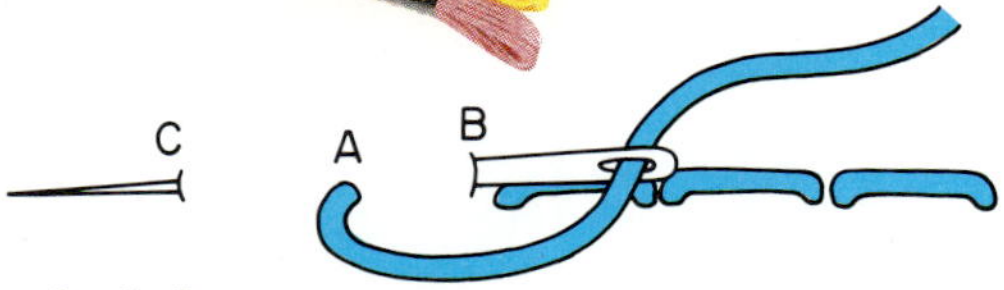

Backstitch

(1) Come up at A. (2) Go down at B. (3) Come up at C. (4) For next stitch, go down at A and come up to the left of C. Make all stitches same size.

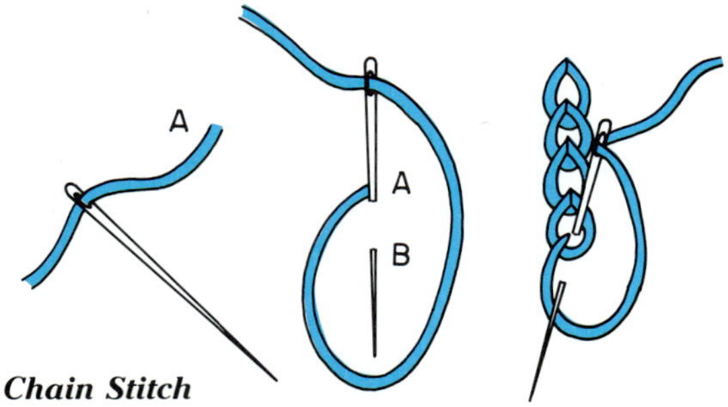

Chain Stitch

(1) Come up at A. (2) Go down in same hole at A, forming a loop. (3) Come up at B, inside loop. (4) Draw loop flat. (5) Repeat, going down at B to form next loop.

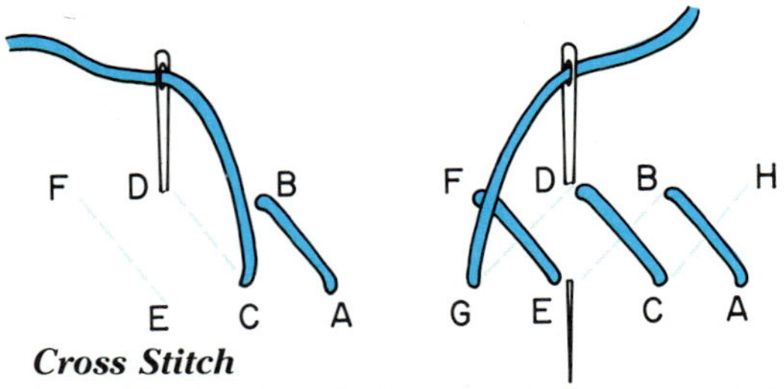

Cross Stitch

***To make a row of stitches:* (1) Come up at A. (2) Go down at B. (3) Come up at C, directly below B. (4) Go down at D, up at E, etc., to end of row. (5) Working from left to right, come up at G, down at D, etc., always working into previous holes. All stitches should cross in same direction.**

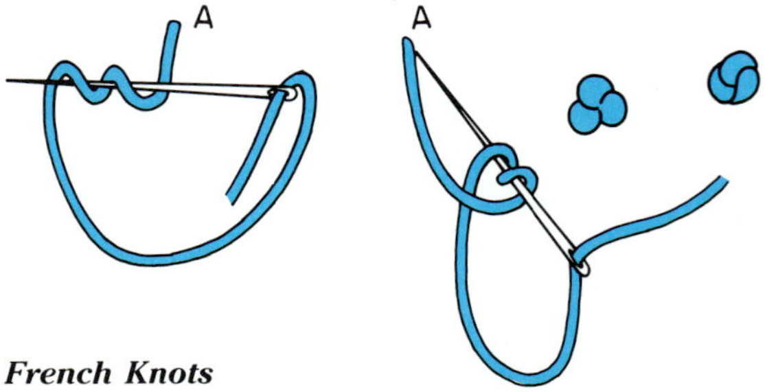

French Knots

(1) Come up at A. (2) Holding thread with opposite hand, loosely wrap thread twice around needle. (3) Return needle to A. (4) Draw yarn tight and push needle through. Last drawing shows finished knots.

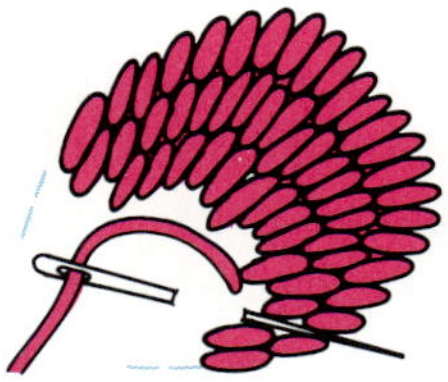

Long and Short

(1) For first row, alternate long and short stitches. (2) For the rows below the first, work in long and short stitches as needed to cover the fabric and give a smooth texture.

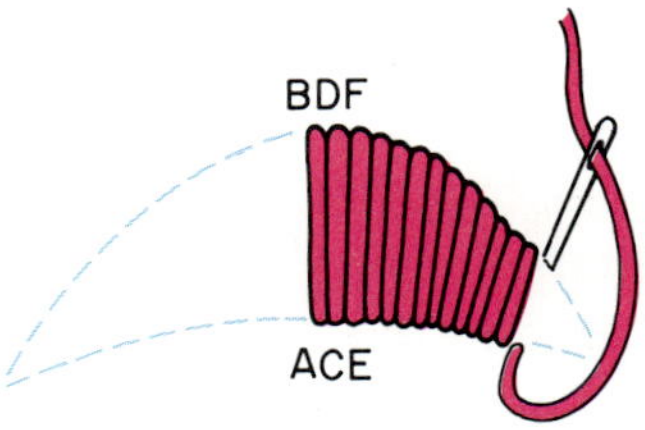

Satin Stitch

(1) Start at widest part of shape. Come up at A. (2) Go down at B. (3) Come up at C, next to A. (4) Go down at D. (5) Repeat until one half of shape is finished; then do other half.

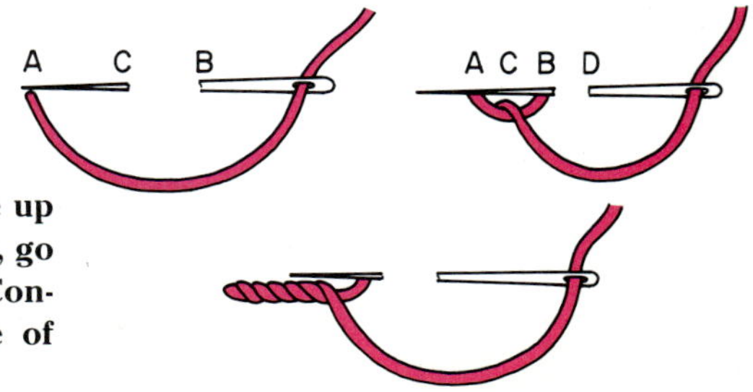

Stem Stitch

(1) Come up at A. (2) Go down at B. (3) Come up at C. (4) Keeping thread to one side of needle, go down at D. (5) Come up at B, in same hole. (6) Continue, always keeping thread to same side of needle.

In *reverse appliqué*, a design is cut out of the top layer of fabric, revealing the layer underneath. The edges of the cut portions are finished with stitching. The piece shown here was sewn by a Hmong craftswoman from Southeast Asia.

APPLIQUES

Appliqué (ap-luh-KAY) is the craft of stitching fabric cutouts into a design. It comes from the French word *appliquer,* "to apply."

Fabric choice is the most important thing to consider in making appliqués. Light- to medium-weight and firmly woven fabrics are the best choices for both background and design areas. Fabrics that stretch or are loosely woven should not be used because they will pucker and lose their shape. Good fabrics to use include linen, denim, kettle cloth, sailcloth, duck, corduroy, velour, seersucker, double knits, and brocades.

Appliqués can be made by machine. Three basic stitches commonly used are:

- *Straight stitch.* This can be used to outline appliqué areas or create shaded effects. But, when used along the edge of an appliqué, straight stitching will not conceal raw edges. It is necessary to hand or machine baste the edges under before pinning the appliqué to the fabric. If the appliqué is made from a fabric that does not fray, basting is not necessary.
- *Zigzag stitch.* A widely-spaced zigzag (open zigzag) can attach the appliqué and is also decorative. Turning edges under is necessary because an open zigzag does not cover raw edges.
- *Satin stitch.* Satin stitching is zigzag stitching with no space between. Edges do not need to be turned under because the stitching will cover edges completely. Generally, a lighter tension is needed for satin stitching to prevent puckering.

TRIMS

Trims can add designer touches to clothes. They can be purchased, or you can make them yourself.

A strip of true-bias fabric tape can turn corners or go around curves, and it lies flat. Bias tape can be purchased at fabric stores and comes in plain or printed varieties. Single-fold tape is a perfect lightweight trim for the top of a garment. Double-fold can bind and trim edges in one easy step.

You can finish an edge with double-fold bias tape. Slip the tape over the edge of the garment with the tape's wider fold on the wrong side. Stitch along the edge of the tape from the right side.

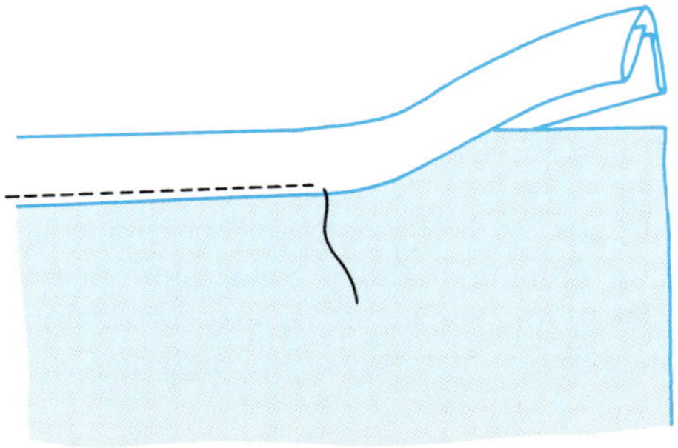

Ribbons, either grosgrain or satin, can be made into roses or bows or be topstitched as a "stripe." Ribbons can also be woven and stitched to collars, yokes, or cuffs.

Lace can be added as a trim, inserted in a seam or tuck, or appliquéd in a pattern.

Braid and rickrack can be used as button loops, drawstrings, or accent trims. Some wider braid can be made into belts.

This sweater is decorated with ribbons that have been woven through it.

Perspective

QUILTING: WARMTH AND PATTERN IN ONE STEP

Quilting is sewing together two layers of fabric with a layer of padding in between. The stitching usually forms a design. Quilting adds warmth to a garment and is often used for jackets.

The quilted items most commonly worn today are made from a layer of cotton blend fabric, a layer of fiber filler, and another layer of cotton blend. The fiber filler is called batting.

Quilted fabrics can be purchased, or you can make your own. The instructions for your sewing machine should include the best stitch length and tension for quilting. Because you sew through several thicknesses, stitches are usually longer.

Be sure to buy a pattern that is designed for use with quilted fabrics. Seam allowances, seam grading, and other details may be different because of the thickness of the material.

Patchwork quilting is done by first sewing scraps of different fabrics together to form a pattern. This layer is then quilted to the batting and the backing fabric.

REVIEW-19

SUMMARY

Finishing touches add a designer look to garments. Belts can be simple tie varieties or made with buckles. Embroidery adds designs with thread. Appliqués are designs made of fabric. Trims can be made by hand or purchased.

CHECK YOUR KNOWLEDGE

1. Name three types of belt materials.
2. What kind of belt can be made without a pattern?
3. What is embroidery? Give two examples of how embroidery may be used tastefully on a garment.
4. When buying embroidery floss, why should you check the care instructions?
5. Name three fabrics good for appliqué.
6. Which three stitches are commonly used with appliqué?
7. Why must appliqué edges usually be turned under?
8. Why are bias strips preferred for trims?
9. Name one way lace can be used as a trim.
10. What is quilting?

EXTEND YOUR KNOWLEDGE

1. Make a report to the class on quilting bees.
2. Plan a design to be embroidered on a shirt. Draw a pattern and label thread colors.
3. Make a poster showing different kinds of trims, such as buttons, beads, and feathers.
4. Make a poster showing magazine pictures of different kinds of belts. Tell which figure type each would flatter.
5. Start a button collection. Report to the class on the different sizes and styles you find. Tell how each might be used.

TAKING CARE OF CLOTHES

Dan was in a hurry. The school bus would arrive in ten minutes, and he was still getting dressed. All his good pants were in the laundry. He had to wear an old pair of jeans that were too short. The shirt he wanted to wear was missing a button. He chose another, but it was wrinkled because he'd left it on the floor. He looked five minutes before finding socks that matched. The bus left without him.

Have you had mornings like this? It's really not hard to avoid these problems. It just takes a little planning and know-how. If you take the time to clean, store, and repair your clothes when they need it, they'll be ready when you need them.

In this unit, you'll learn how to clean and store clothes to keep them looking good. You'll also learn how to repair clothes and how to alter them so that they will fit you better.

Unit 6

CHAPTER 20 Cleaning Clothes

CHAPTER 21 Storing Clothes

CHAPTER 22 Repairing and Altering Clothes

CHAPTER 20

CLEANING CLOTHES

Clean clothes help you look more attractive. Taking good care of your clothes will help them last longer, too. Clothing care is not a big or difficult job if you do it on a regular basis.

In this chapter, you will find answers to the following questions on clothing care:

- How can stains be removed from fabric?
- What is the correct way to wash clothes?
- How are clothes dry-cleaned?
- What are the correct ways to iron and press clothes?

Look for These Terms

preventive care
hard water

PREVENTIVE CARE

Preventive care means stopping problems before they start. For clothing, it means avoiding things which will soil or damage clothes. For example, you could:

- Let deodorant dry before getting dressed
- Use a napkin while eating to catch spills
- Wipe off a dirty chair before sitting down

Preventive care makes it easier to keep clothes clean and in good condition. What other preventive care measures can you suggest?

STAIN REMOVAL

New clothes don't really attract pizza, but sometimes it seems that way! When you get a stain on your clothes—from pizza or anything else—remember two basic rules:

- Treat the stain as soon as possible. Old stains are harder to remove.
- Consider the type of stain and the fabric. Different stains and fabrics require different methods.

Helpful hint: If food or drink spills on your clothing when you're away from home, treat the stain right away with cold water. Later, when you get home, follow regular stain removal procedures, as explained in this chapter.

OILY/GREASY STAINS

These stains are caused by things that contain oil or grease, such as chocolate, gravy, or pizza. For washable fabrics, make a paste of detergent and water. Dampen the stain; then rub on the paste before washing the garment. Or use full-strength liquid detergent on the stain. If the garment must be dry-cleaned, use a spot remover.

WATER-BASED STAINS

Water-based stains are non-oily. They include stains caused by such things as mud, soft drinks, and fruit juice. If the garment is washable, soak it in cool water. If the stain doesn't come out, apply detergent or a mild bleach. For dry-cleanable garments, dab the stain with a damp cloth.

TIPS FOR SUCCESSFUL STAIN REMOVAL

- Treat stains *before* washing or dry-cleaning a garment. Washing or dry-cleaning before treatment could "set" the stain—make it impossible to remove.
- Before heat drying or ironing a garment, check to see if the stains have been removed. Heat sets stains.
- Stubborn stains may need to be treated more than once.
- If you are unable to get a stain out of a dry-cleanable garment, pin a note beside the stain, telling what it is, before you take it to the dry cleaner's.
- Always follow directions on the label of stain removal products. The label will tell you how to use the product, what stains it will remove, and what fabrics it can be used on. As an extra precaution, test the product on a place that won't show, such as a seam allowance.
- A stain removal chart placed in the laundry area is a handy reference.
- If you need special information about stain removal, contact a dry cleaner, home economics teacher, or the Cooperative Extension Service.

Stain Removal for Washable Garments

Stain	Treatment
Blood	Soak in cool water. If stain remains, rub with concentrated detergent solution (full-strength liquid or powder-and-water paste). Rinse. Wash garment.
Catsup	Lift off excess catsup. Soak in cool water. Rub with concentrated detergent solution if stain persists. Wash garment. If needed, include type of bleach appropriate for fabric.
Chocolate	Rub stain with concentrated detergent solution. Wash garment.
Coffee	Soak immediately in cool water. Rub with concentrated detergent solution if stain persists. Wash garment.
Grass	Rub stain with concentrated detergent solution. Wash garment. If needed, add appropriate bleach to wash water.
Grease, Oil	Treat with spot remover or rub with concentrated detergent solution. Wash garment.
Gum	Rub gum with ice to harden it. Chip off the pieces of gum.
Ink	Use spot remover or send to dry-cleaner's. This stain is difficult to remove.
Lipstick, Make-up	Rub stain with concentrated detergent solution. Wash garment.
Mud	Allow mud to dry. Shake or brush away loose particles. If a stain remains, soak in cool water. Wash garment.
Perspiration	Soak in solution of water and detergent. Rub area with concentrated detergent solution if stain remains. Wash garment.
Soft Drinks	Soak immediately in cool water. Rub with concentrated detergent solution if stain persists. Wash garment.

CARE LABELS

Caring for clothes was simpler when there were only natural fibers. New fibers and fabric finishes have changed the way we care for clothes. Today, it is important to read clothing care labels. See the chart on pages 226 and 227 for information about the terms used on care labels.

LAUNDRY

Many of today's clothes can be washed by machine. However, loosely woven, very sheer, or delicate fabrics are usually washed by hand. For example, wool sweaters, fancy lingerie, and hose are washed by hand. These garments are hand washed because machine washing can ruin their shape.

Before you wash clothes, you should check them for needed repairs and stains. Mend the clothes and treat the stains. Close zippers, remove jewelry and non-washable trims, empty pockets, and turn garments wrong side out. Then sort the clothes into the following piles:

- *dark clothes*—clothes that are navy, black, brown, red, or dark green. Wash dark clothes separately so that they won't collect lint from lighter clothes. Also, if some of the colors run, it won't be as noticeable.
- *white or light-colored clothes.* Washing these separately reduces color transfer from darker clothes, which makes light clothes look dull or gray.
- *clothes to be bleached.* Only certain fabrics can safely be bleached. Check the garment's care label.

Turn garments, especially knits, wrong side out before putting them in the machine. This helps protect the right side from wear and tear.

What settings would you choose if you were going to wash a small load of light-colored shirts and blouses?

MACHINE WASHING

Follow the manufacturer's directions for using the washing machine. You'll get better results, and the machine will last longer.

When you put clothes in the washer, pack the tub loosely. If you put too many clothes in the washer, water does not move easily through the clothes. When this happens, dirt and soil are not carried away. Your clothes do not get clean.

The water temperature you select depends upon the type of fabric and the amount of soil. Hot water is best for heavily soiled clothes and colors that won't fade. Hot water helps get rid of germs also.

Warm water is used for lightly soiled clothes. It will remove the wrinkles from clothes made of permanent press fabrics. Warm water is cheaper because it takes less energy to heat it.

Cold water is used to wash clothes that fade. It is used in the rinse cycle to reduce wrinkles in permanent press fabrics. Using cold water to wash or rinse your clothes reduces energy costs.

Label Meanings

When the Label Says:	It Means:
Washable Machine Washable Machine Wash	Item can be washed at home or in commercial laundry and dried.
Home Launder Only	Do not use commercial laundering.
Machine Washable—Cold Water	Wash in cold water only; use cold setting on machine.
Machine Washable—Warm Water	Can be washed in water up to 110°.
Machine Washable—Hot Water	Can be washed in water up to 130°.
No Spin	Remove article from the wash before the final spin cycle.
Machine Washable—Delicate or Gentle	Use gentle wash cycle only or wash by hand.
Machine Wash—Permanent Press	Use permanent press cycle on machine or else use regular wash, cold rinse, and short spin.
Machine Wash—Separately	Wash only with like colors.
Hand Washable	Can be hand washed in cool or warm water; may be dry-cleaned.
Hand Wash Only	Do not machine wash or dry-clean.
Hand Wash Separately	Hand wash alone or with like colors.
Dry Clean Only	Do not wash. Item must be dry-cleaned.
No Bleach	The item cannot be bleached.
No Chlorine Bleach	Do not use chlorine bleach. All-fabric bleach may be used.
Tumble Dry Machine Dry	Item can be machine dried. Follow label directions for dryer temperature setting.
Tumble Dry—Remove Promptly	Remove article as soon as the cycle is over. (This reduces wrinkles.)
Drip Dry	Do not tumble dry; hang the article while still wet and let dry.

(Continued on next page)

Label Meanings (continued)

When the Label Says:	It Means:
Do Not Twist, Wring, or Squeeze	Article must be hung to drip dry, or dried flat.
Dry Flat	Article must be placed on a flat surface to dry.
Block to Dry	Article must be shaped and sized while wet and then dried on a flat surface.
Hang Dry or Line Dry	Hang damp and allow to dry.

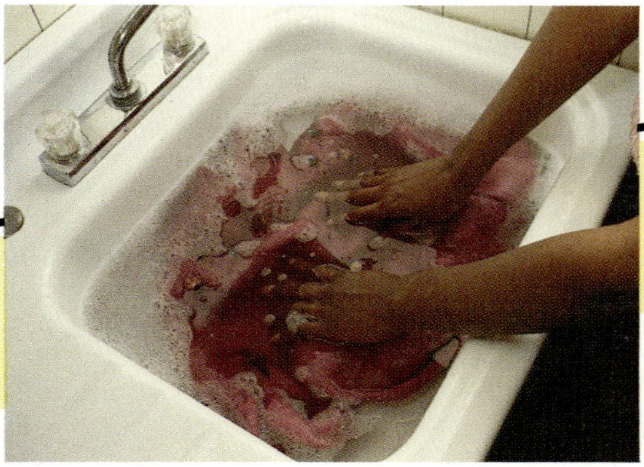

Hand washables are delicate. Don't scrub them; just squeeze water and suds through them.

Sweaters should be dried flat. Place them on a clean, dry towel.

HAND WASHING

Some clothes cannot be cleaned in a washing machine. They must be washed by hand. Hand-washable clothes are usually loosely woven, made of silk or wool, or likely to fade or shrink. These garments require very gentle handling and lukewarm or cool water. To wash clothes by hand:

1. Put the detergent in the water before adding the clothes. This helps to spread the soap or detergent evenly through the water.

2. Gently squeeze the suds and water through the clothes.

3. Rinse thoroughly with cool, clear water.

4. Gently squeeze the water out of the clothes. Do not wring or twist.

5. Use a towel to blot up excess moisture.

6. Sweaters and other loosely woven clothes should be allowed to dry on a flat surface so they don't stretch out of shape.

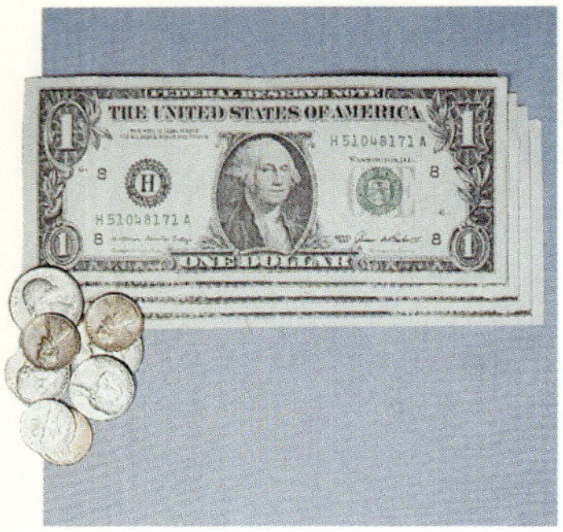

Getting Your Money's Worth

LAUNDRY PRODUCTS

Do you know the difference between soap and detergent? When should you use a pre-wash, and when is it better to use a pre-soak? Knowing about the different kinds of laundry products will help you make better buying decisions.

Soaps and detergents are used in the wash water to clean clothes. Soaps are made from fat, oil, and lye. They are available as bars, flakes, powders, or liquids. Detergents are made from petroleum, fats, and oils. There are heavy-duty detergents for heavily soiled, tough fabrics and light-duty detergents for delicate fabrics. Detergents may be powders or liquids.

Should you use soap or detergent for washing your clothes? It depends on the hardness of the water. **Hard water** is water that contains a lot of minerals. Soap combines with these minerals and forms a scum that is hard to remove. If you have hard water, use detergent rather than soap. If you're unsure about water hardness, contact the local water department.

Water softeners are powders that soften wash water. If you have hard water, a water softener can make it easier for the detergent to do its work.

Bleaches are used along with soaps or detergents to remove soil and stains and to help white clothes stay white. There are two kinds: chlorine and oxygen. *Chlorine bleach* is stronger. It should be diluted with water and added to the wash water after agitation begins. Chlorine bleach will fade colors, and it will harm many fabrics. Check garment care labels to see whether it's safe to use chlorine bleach. *Oxygen bleach* is often called "all fabric bleach." It is very mild but not as effective as chlorine bleach for removing stains.

Pre-washes are sprayed on soiled or stained areas before washing. They are especially good at removing oil and grease stains.

Enzyme pre-soaks are good at removing protein-based stains such as blood or eggs. They are also effective on grass stains and mud. The product is combined with water, and the garment is soaked in this for a while before washing.

Fabric softeners soften fabrics and reduce wrinkles and static cling. They also reduce absorbency, so don't use a fabric softener every time you wash towels. Liquid fabric softeners are added to the rinse water. Fabric softener sheets are used in the dryer. Some detergents have fabric softener in them.

Here are some tips for saving money:

- For best results, follow the instructions on the package.
- Use only the products you need. For example, you don't need a pre-soak for items that aren't stained or heavily soiled.
- Compare cost per ounce for different products. Often the cost per ounce is written on the supermarket shelf. If not, you can figure it yourself. Divide the total cost of the product by the number of ounces. For example, 45 ounces for $2.25 equals 5 cents per ounce.

DRYING

Clothes can be air dried or dried in a dryer. Air drying is cheaper, but it takes longer and leaves clothes stiff. Some people prefer the fresh smell of clothes dried outdoors.

Delicate fabrics and clothes that shrink easily should be air dried. When placing clothes on a line, put the clothespins in a place where the imprint will not be seen. For example, shirts should be hung upside down so that the clothespins will press against the lower side seams. Loosely woven clothes should be laid on a flat surface to dry.

When drying clothes in a dryer, group clothes of the same weight and fiber together. This helps you select the best time and temperature. Too high a drying temperature can damage clothes. The fabrics could shrink or melt. Fabric finishes may be destroyed. Check the care label in the garment for the best drying temperature.

When the dryer stops, check the clothes. If they are still wet, you will have to restart the dryer. However, if the clothes are only slightly damp, remove them. Clothes made of natural fibers will have fewer wrinkles if removed from the dryer while slightly damp. Clothes of manufactured fibers will have less static cling. Put the clothes on hangers and let them air dry before storing them.

For home dryers, one full wash load equals a dryer load. If you overload the dryer, clothes won't dry properly.

DRY CLEANING

Some clothes cannot be washed when they become soiled. They must be dry-cleaned. In dry cleaning, a chemical is substituted for water during the cleaning process.

Wool or silk garments are usually dry-cleaned. Most wool garments shrink when washed in a washing machine or dried in a dryer. Silk garments tend to lose their color if cleaned in a washing machine. Garments with special trims, decorations, or fabric weaves may need to be dry-cleaned. The garment label will indicate which clothes should be dry-cleaned.

Dry cleaning is available at professional cleaning establishments or at some self-service laundries. Do-it-yourself dry cleaning is less expensive than professional dry cleaning but requires you to do more steps.

For self-service dry cleaning:

1. Sort the clothes into piles as you do for washing.

2. Empty the pockets of each garment and brush lint from creases and cuffs. Remove trims and buttons which may be damaged by the dry cleaning chemical.

3. Place clothes loosely in the machine and follow the directions on the machine to begin the cleaning process.

4. When the cleaning process is finished, remove the clothes and place them on hangers. Replace any trims or buttons that were removed. Press clothes with an iron to remove wrinkles.

You may prefer to take your clothes to a professional dry cleaner. Label spots and stains. When you pick up your clothes, check them to make sure the garments have been cleaned satisfactorily. Most businesses will reclean a garment free if spots have not been removed.

IRONING AND PRESSING

As defined in Chapter 18, pressing is done by lifting and setting down the iron, letting steam and heat remove the wrinkles. Ironing is done by sliding the iron over the clothes. Dry heat removes the wrinkles. To avoid stretching the fabric, ironing should be done in the direction of the lengthwise and crosswise yarns.

Most irons today can be used as either steam or dry irons. Turn the iron to the temperature setting recommended on the garment label. Wait about two minutes for the iron to heat before using it.

Safety Tips

- **Make sure the iron is turned to "Off" before you plug it in.**
- **Be sure the iron's cord and plug are in good condition, with no worn spots or breaks. A faulty cord or plug could start a fire.**
- **Before filling a steam iron, make sure that both the iron and the steam button are "Off."**
- **Rest the iron upright on the ironing board. Don't leave it on the garment.**
- **When you have finished, turn the iron off, unplug it, and allow it to cool completely before storing it. Drain steam irons before storing.**

"When will it be ready?" Usually, you have to leave a garment at the dry cleaner's for several days.

REVIEW-20

SUMMARY

Clean clothes last longer and look nicer. To keep clothes clean, remove stains as soon as they occur. Sort your clothes and wash or dry-clean them according to the care labels on the garments. Iron or press clothes as needed to remove wrinkles.

CHECK YOUR KNOWLEDGE

1. Define preventive clothing care. Why is preventive care important?
2. What are the two basic rules for stain removal?
3. What are the two types of stains? Give an example of each. How is each type of stain removed?
4. What types of clothes should be hand washed?
5. How should clothes be sorted for laundering?
6. Why is it important to pack the tub of the washer loosely with clothes?
7. When should hot, warm, and cold water be used for washing clothes?
8. Describe how to wash clothes by hand.
9. What can happen when you use too high a drying temperature?
10. How does dry cleaning differ from washing clothes?

EXTEND YOUR KNOWLEDGE

1. Make a list of five preventive care tips for clothing. Include reasons.
2. Research consumer magazines for articles about washing machines. What features do today's machines have? Which features would be most useful for a young, single person?
3. Visit a supermarket and write down the prices and sizes of five brands of detergent. Which brand and size costs the least?
4. Make note of the television ads for laundry products. What claims do they make? To what emotions do they appeal (such as the desire to be clean, thrifty, accepted by others, etc.)?
5. Pretend you are teaching a younger brother or sister how to iron and press clothes. What advice would you give him or her?

CHAPTER 21

STORING CLOTHES

Between wearings and as seasons change, clothes need to be stored. How you store your clothes determines their condition when you get them out to wear again. Using good storage practices means that your clothes will be in good condition.

In this chapter, you will learn answers to these questions about storing clothes:

- What should you do to clothes before storing them?
- What are the three types of storage places for clothes?
- What kinds of clothes should be stored in each place?

Look for These Terms

lint	mildew
mold	insect repellent

TREATING CLOTHES BEFORE STORAGE

Before clothes are put away, several things should be done. Shoes should be polished or cleaned. Allow the shoes to air out before storing them. Garments should be cleaned or hung up and allowed to air before being returned to the closet. Hanging and airing allows wrinkles to fall out. It also allows odors picked up during wearing to evaporate. Wrinkles that remain in clothes should be pressed out before the next wearing.

Brushing wool or napped garments removes lint. **Lint** consists of small fibers that have come off fabric. Cuffs on pants are a good place for lint and trash to collect.

Clothing repairs made before clothes are put away will help you get ready faster the next time you dress. Replace missing buttons, repair torn hems, and restitch any rips in seams.

If you have been out in the rain, your wet clothes should be allowed to dry before being hung up and put away. Some garments will stretch out of shape if hung up when they are wet. Also, mold and mildew can grow on damp clothes hung in a closet. **Mold** and **mildew** are two types of fungi which discolor and weaken fabrics.

The brush shown here has a napped fabric surface. The fabric picks up lint and hair from garments.

Stuff wet shoes with paper to help them keep their shape as they dry. Dry the shoes away from heat.

PLACES TO STORE CLOTHES

When clothes are not being worn, they should be kept in closets, drawers, and boxes. Clothes worn frequently should be stored in easy-to-reach places. This usually means the front of the closet or in a chest near or in the closet. Clothes worn less often can be kept in the back of the closet or in a box in the attic or under the bed.

HELPFUL HINT: You can buy boxes that are made for under-bed storage. They are made of sturdy cardboard and come with a lid.

CLOSETS

A well-organized closet will make it easier to find your clothes. Your clothes will also stay in better condition.

Clothes which are hung up need a hanger sturdy enough to support the weight of the garment. Jackets and coats need a padded or wooden hanger to support their weight. Some wooden hangers have a wide bar for hanging slacks in a folded position. Slacks can also be hung without a fold on a hanger with clamps. Dresses, blouses, and shirts are lighter in weight. They can be hung on a plastic or lightly padded hanger.

Thin wire hangers do not provide good garment support. They can cause creases to form at the shoulders.

Shoes can be stored on shoe trees, in shoe bags, or in plastic or cardboard boxes. Placing the shoes in a covered container keeps dust away. If the shoes are not visible through the box, label the box.

Arranging clothes in a closet by a plan helps you locate the garments later. Group clothes by type and color. For example, hang all blue slacks together and next to the gray slacks.

Using two rods on one side of the closet allows you to store more clothes. Hang shirts and blouses on a high rod. Hang folded slacks, short jackets, and skirts under the shirts on a lower rod.

Long coats, dresses, and unfolded slacks need a rod high enough to keep them off the floor. You can place shoe racks or a laundry basket for soiled clothes on the floor under the dresses and coats. Place hats, handbags, suitcases, or boxed items on shelves over the hanging garments.

HELPFUL HINT: You can easily add a closet shelf. Buy particle board of the right length and width for your closet. Paint it, or cover it with self-stick paper. Install it on shelf brackets.

When a closet is well organized, it's easier to find things.

DRAWERS

Underwear and garments that stretch if hung, such as sweaters, are stored in drawers. If the drawer is very big, use cardboard dividers to keep the items separated. For example, dividers could separate socks, shorts, and undershirts. Another drawer might use dividers to separate belts, gloves, and jewelry. Small boxes keep earrings, pins, and other easy-to-lose items organized.

When drawer space is not inside the closet, it should be as near the closet as possible. Having to walk across the room or around the bed to get items slows you down as you dress.

STORAGE CONTAINERS

Seasonal clothing needs special protection during the season it is not worn. These clothes need protection from dust, insects, and sunlight.

Out-of-season clothes are stored in garment bags and storage boxes. Garment bags come in various sizes. Choose a size to suit your needs. Look for sturdy construction. Flimsy bags tear easily.

It is not a good idea to use the lightweight plastic covers that come from the dry cleaner's. These covers tend to cling to the clothes and prevent air circulation.

Clothes to be stored should be clean and in good repair. Clean, repaired clothes are ready to wear the next season. Insects, such as moths and silverfish, do not readily attack clean clothes. They prefer soiled spots on clothes.

When storing clothes, fasten all buttons and hooks and close all zippers. This helps the garment retain its shape and keeps it from snagging other garments. Pack the container loosely to reduce wrinkles and allow air to circulate.

Garments which will stretch easily, such as sweaters, should be folded and stored in boxes. Other items suitable for box storage include shorts, socks, pajamas, underwear, and accessories. If hanging space is limited, suits, coats, slacks, shirts, and dresses could be folded and stored in boxes.

Place garment bags and boxes in a dry place. Clothes stored in a damp place pick up musty odors and are more likely to be attacked by insects, mold, and mildew.

Hang garment bags in the back of large closets, in extra closets, or in attics. Place storage boxes on high shelves, under the bed, or in the attic.

What kinds of clothes should be stored in garment bags? What kinds should be stored in boxes?

Insect Repellents

When clothes are stored for a long time, there is the possibility that insects will attack the clothes. **Insect repellents** are substances that keep insects away. Putting mothballs or crystals in each garment bag or box discourages insects. Storing the boxes or bags in cedar closets also helps keep insects away. Moths and silverfish do not like the fumes given off by mothballs or cedar.

HELPFUL HINT: If you don't have a cedar closet, buy some cedar chips. Put them in an old nylon stocking and hang it in the closet to repel moths.

Cedar wood gives off a scent that repels insects.

Perspective

PACKING FOR TRIPS

Traveling is fun, but it's no fun to arrive at your destination and find your clothes too wrinkled to wear. Even worse is finding that your shampoo or mouthwash has leaked and stained your clothes. Careful packing can help you arrive with fresh clothing, ready to wear.

Start by collecting on your bed all of the things you plan to pack. Put the heaviest items, such as shoes, at the bottom of your suitcase or duffel bag. Roll underpants, socks, or hosiery and stuff them inside the shoes. Other undergarments can be rolled and packed into nooks and crannies.

Toiletries and makeup should be in plastic bottles. Even these can leak, so put them in a plastic bag and tie securely. Better yet, put them in a plastic-lined, zippered bag.

Clothes that wrinkle easily should be packed in the top layer of the suitcase or duffel bag. Placing tissue paper or plastic bags between the folds can help keep creases from forming. The plastic bags also come in handy for carrying wet swimsuits or dirty laundry home.

When you reach your destination, put your garments on hangers. Arrange the hangers in a closet with space between the garments so that wrinkles can hang out.

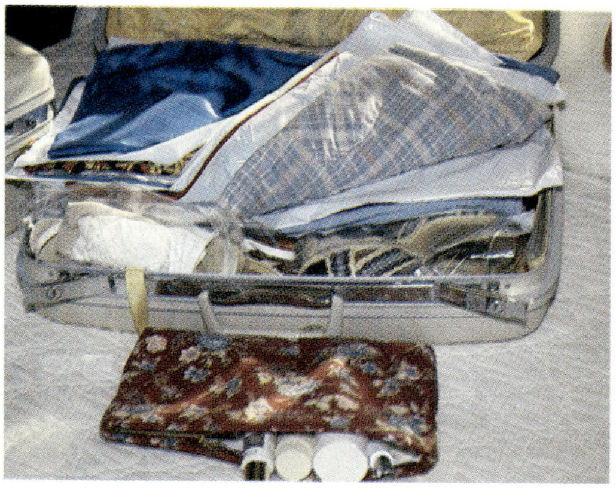

REVIEW-21

SUMMARY

Before clothing is stored, it should be clean and in good repair. How and where you store clothes depends upon the space you have and how long you need to store them. Clothes can be stored in closets, drawers, garment bags, or boxes. Clothes which are hung up should be placed on sturdy hangers.

Containers and closets should be loosely packed to allow air to circulate. Include mothballs or use cedar-lined closets to repel insects. Label containers so you can find your clothes.

CHECK YOUR KNOWLEDGE

1. Describe the care which shoes and garments need before they are put away.
2. Where can clothes be stored? What type of clothes are kept in each place?
3. How does the hanger for a coat differ from one used for a shirt? Why is a different type hanger needed?
4. Where are shoes stored?
5. How should clothes hung in a closet be arranged? Why is this important?
6. How should out-of-season clothes be stored?
7. Why do people put moth crystals in with their stored clothes or use cedar-lined closets?
8. Why is it not a good idea to use the plastic garment bags that come from the cleaner's?
9. Why is it not a good idea to store out-of-season clothes in a damp place?
10. Why are clean clothes less likely to be attacked by insects?

EXTEND YOUR KNOWLEDGE

1. Draw up a plan for organizing your closet. What storage containers would you need to buy? How much would these cost?
2. Write a report on the types of insects that commonly attack clothes. Tell why they are attracted to clothes and what can be done to prevent damage.
3. Demonstrate to the class how to pack a suitcase or duffel bag.
4. Research the various types of luggage. Write a report on their features and cost.
5. Pretend you are about to rent an apartment and you need storage places for your clothes. But you don't have much money? What kinds of inexpensive storage could you obtain?

CHAPTER 22

REPAIRING AND ALTERING CLOTHES

Seams rip. Buttons fall off. Hems tear. Snags occur. Fabric frays. Any of these things can happen to clothing as it is worn. They can ruin the appearance of a garment. Fortunately, most of these accidents can be easily repaired.

Sometimes when new clothing is purchased or made, it does not fit as you would like. Changes in your weight or a growth spurt can also change the fit of your clothes. Being able to alter clothes helps you get the fit you want and a garment that looks attractive on you.

In this chapter, you will learn how to do minor repairs and alterations. You will learn answers to these questions:

- How can you repair holes or rips in garments?
- How can you repair or replace fasteners?
- How can garments be increased or decreased in width or length?

Look for These Terms

fusible web
darning
fusible tape
reinforcing button

REPAIRS

Clothing that is worn often or worn for heavy work soon shows signs of wear. Most people can't afford to throw away a garment if a button comes off, a seam rips, or a hem tears. They repair the clothes so they can still wear them.

Before you repair a garment, ask yourself these questions:

- Can the repair work be done easily, without spending a lot of time or money?
- Is there enough wear left in the garment to justify repairs?

TOOLS AND TECHNIQUES FOR REPAIRS

Repairs use the same basic sewing skills and tools needed in garment construction. If you need to refresh your memory on any of these, refer to Chapter 18.

Ripping Out Stitches

A helpful tool for removing stitches is the seam ripper. (See page 180.) It has a dull point and a sharp blade attached to a handle. The point is inserted under the stitch, and the blade cuts the stitch. Once a stitch has been cut, the next stitch pulls loose when the point is inserted and lifted upward. Repeat this process until the needed amount of seam or hem has been removed. Pull out all loose threads.

Helpful hint: As you work, be careful not to cut or stretch the fabric. Stretching or cutting the fabric increases the repair work needed.

Basic Repair Stitches

Generally speaking, repairs are made using the same machine and hand stitches used in garment construction. Refer to Chapter 18 if you wish to review the information on stitches.

PATCHING

Patches may be functional or decorative. Functional patches are used to cover or fill holes. They are the same color and texture as the garment fabric. Decorative patches contrast with the fabric. They resemble appliqué or use embroidery stitches as part of the design. Patches are either fused or machine stitched in place.

Patches can be part of a garment's design.

Fusible patches have an adhesive on the back. When heated with an iron, the adhesive softens and sticks to the garment. Fusible patches are quick and easy to apply. You may buy them in a variety of fabrics and precut shapes or strips. Follow package directions for applying.

To make a repair that's nearly invisible, you can fill a hole rather than cover it. You will need a piece of matching fabric the size of the hole and a second piece cut larger than the hole. You'll also need **fusible web,** a weblike material that melts when heated with an iron. It is sold in fabric stores.

Working from the wrong side of the garment, place the smaller patch in the hole. Cut a piece of fusible web the same size as the larger patch. Place it over the smaller patch. Put the larger patch on top of it. Fuse the patch in place with a hot iron.

Patches can also be put on with the sewing machine. On the outside of the garment, use chalk to trace a square around the hole. The square should be large enough so that its sides are at least ¼ inch from the hole. Clip the hole to the corners of the square and fold the edges under. Cut a patch slightly larger than the square. Place the patch under the hole and slip-stitch the folded edges of the hole to the patch. Turn the garment wrong side out. Fold in edges of patch and machine stitch to the garment around the fold line.

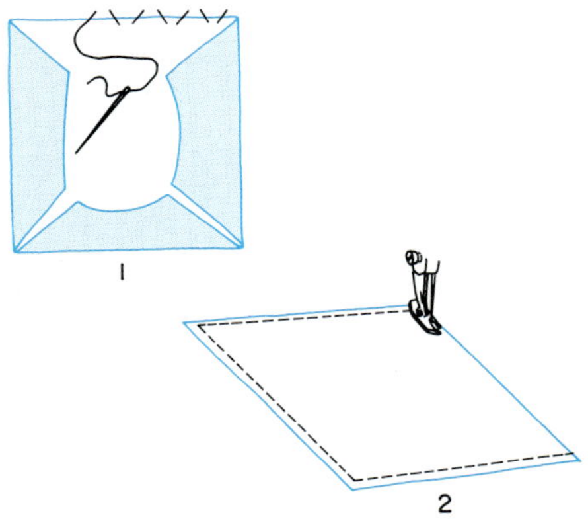

(1) ***Right side of garment.*** **Tuck in edges of hole and slipstitch to patch. (2)** ***Wrong side of garment.*** **Machine stitch patch to garment.**

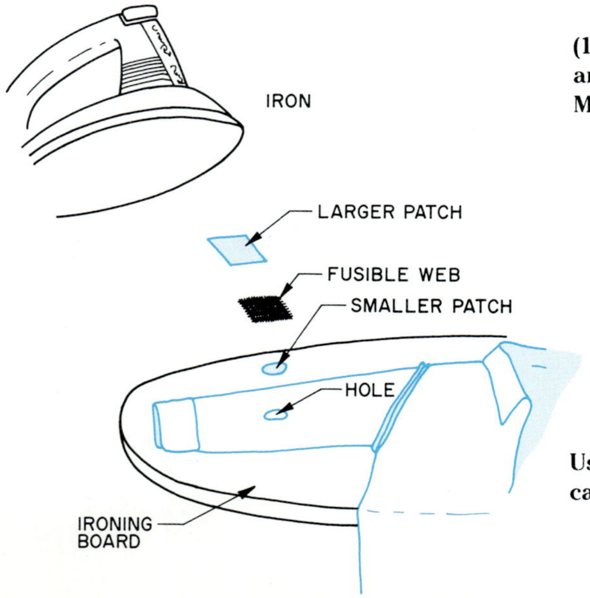

Using fusible web to hold the fabrics together, you can make a nearly invisible patch.

DARNING

Darning is the process of mending tears or filling in holes by interlacing stitches. Darning can be done by hand or machine. Machine darning is done quickly and is strong. It can be seen on the outside of the garment. Hand darning is invisible but takes longer to complete.

When darning by machine, cut a piece of backing fabric that is longer than the tear or larger than the hole. The backing fabric should be a weight and color similar to the garment. It is used to support the weakened area. Place the backing fabric on the wrong side of the garment and pin in place over the damaged area. Turn the garment right side out. Trim frayed edges around the tear. Zigzag over the entire damaged portion. If using a straight stitch, place the stitching in a zigzag pattern. Of course, you should stitch with a thread that matches the garment.

Hand darning is done with a small needle and a thread that matches the fabric. It is done from the right side of the garment.

To repair a tear, insert the needle 1/4 inch above the end of the tear. Weave the thread along the fabric grain, working across the tear. Continue weaving in rows until you are 1/4 inch beyond the end of the tear.

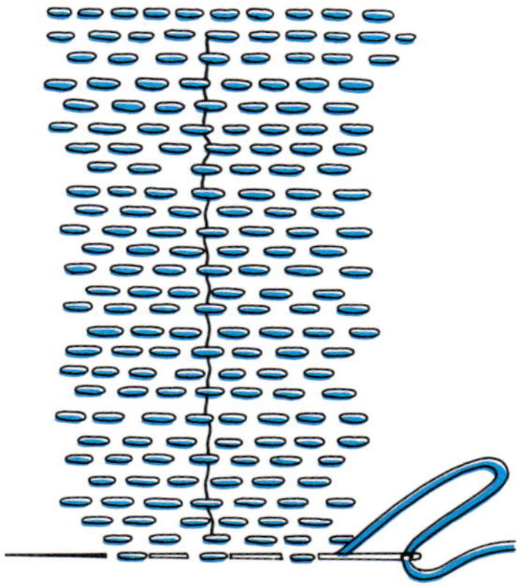

Repeat the weaving process, moving at right angles to the first set of rows.

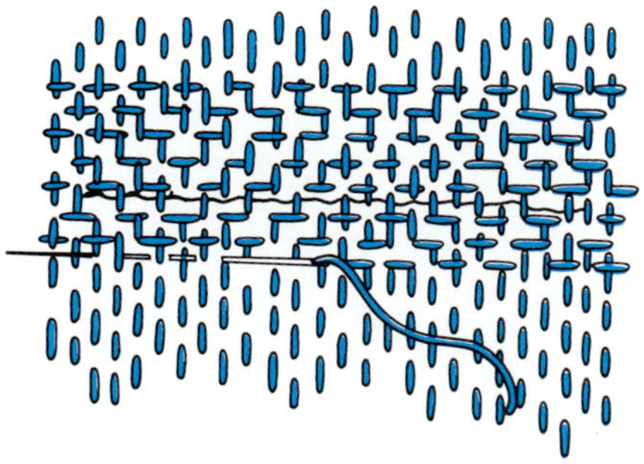

Hand darning can also be used to fill in a hole. Create a boundary for the darning by tracing a circle around the hole with chalk. Fill the circle with rows of thread just as you did for repairing the tear.

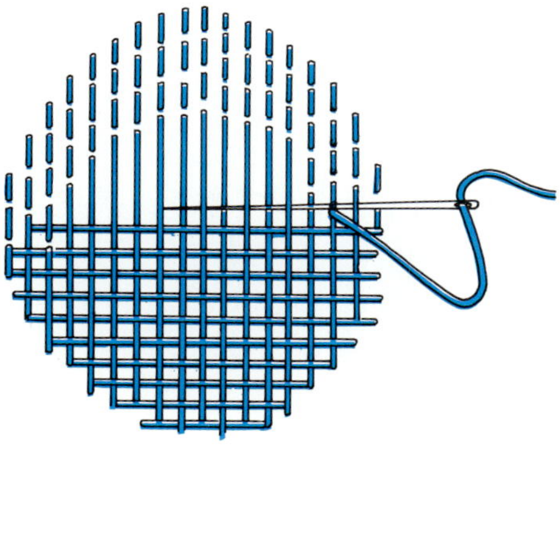

Holes that appear in knitted garments can also be rewoven. Outline the hole with a square as described above. Using yarn to match the garment and a crewel needle, connect the rows on opposite sides of the square.

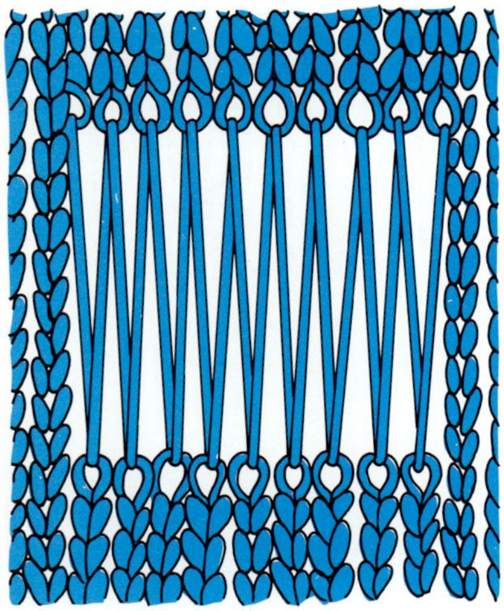

Then work a chain stitch to fill in the hole and connect the remaining two sides.

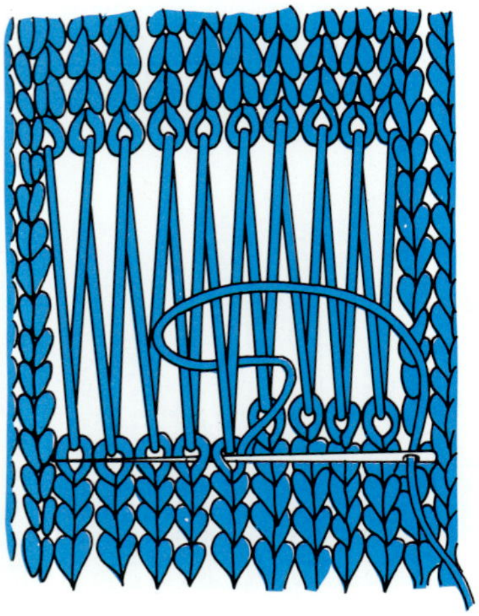

Sometimes, garment fabric is woven very tight or knitted with small stitches. When these garments get holes, it is difficult to see the pattern and reweave it. To repair these holes, seek the help of a professional.

REPAIRING OR REPLACING FASTENERS

Garment fasteners receive a lot of stress and strain. Sometimes they break or become loose and need to be repaired.

When a zipper slide breaks, the whole zipper must be replaced. To replace a zipper, you first remove the broken one. Press the seams flat and follow regular construction procedures for inserting the new zipper. The new zipper should be the same color as the garment fabric.

HELPFUL HINT: If the seam allowances are narrow, extend them by stitching matching seam tape to them.

Loose buttons can be restitched following the same process used for new buttons. Refer to Chapter 18.

When a button is torn off a garment, the hole must be mended before the button can be reattached. Patch the hole with strips of fusible tape between the wrong side of the garment and the garment facing. (**Fusible tape** is a strip of fabric with heat-sensitive adhesive on one side. It is ironed on, like a fusible patch.) As you reattach the button, use a reinforcing button on the facing. A **reinforcing button** is a small, flat button that is stitched on the

A reinforcing button eases the strain on the fabric. Note the toothpick placed across the outer button to obtain a little slack in the threads.

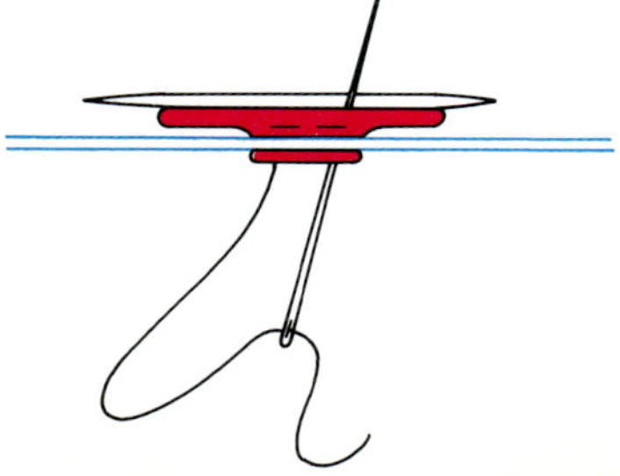

underside of the garment at the same time as the outer button is stitched. A reinforcing button reduces the strain on the fabric when the outer button is fastened and unfastened.

Occasionally, threads around buttonholes come loose, and the buttonhole unravels. The buttonhole can be restitched by hand, using a blanket stitch. (See Chapter 18.) It can also be reworked by machine with a zigzag stitch. Press the opening flat before restitching.

Just as threads break on buttons, they also break on hooks and eyes. Reattach hooks and eyes as described in Chapter 18.

ALTERATIONS

A garment is altered to increase or decrease its width or length. It is easier to decrease garment width than to increase it. Garment width cannot be increased if the seam allowances are too narrow or darts have been clipped or slit open. Garment length can be increased only if there is enough depth in the hem.

HELPFUL HINT: A handy saying to remember is "The ripples point to the problem." When a garment doesn't fit right, it usually pulls or sags, creating ripples. Think of these ripples as arrows that point to the place where alterations are needed.

BODICE LENGTH

The bodice of a dress is the portion above the waist. If the dress has a waistline seam, the bodice can be shortened. It usually cannot be lengthened because the seam allowance is too small.

To shorten the bodice, try on the garment. Tie a string around the waist to indicate the new waistline seam. Mark the string's position with pins.

Remove the garment. Straighten the line of pins if needed. Replace the pin line with a line of basting stitches. The basting line becomes the new seam line of the bodice. Remove the old waistline seam and the lower half of the zipper. With right sides together, reposition the seam line of the lower half of the garment along the basting line of the bodice. Ease in any fullness. Stitch the new seam. Trim the excess seam allowance. Restitch the lower half of the zipper.

BODICE WIDTH

Bodice width can be changed at seam lines or darts. The more seams in a garment, the easier it will be to alter the width.

To increase bodice width, take your measurements. Add about 1 inch for wearing comfort. From this total, subtract the actual width of the bodice. The difference is the amount you need to add.

The ripples point to the problem: the side seams need to be let out.

Check the garment seams and darts to determine which ones can be let out. Divide the amount of width needed among the seams to be used. For example, if you need to add 1½ inches and there are three seams, you will add ½ inch at each seam. Press these seams closed.

Your new stitching line will be in these seam allowances. Divide the amount you want to add in half. If you are adding ½ inch at each seam, your new stitching line should be ¼ inch away from the old one. Stitch the new seams. Remove the stitches from the old seams and press the seams open flat.

To decrease bodice width, try the garment on and pinch out the extra fullness. Evenly distribute the decrease among all darts and seams. Pin folds along the darts and seams to indicate new seam lines.

Remove the garment. Stitch the new seams and darts. Remove the old stitching lines and press.

SKIRT OR PANT LENGTH

Changes in skirt or pant length are the most common alterations. They are also the easiest.

To adjust hem length, remove the existing hem and press out the crease. Try on the garment. For skirts, ask a friend to use a hem marker and put pins where the new crease should be placed. When hemming slacks, ask a friend to fold the hem under and pin in place.

The hem of slacks should touch the top of the shoe or foot in front. In back, the hem should cover half of the heel. This means that slacks are about ½ inch longer in the back.

You can use hem tape (seam tape) to finish the raw edge of a hem. Lap the tape ¼ inch over the hem edge. Stitch it in place with a straight or zigzag stitch. Then blindstitch the hem in place.

If the new hem is too deep, remove the hem tape and shorten the hem depth. Reattach the hem tape and stitch the new hem. If there is too little depth in the hem, remove the hem tape. Replace it with a bias facing, which you can buy in a fabric store or cut from scraps of the garment fabric. Then, restitch the hem and press.

If hem tape is not used and the garment is made of a woven fabric, the raw edge should be finished to prevent raveling. The raw edge may be pinked and machine stitched, machine zigzagged, or turned under and stitched. After the raw edge is finished, the hem can be restitched.

HIP WIDTH

Occasionally, skirts and slacks need to be altered along the hipline. Changes should be made to both sides or to the front and back of the garment so the garment will hang on grain. Changes in skirt width may also mean that a portion of the hem is removed and replaced.

When increasing the hip width, take your hip measurement. Add about 2½ to 3 inches for ease. From this total, subtract the actual width of the garment. The difference is the amount you need to add. Decide which seams can be released. Divide the necessary increase evenly among those seams. Then divide that amount in half. For example, if you are adding ¾ inch at each seam, your new stitching line should be ⅜ inch from the old seam line. Remove the waistband. Press the seams closed. Stitch the new seams. Rip out the old seam lines. Press the new seams open flat. Replace the waistband.

When decreasing the hip measurement, try the garment on and pin tucks along the seam lines. Be sure to evenly distribute the decrease among the seams. Keep some fullness for wearing ease. Take off the garment, remove the waistband, and stitch the new seams. Remove the old stitching, trim seam allowances, and press. Replace the waistband.

When decreasing hip width, you may want to take in the darts as well as the seams to get a better fit.

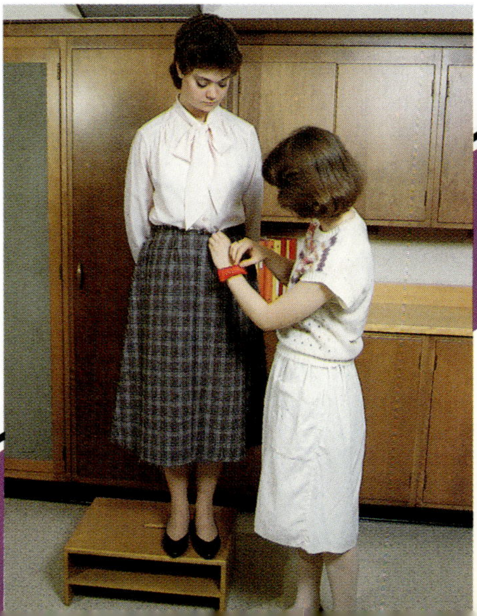

WAISTBANDS

Minor changes in the waistband length can be made by moving the button or hooks and eyes. Generally, the fastener can only be moved ⅛ inch to ¼ inch. Moving the fastener more than this amount will create a gap or bulge above the zipper.

Adding or removing more waistband length requires removal of the waistband. Changes in waistband length also require changes in gathers, darts, or seams.

Lengthening the Waistband

After removal of the waistband, release darts, seams, and gathers. Press darts and seams open flat. Stitch a new gathering thread if there are gathers. Try on the garment. Pin the new seam lines in place or draw the gathering thread as much as needed. Remove the garment and stitch the new seams.

Divide the waistband as shown, then pin it to the garment, aligning it at the side seams, center front, and center back.

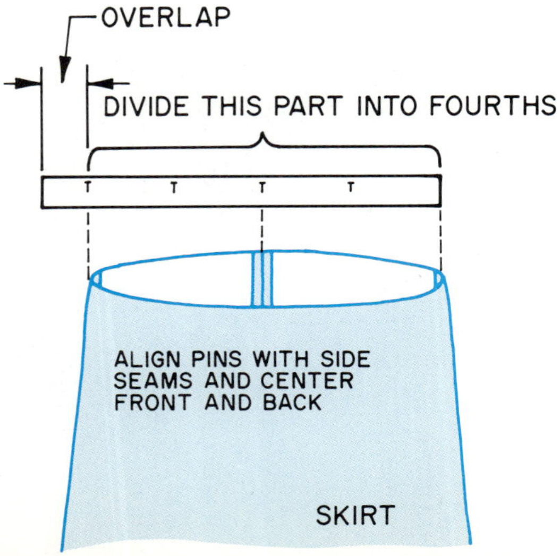

Compare the new waistline measurement with the length of the waistband. If the waistband is too short, sew an extension onto it. The extension fabric should match the garment fabric as closely as possible or be concealed by the waistband overlap or by a belt.

To reapply the waistband, place a pin indicating the length of the overlap. Fold the remaining waistband length in half, lengthwise, and mark the crease with pins. Next, fold each end to the center and mark the creases with pins. This procedure divides the waistband into fourths that can then be aligned with the side seams and center front and back. After pinning these points, ease fullness in between the points. Restitch and press the waistband.

Shortening the Waistband

If the waistband is to be shortened, it must first be removed. If gathers are present, stitch new gathering threads. Try on the garment. Draw up the gathering threads the needed amount or pin tucks along dart and seam lines. Remove the garment and restitch the gathers, darts, or seams. Remove old stitching as needed. Press the seam lines.

Compare the new waistline measurement with the waistband length. Shortening the waistband increases the overlap on the band. If the overlap is more than 1 inch long, the waistband needs to be shortened before it is reapplied. Determine seam and center front and back placement as described under "Lengthening the Waistband." Pin the waistband in place, stitch, and press it.

SLEEVE LENGTH

Long sleeves should end just beyond the wrist bone. Three-quarter-length sleeves should cover the elbow. Short sleeves should end above the elbow.

Sleeves that are too long are easy to alter. To shorten sleeves with a hem, you will need to remove the old hem. Press out the crease. Put the garment on. Have a friend fold the hem under until the sleeves are the proper length. (Be sure to check long sleeves with the arm bent.) Have your friend pin the hem in place. Remove the garment. Measure the hem depth. If it is more than 2 inches, trim off the extra fabric. Stitch the new hem and press.

To shorten sleeves with a cuff, you will first need to remove the cuff. Put the garment on. Pin the cuff in its new place. Measure and mark a new seam line. Remove the garment. Restitch the cuff. Trim away all excess length. Press.

Lengthening sleeves that are too short sometimes is a challenge. The easiest way to lengthen sleeves is to let out the hem.

Other ways to lengthen sleeves require some creative thought. Sleeves can be lengthened by adding contrasting cuffs, a lace or eyelet ruffle, or a matching or contrasting braid. Long sleeves that are too short can always be restyled into three-quarter-length or short sleeves.

(1)
If the sleeves are too short . . .

(2)
. . . add contrasting cuffs. A new collar of the same fabric gives the shirt a coordinated look.

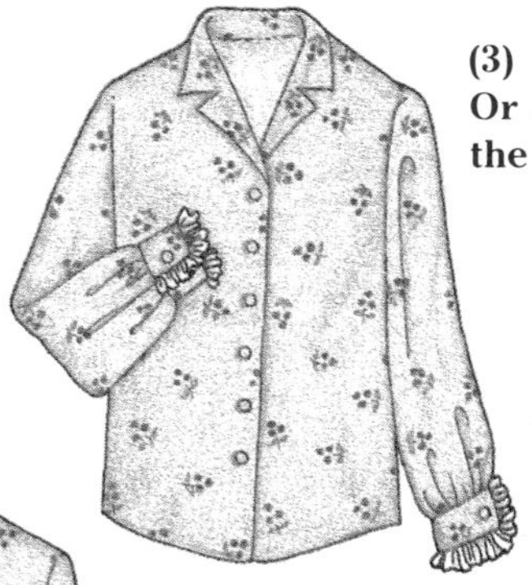

(3)
Or add ruffles or lace to the cuffs

(4)
or cut and re-hem to make short sleeves.

Getting Your Money's Worth

RECYCLING CLOTHES

Are there clothes in your closet which you no longer wear? Perhaps they're out of style or you've outgrown them. Maybe they need repair. Take a close look at these clothes. You may be able to recycle them into useful garments. Listed below are some ideas for redesigning clothes.

- Cut the legs from pants to make the pants into shorts.
- Sew leather or suede patches on worn elbows of jackets or sweaters.
- Shorten a dress with no waistline into a blouse-length garment.
- Taper the legs of flared pants into straight-leg pants.
- Recut a full skirt into a straight skirt.
- Remove the collar and sleeves from a jacket to make a vest.
- Extend the length of sleeves, pants, or skirts with contrasting bands or cuffs or insert a row of lace or braid.
- Cut the top from a short slip to make a camisole, or add rows of lace to the bottom to make the slip longer.
- Dye a faded shirt to restore or change its color.

REVIEW-22

SUMMARY

Alterations and repairs help keep the clothes in your wardrobe usable. The tools and techniques used for repairs are basically the same as those for constructing a new garment. Alterations are made to change garment width or length. Alterations in hem length are the easiest and most common ones made. Other alterations require more sewing skill.

CHECK YOUR KNOWLEDGE

1. Before beginning a garment repair, what things should you consider?
2. What is the difference between a functional patch and a decorative patch?
3. What is fusible web?
4. What are two ways to fill a hole in fabric?
5. List two ways to darn fabric. Which way is more durable? Which is invisible?
6. When replacing a zipper, what should you do if the seam allowances are too narrow?
7. What must you do before replacing a button that was torn from a garment?
8. What is a reinforcing button? Why is it used?
9. Which is easier—increasing or decreasing garment width? Why?
10. Describe how to alter skirt or pant length.

EXTEND YOUR KNOWLEDGE

1. Are there places in your town where clothes can be professionally altered or repaired? If so, find out the normal charges for altering a hem, increasing hip width of pants, and mending tears.
2. Make a poster titled "A Stitch in Time." On the poster, show techniques for patching or darning or for replacing fasteners.
3. Choose an old garment. Repair or update it using decorative patches. Bring the garment to class.
4. Bring to class a garment you no longer wear. Discuss what could be done to make the garment usable again.
5. Pretend you are preparing a "repair kit" for making common clothing repairs. What items would you include? Why?

CLOTHES AND CAREERS

Have you thought about what you want to do after you graduate from school? It's not too early to begin making your career plans.

The first step in career planning is to learn about yourself. What are your abilities? Are you good at math? Do you do well in English or science? Perhaps you have artistic talent. Knowing what your abilities are can help you find out what sort of career would be right for you. You should also think about your likes and dislikes. Do you enjoy working with people, or do you prefer to work on your own? Do you like an active, outdoor life, or are you happier indoors? Do you enjoy making things? Your likes and dislikes are clues about what type of work you would enjoy.

The second step in career planning is to learn about the careers that are available in today's world. This unit will help you do that. It tells about the clothes industry. You'll learn about careers in clothing. You'll also find some good tips for getting and keeping a job.

Unit 7

CHAPTER 23 The Clothes Industry

CHAPTER 24 Careers

CHAPTER 25 How to Get and Keep a Job

CHAPTER 23

THE CLOTHES INDUSTRY

An industry is a group of related businesses. The automobile industry, for example, includes all the auto manufacturers and dealers. You could break down the automobile industry into smaller industries. For instance, you could talk about the auto parts industry or the used car industry.

The clothes industry is also made up of several industries. The major ones are the textile, apparel, and retail industries. The **textile industry** takes the raw materials and makes fibers, yarns, and fabrics. The **apparel industry** uses the yarns and fabric to make clothing. The **retail industry** gets the clothing to the consumers.

In this chapter you'll find answers to the following questions:

- How does the clothes industry affect our economy?
- What is the role of government in the clothes industry?
- How are clothes designed, produced, and sold?

Look for These Terms

textile industry
apparel industry
retail industry
union
line of clothing
market research
assembly line
merchandising plan
fashion promotion

CLOTHES ARE BIG BUSINESS

New York City is the clothing capital of the world. In this city 20,000 people are employed by the textile industry, 140,000 by the apparel industry, and over 250,000 by the retail industry. Nationwide more than 2.6 million people work in the textile and apparel industries. And the retail industry is too large to count!

Because they are so big, these industries have a big influence on our country's economy. The textile industry alone is the nation's 10th largest employer. The total income of all the textile employees is more than $10 billion each year. These employees use their money to buy homes, cars, food, and thousands of other consumer goods. What would happen if the textile industry shut down? A lot of people would be out of work. They would not be able to afford many consumer goods. Therefore the people who make and sell the consumer goods would have problems. *They* might lose *their* jobs.

In the apparel industry, a lot of people have already lost their jobs. A great deal of labor is needed to make clothing. The cost of labor in the United States is increasing. In foreign countries, people work for less money. Clothes can be made at less cost. Therefore many American apparel manufacturers are moving their factories to other countries. What effects do you think this has on the American economy?

On the other hand, the retail industry in the United States is growing. Retail sales of apparel are over $97 billion a year. This means new jobs are opening up in sales, advertising, customer service, and mail order.

Check the labels on your clothes. How many of them are imported? From which countries do they come?

THE ROLE OF GOVERNMENT

Clothing has become such a big business that the government has stepped in to help regulate (control) some of the problems. In the beginning the government acted to protect the workers. Safety standards were set. Workers' hours were limited. In the past twenty years the government has switched its attention from workers to consumers. Today there are many laws and regulations to protect consumers. Most of them relate to truth in advertising and honesty in selling. See Chapter 15 for information about consumer rights.

In the late 1800s many women and children did piecework for garment manufacturers. They sewed in their homes or in small, unhealthy "sweat-shops" for long hours and low rates of pay. In 1883 striking garment workers asked that the rate for piecework be made high enough to enable workers to earn $15 per week.

THE ROLE OF UNIONS

A **union** is a group of workers in similar jobs who have joined together to promote workers' rights. The purpose of unions is to obtain better working conditions, better pay, and better benefits for workers.

The largest union in the clothing industry is the International Ladies Garment Workers Union (ILGWU). It is for workers employed in the manufacture of women's and children's clothing. Workers employed in the manufacture of men's and boy's clothing may belong to the Amalgamated Clothing Workers of America (ACWA).

Unions have worked hard and have had a great deal of power in the past. As a result, garment workers in America are the best paid in the world. Unfortunately, the high wages of workers have influenced many factory owners to build their plants in other countries.

The ILGWU has begun a campaign to encourage consumers to buy American-made clothing. Their slogan is "Look for the union label." The ILGWU label is placed in every garment made by the union workers.

When you see this label in a garment, you know it was made by union workers.

—Perspective

TEXTILES: MORE THAN JUST CLOTHES

You know that the textile industry makes fabrics for clothing. Did you know that it also makes hundreds of fabrics for other uses? Here is a sampling. What others can you name?

For the home, office, or school
- upholstery fabrics
- curtains and drapes
- carpeting
- towels
- some kinds of typewriter ribbon
- points for felt-tip pens
- some types of book covers

For transportation
- filters
- tire cord
- parachutes
- hot-air balloons

For industry
- fish nets
- conveyor belts
- fire hoses

For health care
- artificial blood vessels
- sutures for sewing together wounds and surgical incisions
- masks
- medical dressings

For defense
- bulletproof vests
- rifle slings
- flame-resistant flight suits

THE TEXTILE INDUSTRY

The textile industry is made up of all the makers of the materials used in clothing. These materials include fibers, yarns, and fabrics, as discussed in Unit 3. They also include trimmings, such as ribbons and lace, and functional items like zippers and elastic.

The textile industry begins with fibers. Natural fibers come from farms and ranches. Manufactured fibers are made in factories. Textile mills turn the fibers into yarn and fabric. There are over 7,000 textile plants located in 42 states. These plants produce over 17 billion yards of fabric each year for the apparel industry.

THE APPAREL INDUSTRY

The fabric produced by the textile industry is sold to designers, clothing manufacturers, or fabric stores. The apparel industry is made up of all the people that take the fabric and turn it into clothing. Some people refer to this industry as the garment industry or the "rag trade."

New York City is the center of America's garment industry. Most clothing manufacturers have offices here.

The process of making clothing begins with designers. Designers use research and creativity to develop ideas for a new line of clothing. A **line of clothing** is a collection of garments for a particular season of the year. Designers must understand the needs and wants of consumers. They must also consider how to produce and market the new line. They must estimate costs and predict sales to determine if a profit can be made. They must find out what other clothing companies are doing. Gathering information about consumers' needs and wants, production costs, and competition is called **market research.**

If market research indicates that the new line of clothing will sell, then the clothing goes into production.

- A production schedule is set. This shows when each stage of production is to be completed, from fabric delivery to the shipping date of the finished garments.
- The manufacturer buys the materials needed to make the garments.
- The production patterns are made. A production pattern is a master pattern that shows the shapes of the garment pieces.
- The production pattern is graded. This means that different sizes are developed from the production pattern.

- The marker, or pattern layout, is made by arranging the pattern pieces on the fabric. Because fabric costs money, the layout is designed to avoid waste.
- The fabric is layered so that many identical pieces may be cut at one time.
- The marker is put on top of the fabric layers. A machine cuts the fabric. Today some factories use lasers to do the cutting. Lasers are fast and accurate.
- The cut pieces are bundled and sent to the sewing machine operators.
- The pieces are sewn together.
- Trims and fasteners are applied.
- Garments are pressed.
- Garments are inspected for quality. Most garments carry an inspection number or stamp. This shows that the garment has passed the quality inspection. Garments that have defects are called "seconds" or "irregulars." They may be sold in stores, but they must be labeled as seconds or irregulars.
- Garments are packed and shipped to the retailer.

Have you seen labels like this? It means the item has passed the quality control inspection.

ASSEMBLY-LINE PRODUCTION

You have already learned about the construction of garments sewn at home. In a factory, many of the same processes are used. However, many people work on the garment. Usually each person does only one task, such as sewing on a pocket. The person does that same task over and over throughout the work shift. He or she becomes very skilled and fast at that task.

After the pocket is sewn, the garment piece is passed to the next worker. This worker also does one task, such as sew one side seam. The garment piece is then passed to still another worker, and so on until the garment is finished. This organization of people and tasks is called an **assembly line.**

In assembly-line production, each worker makes only part of the garment. Why do you think it's important for each part to be made exactly as specified?

Another difference between factory and home sewing is the equipment. Factory machines look different from the home sewing machine. Some are designed for a specific construction need. For example, there are machines that only finish seams. These machines, called sergers, encase the raw edge of the fabric with an interlocking thread. Specialized equipment allows a factory to operate faster and more efficiently.

To make a profit, factories must produce goods quickly, with little waste of time or material. Specialized equipment helps them do this. So does assembly line production. Factories may produce several hundred garments in one day.

THE RETAIL INDUSTRY

Retailing is the business of selling merchandise to consumers. A clothing retailer buys garments from the manufacturer and sells them to us, the consumers.

Retailers must know a lot about clothing. They must stay informed about the latest fashions. They must understand consumers' needs and wants.

Retail selling is done in stores and through catalogs. Either way, the goal is to keep the merchandise moving—coming in from the factories and going out to the consumers.

To keep merchandise moving, the retailer develops a selling plan. Often this is called a **merchandising plan.** To develop the plan, the retailer considers the store's customers. What do they like? What can they afford? The retailer also considers the store's image. Bill's Sporting Goods would probably not do well if it tried to sell tuxedos. But it could sell ski jackets.

The merchandising plan tells how much and what kind of merchandise to buy. The plan also tells how to promote and advertise the merchandise.

Buyers then select the desired merchandise. The promotion department makes the public aware of the merchandise. This is done through advertising, store displays, and special events such as fashion shows. Salespeople sell the products to the customers.

There are also many behind-the-scenes people in the retailing industry. Artists and copywriters prepare ads. Receiving clerks check in new merchandise. Accountants, stock clerks, office clerks, security workers, maintenance staff—all these people and more are needed in the retail business.

The next time you're in a store, think about how the store encourages people to buy. Are there attractive displays? Frequent sales? Product demonstrations?

Fashion ads are usually designed to appeal to a particular age and income group. To what group does this ad appeal?

FASHION PROMOTION

Fashion promotion is any activity designed to help sell a fashion item. It includes advertising, publicity, special events, and displays. You've already read about fashion promotion in stores. Fashion promotion also is done in fashion magazines and other publications. Fashion promoters supply photographs and written information to the magazines. Sometimes fashion promoters write articles for magazines and newspapers.

Fashion promoters also handle the publicity for their products at trade shows. A trade show is a large gathering of the people in an industry. They come together to show their products and to see what others have to offer.

"Fashion communication" is another name sometimes used to mean fashion promotion. People in fashion promotion are communicating fashion news. They write about fashion. They speak about fashion. Fashion photographers are also part of the effort to communicate fashion news. People who are in the business of communicating fashion news may work for manufacturers, pattern companies, stores, advertising agencies, newspapers, or magazines. Think about all the ways you learn about new fashions. What source do you rely on the most?

OTHER CLOTHING INDUSTRIES

At the beginning of this chapter you learned that the major clothing industries were textiles, apparel, and retailing. There are also several smaller industries.

FABRIC CARE

The fabric care industry has become big business. Consumers want help caring for their clothing. Specialists in clothing care include dry cleaners and commercial laundries.

In dry-cleaning plants, workers inspect garments for stains, rips, and damaged areas. These get special attention. Garments are then sorted according to color and fiber content. The clothes are cleaned and pressed. Each task requires handling and treating clothing. Therefore knowledge of fibers and fabrics is essential.

Many dry cleaners offer other services also, such as alterations and repair. They may also store out-of-season clothing.

People who work in commercial laundries also must have knowledge about fibers and fabrics. They handle clothing in much the same way as in the dry-cleaning plant. Garments are sorted. Stains, rips, and damaged areas are treated or repaired. After the clothing is cleaned, it is pressed.

ALTERATION AND REPAIR SERVICES

Alteration and repair services are needed by many people who don't have the skill or the time to do the work themselves. Department stores, specialty shops, and dry cleaners usually have alteration and repair departments. Dressmakers and tailors may do alterations and repairs in addition to making new garments. Some even specialize in alterations and repairs.

People who alter or repair clothes must have clothing construction skills. A knowledge of fibers and fabrics is also essential. They must be prepared to work on different types of garments and with different types of fabrics. Speed and quality of workmanship are important.

DRESSMAKING AND TAILORING

Dressmakers and tailors are in the business of custom sewing. They make garments for individuals. A person may be hard to fit or may want a certain style of garment that cannot be found in a store. A dressmaker or tailor will make the garment to order. Dressmakers generally sew women's clothes. Tailors usually sew men's clothes. Some tailors and dressmakers specialize in a certain type of garment. For example, they may tailor only men's suits or make wedding dresses.

REVIEW-23

SUMMARY

The clothing industry consists of three major industries and several smaller ones. The major industries are the textile, apparel, and retail industries. Some of the smaller ones are fabric care, alteration and repair, and dressmaking and tailoring.

The clothing industry is large and has a big influence on our nation's economy. Because clothing is such big business, government has passed laws and regulations to protect workers and consumers. Unions also help workers by obtaining better pay, benefits, and working conditions.

CHECK YOUR KNOWLEDGE

1. Briefly describe what the textile, apparel, and clothing industries do.
2. Why have many clothing manufacturers moved their plants to other countries?
3. Name two ways the government has protected workers in the clothing industry.
4. What is the purpose of a union?
5. What do the letters ILGWU and ACWA stand for? Which workers are in each organization?
6. Besides fibers, yarns, and fabrics, what does the textile industry make?
7. What is market research?
8. What is assembly-line production? What is its advantange?
9. What does a merchandising plan include?
10. What is fashion promotion?

EXTEND YOUR KNOWLEDGE

1. Design a flow chart that shows the progress of clothing, from the textile mill to the consumer.
2. Research the founding of the ILGWU. Write a report on what you learn.
3. Look in recent issues of newspapers and magazines to learn about the imported clothing issue. Do you think the United States should limit clothing imports? Why or why not?
4. Analyze fashion promotion in two different fashion magazines. Which appealed to you more? Which provided more consumer information?
5. What types of fabric care, alteration and repair services, and custom sewing are available in your area? Why do you think people need these businesses?

CHAPTER 24

CAREERS

When you were a small child, you probably had many thoughts about what you wanted to do when you grew up. A baseball player, a nurse, a computer programmer, a teacher—these may have interested you. But now that you'll soon be an adult, you may be confused as to what your career choice really should be.

As you read in the introduction to this unit, knowing yourself is the first step to choosing the right career. If you know your likes and dislikes, you will be able to choose a career you will enjoy. Write down on a piece of paper everything you like to do. Look at the list. Does it include anything that has to do with clothing? If it does, maybe you would enjoy a career in making, buying/selling, designing, or teaching about clothes.

In this chapter, you'll find answers to the following questions about careers:

- What kinds of careers are available in the clothing industry?
- What kind of training and education are required?
- What personal abilities are needed?

Look for These Terms

entry-level job
draping
custom-made garments

STARTING OUT: PART-TIME AND SUMMER JOBS

You may be able to start on your way to a career while still in high school. A part-time or summer job that gives you on-the-job training is a good start. Whether you begin this way or not, remember that you will probably have to start at the entry level.

An **entry-level job** is a job for beginners. It is for people who have not had experience in that line of work. For example, to get a part-time job as a salesclerk, you usually don't need to have worked before as a salesclerk. However, you do need to have some basic skills and interest in the clothing field.

Many high school students find part-time or summer jobs in department stores. If you land a job in a department store, it will probably be one of the following entry-level jobs:

- *Stock clerk*—keeps track of the goods that are in stock; tells the boss (head of stock) how much stock there is to help him or her in reordering.
- *Receiving clerk*—checks all goods that come in from other places; makes sure that what was ordered was what came and that it was not damaged.
- *Marker*—puts price tags and labels on the new merchandise; checks everything to make sure it goes to the selling floor with the right tag.
- *Packer*—packs items to be sent to customers by mail or truck.
- *Wrapper*—wraps gifts in the store for customers.
- *Mail-order clerk*—handles paperwork for orders that come in through the mail or by telephone; must make sure customers get what they ordered.
- *Office clerk*—files, types, keeps records; always plenty to do.

These are behind-the-scenes jobs. Now let's go to the selling floor. There are some people there who have entry-level jobs:

- *Salesclerk*—helps people select items; operates the cash register; knows how to handle cash, check, and credit card purchases; makes change; puts merchandise in boxes or bags for customers.
- *Cashier*—similar to salesclerk, but cashier stays at cash register, ringing up sales.

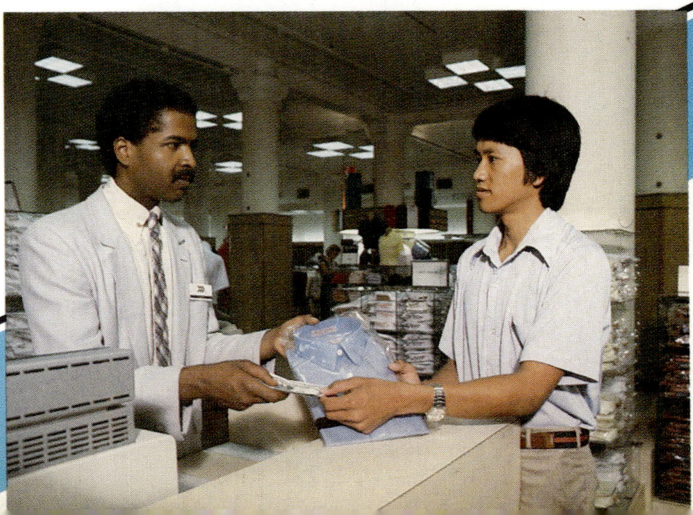

Do you enjoy helping people? The ability to deal with the public in a helpful and courteous way is important for a salesclerk.

With most entry-level jobs, training is provided on the job. The training may last just a few hours, or it may take several days. It depends on the kind of job and the kind of training program the store offers. Salesclerks, for example, are taught not only how to run the cash registers and make out sales slips, but they also are given instructions about dress, grooming, and behavior. This is important. Salespeople come in direct contact with the public. They must present a good image for the store.

Entry-level jobs are like the first rung on a ladder. If you do well in the entry-level job, you can advance up the ladder to jobs that have more responsibility and higher pay. That's why part-time and summer jobs are a good way to begin. When you're ready for a full-time job, you will already have experience. You can get a job that's higher up on the career ladder.

CAREERS IN THE TEXTILE INDUSTRY

The textile industry takes raw fibers and converts them into finished fabrics. There are careers in design, research, production, and selling.

DESIGN

A *textile print designer* develops new patterns and designs to be printed onto fabrics. Designers must predict what the public will like and buy. They must keep in mind that they are designing for the public's taste and not for their own likes. What will the public buy? Butterfly prints? Calico prints? Indian prints?

A *fabric designer* designs the construction of the fabric. Fabric designers do not create patterns to be printed on fabric. Instead, they weave sample designs on a hand loom. The design and the colors are woven right into the fabric.

Both print and fabric designers must understand how fibers are made and how they behave. They must also be creative. Most of these designers receive their training in technical schools or colleges.

This fabric designer is using a computer-aided design system to "weave" new fabric designs. Because the system can imitate the different types, textures, weights, and colors of yarn, the designer can create an endless number of patterns, and she can do it much faster than by hand.

RESEARCH AND DEVELOPMENT

Competition in the textile market is keen. Textile makers are always coming out with new fibers and fabrics to meet the changing needs and wants of consumers. Ideas for new products start in the research and development department.

Scientists, engineers, and *lab technicians* create new products and figure out how to mass-produce them. They also look for ways to improve present products and manufacturing processes.

As a textile researcher you might be involved with the design or improvement of textile machinery. You may help develop new dyeing or finishing techniques. You might even invent a new fabric. It's an exciting field. Textile researchers created the knitted replacement arteries which are used in heart surgery. Space suits also were designed and developed by textile researchers.

The lab technician is mixing dye for fiberglass fabric.

PRODUCTION

The jobs of *machine tender* (operator) and *machine repairer* are very important in the textile industry. Many tasks are done in a textile plant, beginning with the opening of bales of fiber and ending with making the yarn into fabric and finishing the fabric. Each task requires special machinery. The textile industry depends on the people who operate and maintain these machines.

Production supervisors direct the machine tenders and repairers. The production supervisors must be able to handle responsibility. They need to motivate others to give their best efforts on the job. Production supervisors often move on to higher levels of management.

These machine operators are inspecting an open-end spinning frame in operation.

SELLING

You've seen that the textile industry needs people who can design and produce products. The industry also needs people to sell its products. *Sales representatives* contact possible buyers and tell them about the products. They also communicate the buyers' wants and needs back to the textile manufacturer.

Travel is a part of almost every sales representative's life because there must be constant contact with customers. Willingness to travel and the ability to get along with people are essential for a sales representative.

Sales representatives for textile companies visit clothing designers and manufacturers to show them the latest products.

CAREERS IN THE APPAREL INDUSTRY

The apparel industry uses fabrics to make clothing. First a garment is designed; then it goes to the factory for production. The clothing made in factories is mass-produced. That is, many garments of one type are sewn at the same time. Mass-produced apparel is referred to as ready-to-wear.

FASHION DESIGN

A *fashion designer* creates a garment from an idea. Sketches are made until the designer is satisfied with one. Then fabric is cut and fitted to a model form according to the design lines. This process is called **draping.** The fabric pieces are removed from the form and sewn together.

Fashion designers must have artistic ability as well as practical knowledge of textiles and garment construction.

A live model will then show the sample garment to production managers. They consider the design itself, the latest fashion trends, and the cost of making garments from the design. If the design is accepted, the garment is put into production.

If you want to be a designer, you should have a flair for clothes and an interest in fashion. A designer should have a feel for fabric and a lot of color sense. It is also important to have skill in fitting and constructing garments. A designer needs to be creative and imagine from an idea what a garment will look like on a person.

Wages for the beginner are not very high. But, as a reputation is earned, income increases. Most of the jobs are in large cities. Sixty percent of them are in the New York area.

Perspective

PICTURE PERFECT

Being a model is an exciting, glamorous job. It's also hard work. A model has to look fresh and energetic, even after many hours on the job. Standing on a city sidewalk for several hours in order to get the right shots can be tiring. Posing under hot studio lights or in shorts in the middle of winter can be uncomfortable. Yet a model must not look tired or irritated.

Modeling requires a lot of discipline. Successful models take good care of their bodies. They exercise every day and eat the right kinds of food. They get plenty of sleep (baggy eyes can ruin a photo). They take good care of their skin and hair.

Of course, models must be attractive. Good coordination and gracefulness are also desirable. Female models usually must be between 5′5″ and 5′10″ tall. Male models generally must be between 6′ and 6′2″ tall and wear a size 40 or 42 Regular suit.

How does one get a modeling job? It's best to contact a reputable agency. Photographers, advertising agencies, retail stores, and magazines almost always use agency models. The modeling agency charges the model a fee for every job it arranges. Usually the charge is 10 to 20 percent of the modeling fee.

Adapted from an article by the American Home Sewing Association. The American Home Sewing Association is a nonprofit organization representing the home sewing industry's efforts to encourage the development of sewing skills.

PRODUCTION

After a garment design is accepted, it goes into production. Many people are needed to produce the clothing we wear.

Sample stitchers follow a designer's pattern or sketches to make sample garments. This person checks the fit and hang of the garment on the model form. Positions of fasteners and trimmings are marked.

The *patternmaker* uses a designer's sketch or the sample garment to develop a master pattern for each piece of the garment.

Pattern cutters, or *fabric cutters,* cut as many as one hundred layers of fabric at one time. Laser beams are used in some plants for the cutting. The cut pattern pieces are sorted and tied into bundles by the *assorter.* These bundles go to the sewing machine operator.

Sewing machine operators sew pieces together. These workers might make only certain parts of a garment, or they might put all the completed parts together.

Finishers add outside stitching, trims, buttonholes, or buttons. These workers need to sew rapidly and accurately by hand.

Pressers iron out wrinkles and press creases and pleats in place.

Garment production involves many different jobs.

CAREERS IN DRESSMAKING AND TAILORING

Not all garments are mass-produced. Some are custom-made. **Custom-made garments** are made especially for an individual by a *dressmaker* or *tailor*. These experts in custom sewing work in businesses or in their homes. They may make entire garments, or they may specialize in alterations and repairs.

Custom sewing requires a high degree of skill. People who go to a tailor or dressmaker expect better fit and better workmanship than they would find in ready-to-wear garments.

Accuracy and willingness to work with details are necessary for success as a dressmaker or tailor. You must also be able to work well with people and be tactful when making suggestions to the customer. Sometimes you might have to work under pressure to complete a garment in a short time. Of course, you must know fabrics and how they can be used in a garment. You must have good construction skills.

Custom sewing requires good construction skills and careful attention to detail.

CAREERS IN RETAILING

The clothing retailing industry sells merchandise to consumers. Retailing is a very large industry. New stores are opening everywhere, every day. This means lots of career opportunities. You've already read about the entry-level jobs. This section describes some higher-level jobs.

BUYING

A *buyer* purchases the merchandise that the store will sell. A large store has a buyer for each department.

In this job, you would work closely with the department or store manager. You might work for one store, for a large central store that buys for other stores in a chain, or for several small stores. You would visit showrooms in large cities and select those items you feel the customers would buy. Many times there is an assistant buyer who helps get the job done.

To be a buyer you need to:

- have organizing ability
- be somewhat aggressive
- be diplomatic in dealing with wholesalers and salespeople
- have good taste and the ability to predict fashions
- be able to tell when interest in a trend has reached its peak

Positions as buyers are limited. There is competition for those positions. Therefore only the more successful people in retailing reach this level.

DEPARTMENT/STORE MANAGEMENT

The *manager* is in charge of the workers in a department. The manager also keeps track of the sales. If something is not selling well enough, the store may stop offering it.

Managers need special skills. Because they must supervise the store workers, they must be able to motivate others and get along well with people. The money tasks expected of them require that they have organizational skills, and they must have a good business sense. It is the manager's responsibility to make the store profitable.

A manager in a department store must keep track of which items are selling and which are not.

CAREERS IN FASHION PROMOTION

Fashion promotion is the art of letting people know what is new in clothing and convincing them to buy it. This is done through various communication jobs.

Fashion illustrators must catch people's attention with a pleasing picture. If you have artistic ability, are creative, and have an interest in clothing, you may enjoy a career as a fashion illustrator. You would work for retail stores, pattern companies, or advertising agencies. The work is complex. In each illustration you need to show construction details, fabric textures, fabric designs, and accessories. The total picture must be eye-catching to the viewer.

High school courses in art, history, psychology, and clothing are helpful. Usually further education at a university or at an art or fashion institute is needed.

Fashion photographers help promote fashions by capturing the right pose with the right props on film. They take photos of models showing fashions and accessories. In addition to still photography, they may work with film and videotape.

Fashion writers usually need a college degree in journalism or in textiles and clothing. Some of the duties of a writer are to write columns or feature stories for newspapers, to write newsletters, and to write articles for magazines and prepare news releases. Pattern companies hire writers to write the guide sheets that are included with the patterns. Mail-order companies employ writers to write the catalog descriptions of their products.

There is strong competition for jobs in the communications field. People who are ambitious and have the ability to convince others are likely to get the jobs.

A fashion photographer must have artistic style as well as technical know-how.

CAREERS IN EDUCATION

Teaching about textiles and clothing can be very exciting and satisfying. However, contrary to what people think, teaching is not an easy job. It requires a willingness to give of yourself. It requires a lot of knowledge and the ability to transfer that knowledge to students.

Many home economists are teachers. Some teach all areas of home economics; others specialize in one area, such as clothing and textiles. There are different levels of teaching. In almost every state, textiles and clothing courses begin at the junior high level. Courses in textiles and clothing are also taught in most high schools and colleges. College teachers must be experts in their field. Besides giving instruction, college teachers have to do a lot of research. Many of them write textbooks and/or articles for professional publications.

Clothing teachers help their students understand the meaning of clothing and teach them how to make good clothing decisions.

CAREERS IN RETAIL SERVICES

Customers may want help shopping for garments. Or they may need help maintaining them. There are jobs to meet these needs.

PERSONAL SHOPPERS

Many department stores employ *personal shoppers* to meet the needs of busy people. As a personal shopper, you would ask about the lifestyle and tastes of the customer and then choose clothing for him or her. You must always keep the customer's likes and needs in mind. The customer reviews the clothing you have selected and may choose to buy or not to buy it.

In larger cities there are independent personal shoppers. They don't work for any store, but they may visit several in search of garments for their customers.

ALTERATIONS

An *alterer* is a person who alters ready-to-wear clothing. The person repairs garments and also solves fitting problems for customers. Altering clothes is more difficult than doing the first construction. To do alterations, you must sew well, work fast, and recognize proper fit. Alterations people may work for stores, laundries or dry cleaners, or for themselves.

Beginning alterers are usually paid on an hourly basis. Those who have experience, however, may be paid a salary (a fixed monthly rate). Those who are self-employed set their own rates and earn according to the amount of work done. Trained people in this area are in demand.

LAUNDRY AND DRY CLEANING

These businesses are usually small neighborhood shops. They may be independent or part of a chain. Employees need basic skills in laundry and dry-cleaning procedures. They must keep up to date on fiber and fabric care. They may also be responsible for storing customers' out-of-season garments. Many laundries and dry cleaners also provide clothing repair and alterations for a fee.

Chances for advancement are limited. In this area, you may advance to being in charge of other workers or may open your own business. The pay is usually on an hourly basis.

—Perspective

CAREER PROFILE: FASHION DIRECTOR

Job Description: A fashion director keeps abreast of the latest fashion trends, relates them to his or her company's products, and communicates fashion information within and outside of the company.

Training: A two-year degree from a fashion school or community college or a four-year degree from a college offering programs in clothing and textiles, fashion marketing, communications, or business is recommended.

Personality Profile: A fashion director needs to have a flair for fashion and style and an interest in fabrics, trends, and design. The ability to work well with others, accept new ideas, and communicate effectively is essential.

Related Opportunities: Fashion or fabric editor; assistant fashion or fabric editor; fashion promotion assistant; publicity assistant; copywriter.

Career Close-Up: Carlos Martinez, Director of Fashion Services

As Director of Fashion Services, Carlos Martinez acts as a fashion clearinghouse for an entire company. In charge of a large pattern company's Fashion Information Center, Carlos researches all information on fabric and fashion trends each season and distributes it throughout the company. Research may sound dull, but in Carlos' case it's an exciting part of his job. He covers two European trade shows each season to find out the very hottest fashion trends from Paris, Milan, London, and other fashion centers. Back in his New York office, aided by two accessories editors, two fabric editors, and one senior editor, Carlos puts together his fashion forecast for the season. He's often called upon to present this information to the press, pattern designers, and customers.

Reporting the latest trends may sound like an easy job, but it isn't. Carlos first has to adapt and temper the information for a variety of different markets. He works with many different people both within and outside the company and sees people skills as an important qualification for his job. "In this job," he says, "you have to be able to communicate with people and get along with them. Most importantly, you must be willing to accept new and different ideas."

Adapted from an article by the American Home Sewing Association. The American Home Sewing Association is a nonprofit organization representing the home sewing industry's efforts to encourage the development of sewing skills.

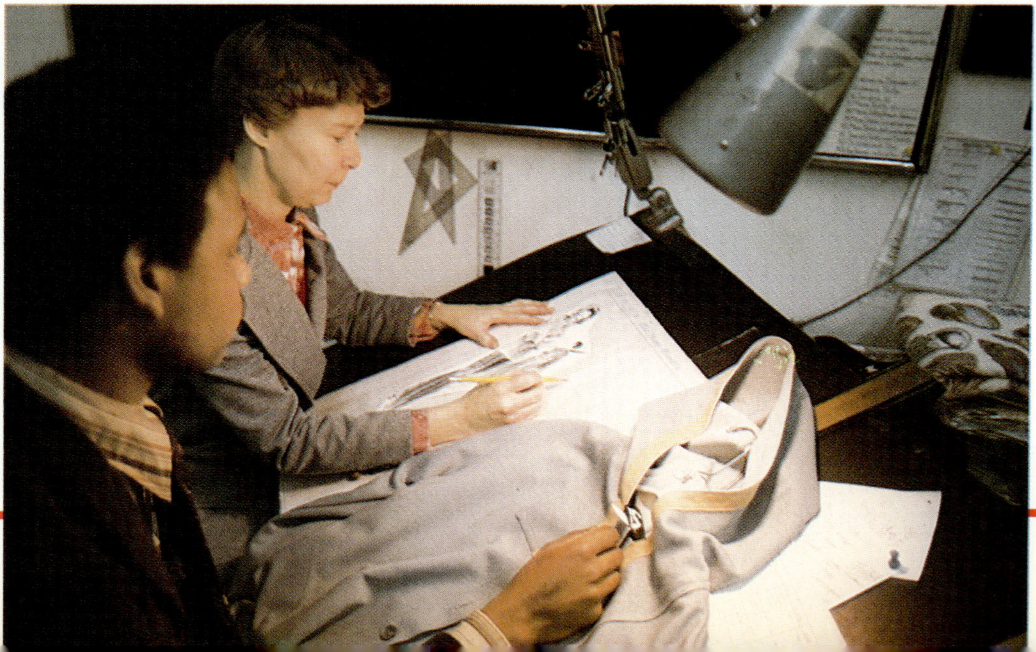

—Perspective

CAREER PROFILE: RETAIL EDUCATION COORDINATOR

Job Description: A retail education coordinator directs his or her company's promotion activities and educational programs and works with company stores throughout the country to carry out the programs. The job usually involves working closely with educators and consumers to help promote proper use of the company's products.

Training: A four-year degree in home economics is recommended, with concentration in clothing and textiles and in education. Business courses are also helpful.

Personality Profile: A retail education coordinator should be creative and have a strong commitment to education. The ability to write and communicate effectively is essential.

Related Opportunities: Editor, copywriter, educational director, traveling educational representative.

Career Close-Up: Charlene Johnson, Fashion and Education Coordinator

Charlene Johnson coordinates the fashion and educational activities of all the fabric stores for a retail fabric chain. Her responsibilities include planning craft and sewing workshops for educators and consumers. The workshops are designed to keep their customers up to date on the latest craft and sewing techniques. Charlene works closely with the chain's buyers and the merchandising department in deciding on the workshops they will offer. Local stores then have a choice in selecting the workshops that address the interests within their communities. Charlene also plans programs that stores present to teachers and students who visit during field trips. These programs include store tours; updates on fabrics, fibers, notions, and crafts; and hints on pattern selection. The actual presentation of the program is done by each store's home economist.

In the area of fashion and special promotions, Charlene plans and coordinates special events such as fashion shows or craft boutiques for the stores. That includes publishing a book to be distributed at the stores, complete with patterns, ideas, and new products and fabric information.

Charlene, who has a degree in textile and clothing design, has a strong background in art and design and loves the creative part of her job. She recommends that students interested in a job like hers have creativity, a good sense of organization, perseverance, and lots of enthusiasm!

Adapted from an article by the American Home Sewing Association. The American Home Sewing Association is a nonprofit organization representing the home sewing industry's efforts to encourage the development of sewing skills.

Perspective

CAREER PROFILE: SERVICE TRAINING MANAGER

Job Description: A service training manager is in charge of planning, conducting, and supervising educational programs for the people who service his or her company's products.

Training: A high school diploma is essential; a college degree is helpful. A service training manager needs a thorough knowledge of the company's products and how to service them. On-the-job training is common.

Personality Profile: Students interested in the service field should have an understanding of mechanics and electrical theory, have manual dexterity, and patience. In addition, a service training manager needs to be able to communicate his or her ideas effectively and be well organized.

Related Opportunities: Repairman, service manager, technical writer, dealer.

Career Close-Up: Joseph Woldarski, Service Training Manager

Adapted from an article by the American Home Sewing Association. The American Home Sewing Association is a nonprofit organization representing the home sewing industry's efforts to encourage the development of sewing skills.

Joseph Woldarski has always loved working with mechanical things, and that's a real asset in his job as a service training manager. Joe is constantly on the go around the country holding service seminars for sewing machine dealers. It's Joe's job to make sure that the people who service his company's machines know the machines inside and out. And Joe plans the programs, puts together the materials, and conducts the seminars that help them do that.

Joe had never used a sewing machine at all when he applied for a job at a local sewing machine service center during high school. But he knew that he liked being involved with machines. He got the job and eventually advanced to assistant manager and then manager of the center. When the company asked him to train other service managers on a new machine, Joe had a chance to demonstrate his abilities. After that, he moved to corporate headquarters and became national service training manager.

Joe attributes his success to his "dedication, time, and willingness to work my way up." Most importantly, he loves his work. "It's very rewarding to teach people new skills and help them become the best they can be."

REVIEW-24

SUMMARY

There are many career opportunities in the clothing field. In the textile industry, there are jobs in design, research and development, production, and selling. In the apparel industry, there are jobs in design and production. The custom clothing area includes jobs in dressmaking and tailoring. Careers in retailing include buying and management as well as entry-level jobs such as salesclerk. The fashion promotion field offers jobs in communications. Teaching about clothing and textiles can be a satisfying career. Careers in retail services include personal shopping, laundry service, and dry cleaning.

CHECK YOUR KNOWLEDGE

1. What is an entry-level job?
2. What is the difference between a textile print designer and a fabric designer?
3. What department of a textile company is responsible for creating new products and improving present ones?
4. Why are the jobs of machine tenders and repairers very important in the textile industry?
5. Name three jobs in apparel production.
6. Name the qualities needed to be a good tailor or dressmaker.
7. What does a buyer for a department store do?
8. Name three jobs that a fashion writer might have.
9. At what grade level do courses in clothing and textiles usually begin?
10. What is an alterer?

EXTEND YOUR KNOWLEDGE

1. Choose one of the careers mentioned in this chapter and research it. Find out what type of education is needed, what the average pay is, and how much of a demand there is for the job.
2. Interview someone in a clothing-related job. How did the person get started? What does he or she like and dislike about the job?
3. Make a chart listing at least five clothing-related careers. Under each career list qualities needed to work in that area, such as "creativity" or "willingness to travel." Which set of qualities most closely matches your own?
4. Make a list of the clothing-related businesses in your community. Divide the list into textile industry, apparel industry, custom sewing, retailing, and retail services.
5. If you were to choose a career in clothing, which one would it be? Why?

CHAPTER 25

HOW TO GET AND KEEP A JOB

Let's suppose you choose a career and obtain the education you need. Is that all you'll have to do to be successful in the world of work? Not quite. Remember, there will be lots of other people in the same career as you. To be successful, you'll have to know more than how to do your work. You'll also have to know how to get and keep a job.

This chapter will help you find answers to these questions:

- Where can you look for a job?
- How should you apply for the job?
- How can you be successful on the job?

Look for These Terms

cooperative education programs
wage
salary
resumé
references
job application
entrepreneurs

LOOKING FOR A JOB

Jobs are everywhere—if you know how to look. Your school and the people around you can be a good source of job information. Tell your parents' friends, your neighbors, relatives—everyone you know—that you are looking for a job. This "word-of-mouth" method has helped many people find jobs.

COOPERATIVE EDUCATION PROGRAMS

Cooperative education programs are offered by many high schools. These programs helps students find part-time jobs while they are still in school. Students receive both wages and school credit for their work. The cooperative education teacher works with the job supervisor to help the student be successful on the job. Ask your clothing teacher or school counselor about cooperative education.

SCHOOL PLACEMENT OR VOCATIONAL OFFICE

Most schools employ trained counselors to help students find jobs. Sometimes their office is called the placement office. Sometimes it's the vocational or guidance office. The counselors can help students find part-time jobs. They also help locate full-time, entry-level jobs for those who have finished school. For students who aren't sure what career they want, there are tests to help them discover their interests and abilities.

"HELP WANTED" ADS

Most newspapers have a classified ad section which lists jobs that are available. These job ads are placed by employers looking for workers. Usually, ads for similar jobs are grouped together. For example, if you are interested in a sales job, you would look under "Sales." The ads usually give a brief description of the job and what kind of person the employer is looking for. Sometimes they state the wages or salary. A **wage** is payment on an hourly, daily, or piecework basis. The more hours you work or products you produce, the more you get paid. A **salary** is a fixed amount paid regularly. No matter how many hours you work, your paycheck remains the same.

Newspaper want ads can be a good source of job information. These ads change often, so check them every day.

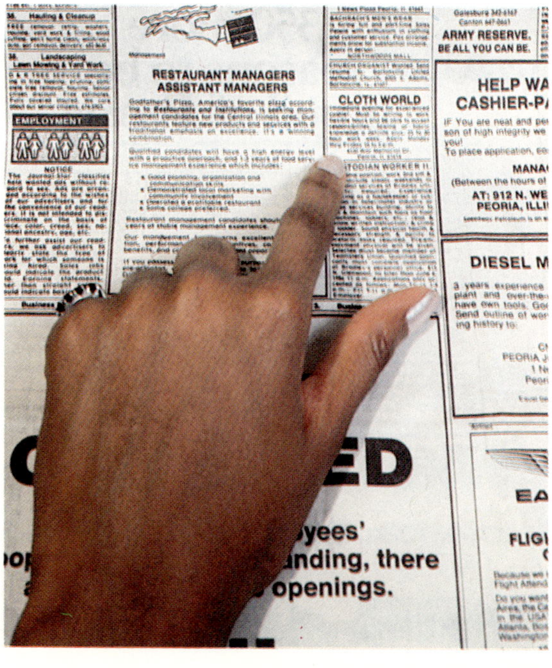

OTHER SOURCES OF INFORMATION

State employment services provide job information, counseling, training, and placement. Some states have a computerized list of job openings. Check for special employment programs for teens. You'll find the employment service listed in your phone book, under your state's name.

Private employment agencies also can help you find a job. However, these agencies charge money for their services. Sometimes the employer pays the fee, and sometimes you do. Often, the fee is a large percentage of your first month's wages or salary. If the agency asks you to sign a contract, be sure you understand it before signing. Know what the fee is and when you will be expected to pay.

Stores or factories may post notices of job openings. You could also call their personnel office to find out what jobs are available.

When you visit an employment agency, you will be asked about your education, previous jobs, and career interests. The agency will then try to match you with a suitable job.

GETTING THE JOB

After you've found out what jobs are available, the next step is prepare yourself to apply for the job. Are special permits required? Is special skill or experience needed? Find out what's needed before you apply.

GATHERING INFORMATION

If this is your first job, you'll need a social security card. You can apply for one at your local Social Security office. This card establishes a social security "account" in your name.

Social Security is a federal retirement and benefits program. A portion of your paycheck will be deducted (taken away) and deposited in this account. On your paycheck, the amount deducted may be listed under FICA (Federal Insurance Contribution Act). Your employer also contributes to your social security account. Your employer needs to know your social security number so the money will go to your account.

The number on your Social Security card is yours alone—no one else has one exactly like it. Your number stays the same throughout your life.

Some state laws require teenagers to have a work permit if they are still in school. Ask your school counselor if you need a work permit. Your counselor can also tell you how to get the permit, if one is needed.

A personal information sheet is needed for most jobs when you apply. This information sheet is called a **resumé** (REZ-uh-may). It lists facts your employer may want to know, such as your education, job experience, and interests.

Think of a resumé as a written advertisement for you. It should tell people about your background and interests. Be sure to include previous work experience, awards, special courses, and any other facts that qualify you for the job.

A resumé may include references. **References** are the names, addresses, and phone numbers of people who know your character and abilities. The people could be teachers or former employers, or they could be people you know socially, such as a minister or family friend. Avoid listing relatives as references. Always ask a person for permission before you include him or her as a reference.

Your resumé should be typed. It should contain no misspelled words or other errors. Your resumé should be no more than two pages long. One page is even better. You don't want to sound as though you are bragging.

Jennifer Dawson
5607 North St.
Creve Coeur, IL 61611
(309) 555-6748

Career Objective:	To develop knowledge and skills leading to a career in fashion merchandising.
Education:	Student at Central High School. Enrolled in vocational education program.
Honors and Activities:	Dean's Honor List Student Career Day leader Yearbook photographer
Work Experience:	Adrianne's Dress Shop, Creve Coeur, IL Salesclerk, June-August, 1986 Assisted customers, operated cash register, assisted store owner with inventory and ordering of merchandise.
Special Interests:	Traveling Photography Art
References:	Mrs. Adrianne Cole 4901 Prairie Drive Westlake, IL 61571 (309) 961-8293 Mr. Robert Wiston 1809 W. Gibson Ave. Creve Coeur, IL 61611 (309) 555-2953

MAKING CONTACT

Your first contact will probably be by phone or letter. If you are answering an ad, be sure to follow the directions in the ad. For example, if the ad says, "Send resumé and two letters of reference," don't call. Send the information requested. Also include a letter explaining that you are answering the ad in the newspaper. Tell when you will be available for an interview. Remember to include your address and phone number so you can be contacted.

If you phone a potential employer, do so from a quiet room so that you can make your call without being disturbed. Be polite but brief. State your name and why you called. Keep a calendar in front of you. Know the times you will be available for an interview over the following two weeks. Try not to schedule more than three interviews in one day. Allow plenty of time to research the company and the position before your interview.

Even if you have already sent a resumé, the company may ask you to fill out a job application. A **job application** is the official form a company uses to collect and record information about all applicants.

Read the application form thoroughly before you begin to fill it out. This way you know what is asked for and are less likely to list information in one place and then find out it is requested in another place. Be sure you understand the directions. If you have questions, ask for help. It's better to ask for help than to fill out the application incorrectly.

If you are sent the application form, be sure to type your responses. If you are asked to fill out the application at the job site, write neatly or print. Employers sometimes judge applicants by the way they fill out the form.

If you will be filling out the application form at the job site, be prepared. Bring along your resumé and social security card so you will have the information you need.

If the company is interested in you, you will be asked to come in for an interview. Be sure to be on time! You can make a bad impression on a potential employer by being late. If you have a good reason to be late, phone and explain your tardiness. Allow yourself plenty of time to get to your interview. If you are not sure of the location, allow extra time to find it.

Arriving late for a job interview creates a bad impression. People may think you are not well organized, or that you don't really care about getting the job.

Remember, a potential employer will judge you by your appearance and manner as well as your resumé.

Check your appearance. Be neat, clean, and well-dressed. A suit, dress, slacks and shirt, or skirt and blouse are appropriate. Jeans and a T-shirt are not. The company will have only a short time to judge you. Your appearance and behavior help the company decide if you are the type of employee they are seeking.

When you arrive, give your name and the reason you are there to the receptionist. While you wait, review in your mind the questions you want to ask and the points you want to make.

When you enter the interviewer's office, be prepared to shake hands. Wait for the interviewer to offer his or her hand. Return the handshake with a firm clasp, but don't squeeze too hard. Look at the interviewer while you are shaking hands. Do not sit down until you are invited to sit.

You will probably be a little nervous. That's understandable and expected. The interviewer may try to "break the ice" by chatting about the weather or other things for a few minutes. Try to be relaxed. Look at the interviewer as much as possible. Eye contact is important.

When you are asked questions, answer them honestly. And answer with more than a yes or no. Give reasons. However, don't talk too long about yourself or your interests. Show an interest in the company. You can ask about job benefits, such as vacation or insurance, but it's better not to bring up money. Let the interviewer be the first one to mention wages or salary.

When the interview is over, thank the person for taking the time to talk with you. A follow-up thank-you letter is also a good idea.

Ten Tips for a Successful Interview

1. Be neat and well-groomed. Your clothes don't have to be expensive, but they must be clean and unwrinkled. Don't overdo make-up, perfume, or cologne. Dont' chew gum or smoke.
2. If the interviewer shakes hands with you, make your handshake firm but not a "crusher."
3. Look at the interviewer. Eye contact shows you are alert and paying attention.
4. Stand and sit tall. Don't slouch.
5. Speak up. Pronounce your words clearly; don't mumble. Remember, an interview is a two-way conversation. The interviewer wants to learn about you, and you want to learn about the company.
6. Ask questions about the job and the company. It shows you are interested. If possible, find out some facts about the job and company *before* the interview. That shows you're interested enough to do some research.
7. Talk about your experience. What have you done that helps qualify you for the job? Don't limit yourself to mentioning previous jobs. Volunteer work or school activities may also count.
8. If you're asked why you want the job, reply honestly, but in a positive way. For example, say "I want to become independent and live on my own," not "I need money so I can get away from my folks."
9. Be prepared to talk about your long-range plans. What are your career goals?
10. Don't worry about being nervous. Everyone who goes on a job interview is nervous. Your interviewer will understand.

KEEPING THE JOB

"You're hired!" At last, the words you've been waiting to hear. You got that job. *Now* you are an employee. And you want to remain with this job—at least for the time being. Keeping a job requires consideration for others—your employer, your co-workers, and your customers.

BEING PROFESSIONAL

Being professional means doing your best. No matter what job you have, you should give it your best efforts. Be dependable. Come to work on time and don't leave early. Employers value employees they can count on. No matter what job assignments you are given, do them promptly and well. Don't goof off or waste time when you're on the job.

Dress properly for the job. If a uniform is required, keep it as clean as possible. Press it before each wearing. If there's an employee dress code, observe it. Above all, be clean and neat in your appearance.

Follow the company rules. If you're required to sign in and sign out, do so. Follow company procedures when you need to ask for supplies, time off, etc.

If you have complaints about the job, talk with your supervisor. Do not complain to co-workers. Complaining to those who work with you won't solve the problem. It will only earn you a reputation as a complainer. Talk with your supervisor instead. Explain the problem. Offer to help solve it. If your supervisor *is* the problem, go to his or her supervisor or to a union steward.

GETTING ALONG WITH OTHERS

No matter what job you have, other people are involved. Most people will treat you the way you treat them. If you are grumpy and uncooperative, don't expect others to be cheerful and helpful to you. Be considerate of other people's feelings. Remember, they're trying to make a living, just like you.

Inability to get along with the boss or co-workers is the most common reason for losing a job. Treat your co-workers with respect. Do your share of the work. Pitch in when others need help. Avoid gossip and disagreements between others. If you maintain a positive, pleasant attitude, your work will be more enjoyable and others will appreciate your contributions.

Perspective

PROFILE OF AN ENTREPRENEUR

While most people work for others, some venture out on their own and become **entrepreneurs** (ahn-truh-pruh-NURS)—people who organize and manage a new business. Marie Lewis is a good example of an entrepreneur. She has started her own pattern company.

Marie began by doing custom sewing and pattern drafting out of her home for a local fabric store. For example, a woman would come to see her and Marie would customize her pattern, draft the pattern, figure out the new yardage and layout, and write the sewing directions. The next day she would start all over with a different woman. It occurred to Marie that she could do the same thing on her own, package it, and sell the patterns for much more than her employer was paying her. Thus Marie's business was born!

The business has been so successful that it has outgrown Marie's home office and moved into a real office with a design room and one full-time and three part-time employees.

Marie credits home economics with giving her the confidence to do something on her own. She admits that running your own business is hard work. "You must be willing to work long hours, and there's no guarantee of success. On the other hand, you are your own boss. You can do what *you* want to do."

Getting Your Money's Worth

WHAT TO DO UNTIL THE PAYCHECK COMES

You're feeling great because you've just been hired for an office job. Now you look in your closet and realize that none of your school clothes would look right at work. You don't want to go into debt by charging a new wardrobe, but your first paycheck is three weeks away. What can you do?

Don't panic. It's possible to put together a good, working wardrobe without going broke. The key is to stick to basics—colors and styles that you can easily mix and match.

For example, a young woman could buy two skirts and a pair of pants in basic colors. She might choose gray and black or red and navy. She could then select tops that coordinate with all three. Here are some possibilities:

gray skirt	lilac blouse
black skirt	blue-striped oxford shirt
black pants	cream turtleneck sweater
red skirt	light blue blouse
navy skirt	red-striped oxford shirt
navy pants	gray turtleneck sweater

Because the colors coordinate, the clothes in each of these wardrobes can be combined to make nine different outfits. By using different accessories—belts, scarves, jewelry, etc.—the look of each outfit can be varied. Later, after that first paycheck comes, a blazer can be added to the wardrobe for even more variety.

What about shoes? One pair of pumps in black or navy could be worn with any of these outfits.

Guys can use the same principles to create a basic wardrobe. One jacket and two pairs of pants in a neutral color can be combined with a variety of shirts and ties.

As always, you should look for quality construction and good fit. The clothes can be inexpensive, but they shouldn't look cheap. See Chapter 14 for tips on how to judge quality and fit.

Your basic wardrobe will get you through the first few weeks on the job. You'll be off to a good start—wardrobe-wise and money-wise!

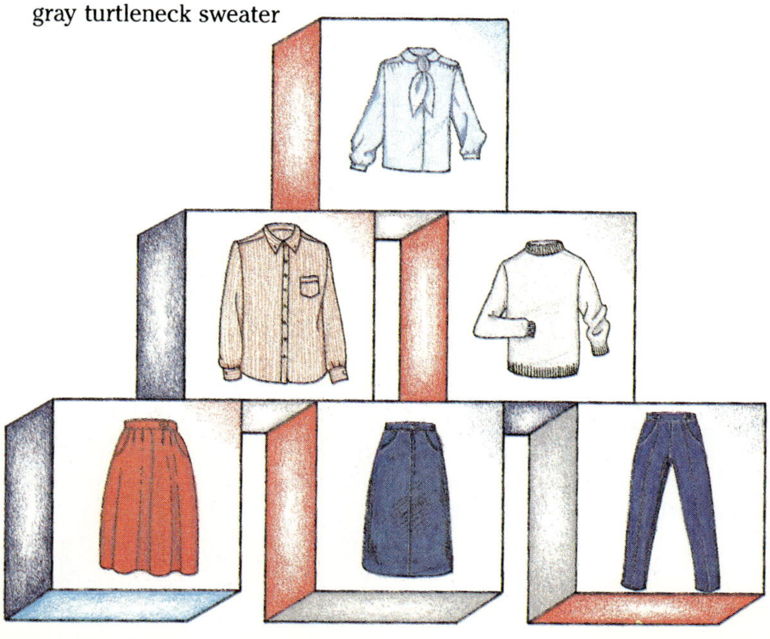

REVIEW-25

SUMMARY

To find a job, you need to know where to look. Friends, relatives, your school, want ads, and employment agencies are all sources of job information.

To get the job, you need to be prepared. Obtain a social security number and any required work permits. Prepare a resumé. When you fill out a job application, be thorough, neat, and honest. Prepare for a job interview by dressing appropriately and deciding ahead of time what questions you want to ask. Be on time for the interview.

To keep a job you must be dependable and able to get along with others. Treat others as you like to be treated.

CHECK YOUR KNOWLEDGE

1. Name two ways a school can help its students find jobs.
2. What is the difference between a wage and a salary?
3. Who pays the fee that private employment agencies charge for finding a job?
4. Why does your employer need to know your social security number?
5. What is a resumé?
6. What are references?
7. What information should you bring along with you if you are going to fill out an application?
8. How should you dress for an interview?
9. Why is it important to be dependable on the job?
10. What should you do if you have complaints about the job?

EXTEND YOUR KNOWLEDGE

1. Check the want ads of a local newspaper. List all of the jobs you find that are related to the clothing industry.
2. Pretend you are writing a book called *How to Look for a Job.* What advice would you give your readers?
3. Prepare a resumé for yourself. Include your education, any jobs you have had, your hobbies, and three references.
4. Write a brief report on how the social security system works.
5. Interview five people to find out how they got their jobs. How many found their jobs through friends or relatives? How many used an employment agency?

The Metric System

The United States uses a measurement system based on inches, pounds, and gallons. It is called the *customary system.* Most other countries use the *metric* measurement system.

The metric system uses meters to measure length, grams to measure weight, and liters to measure volume.

1 meter = 39.37 inches
1 gram = 0.03 ounce
1 liter = 1.06 quarts

In the customary system we convert to larger or smaller units by using various multipliers and divisors. For example, we multiply a foot by *3* to make yards, but we divide it by *12* to make inches. In the metric system all the multipliers and divisors are based on *10,* and they each have a name. Three of the most common are *milli, centi,* and *kilo.*

"milli" means one-thousandth
"centi" means one-hundredth
"kilo" means a thousand times

For example, a meter can be divided into one hundred parts. Each of those parts is a centimeter. If the meter is divided into one thousand parts, each part is a millimeter. And if the meter is multiplied by one thousand, it becomes a kilometer.

Sewing patterns use both metric and customary units. You'll see the symbols for meter (m), centimeter (cm), and millimeter (mm) on the envelope, guide sheet, and tissue paper. This is done because the patterns are sold in foreign countries which use the metric system.

On the pattern envelope, metric measurements are listed in a shaded area to avoid confusion with the customary measurements.

(8	10	12)	(14	16	18)	SIZE	TAILLE	(8	10	12)	(14	16	18)
DRESS A						INS	CM	ROBE A					
4⅞	4⅞	5	5¼	5½	5½	35*/**	90	4.50	4.50	4.60	4.80	5.10	5.10
3⅞	3⅞	3⅞	3⅞	4	4⅛	45*/**	115	3.60	3.60	3.60	3.60	3.70	3.80
3	3	3	3	3⅛	3⅛	60*/**	150	2.80	2.80	2.80	2.80	2.90	2.90
DRESS B								ROBE B					
3	3⅛	3¾	3¾	3⅞	3⅞	45*/**	115	2.80	2.90	3.50	3.50	3.60	3.60
2½	2½	2¾	2¾	2⅞	2⅞	60*/**	150	2.30	2.30	2.60	2.60	2.70	2.70
INTERFACING A,B (Fusible)								ENTOILAGE A,B (thermocollant)					
1	1	1	1	1⅛	1⅛	18,24	46,61	1.00	1.00	1.00	1.00	1.10	1.10
						WIDTHS	LARGEURS						
Lower edge						Dress	robe						à l'ourlet
117	117	117	117	117	117	A	A	297	297	297	297	297	297
40	41	42½	44½	46½	48½	B	B	101	104	108	113	118	123
Finished back from base of neck						LENGTHS	LONGUEURS						nuque à ourlet
(excl. blousing)						Dress	robe						(blousant non compris)
45¼	45½	45¾	46	46¼	46½	A	A	115	116	116	117	117	118
41¾	42	42¼	42½	42¾	43	B	B	106	106	107	108	109	109

How do the two systems compare? Look at the drawings below, which show sections of tape measures.

You can see that one centimeter is a little less than half an inch long.

Many American industries are switching to the metric system. Others are using both systems. The next time you're at the supermarket, notice how most of the labels list both metric and customary amounts.

The following tables show how to convert from one system to the other.

CONVERSION CHARTS

Length

When you know:	You can find:	If you multiply by:
inches	millimeters	25
feet	millimeters	300
yards	meters	0.9
miles	kilometers	1.6
millimeters	inches	0.04
meters	yards	1.1
kilometers	miles	0.6

Mass (Weight)

When you know:	You can find:	If you multiply by:
ounces	grams	2.8
pounds	kilograms	0.45
tons	metric tons	0.9
grams	ounces	0.04
kilograms	pounds	2.2
metric tons	tons	1.1

CONVERSION CHARTS (Continued)

Liquid Volume

When you know:	You can find:	If you multiply by:
ounces	milliliters	30
pints	liters	0.47
quarts	liters	0.95
gallons	liters	3.8
milliliters	ounces	0.03
liters	pints	2.1
liters	quarts	1.06
liters	gallons	0.26

Temperature

When you know:	You can find:	If you multiply by:
degrees Fahrenheit	degrees Celsius	0.6 (after subtracting 32)
degrees Celsius	degrees Fahrenheit	1.8 (then add 32)

GLOSSARY

This glossary defines common terms used in the clothing field. See also pp. 118–119 for definitions of fabrics, pp. 208–209 and 216 for descriptions of hand stitches, and pp. 190–191 for types of machine stitches. If you want to learn more about a term, look in the index to find out which pages of the book discuss that term.

accessory: In clothing, an item in addition to the basic outfit, such as a belt or scarf.

adolescent: (add-ul-ES-unt): A person between the stages of childhood and adulthood.

adornment: Decoration; adding something in order to increase attractiveness.

aerobic (air-RO-bik) **exercise:** Activity that makes your body use oxygen as you exercise.

analogous (uh-NAL-uh-gus) **color scheme:** A color group formed from colors next to each other on the color wheel.

apparel industry: Part of the clothing industry. The apparel industry uses yarns and fabrics to make clothing.

apparel: Clothing.

appliqué (ap-luh-KAY): The craft of stitching fabric cutouts into a design.

assembly line: An arrangement of people and equipment in which work passes from one person to the next, with each person doing a particular task.

assorter: A worker in a clothing factory who sorts the garment pieces after they have been cut out and ties into bundles the ones which belong together.

balance: In clothing, an equal distribution of design elements on both halves of a garment. Balance is one of the principles of design, and it can be formal or informal.

basting: Sewing long, loose stitches to hold fabric together temporarily. Can be done by hand or machine.

bleach: A laundry product used along with soap or detergent to remove soil and stains and to brighten whites.

bodice: (BAHD-us): The part of the garment above the waistline.

body: In fabric, a quality of stiffness.

bolted fabric. *See* **nonwoven fabric.**

bonded fabric: Two fabrics permanently attached to each other with an adhesive.

boutique (boo-TEEK): A small shop, or a department within a larger shop, that specializes in fashionable items.

budget: A spending plan that matches expenses to income.

buyer: In the retail industry, a person who buys the merchandise that a store will sell.

carding: A process similar to combing. It cleans, untangles, and gathers together fibers so that they can be spun into yarn.

casing: A fabric tube that holds a drawstring or elastic in place.

cellulose (SELL-you-lows): The major ingredient in the cell walls of plants.

cellulosic fibers: Manufactured fibers made from cellulose.

characteristic: A trait, feature, or quality that makes someone or something different from others.

clip: To cut evenly spaced slits into fabric seam allowances. Often done on inside curves.

colorfastness: The ability of a fabric's color to remain the same after wear, cleaning, or storage.

color scheme: A cluster of colors used together.

comparison shopping: Visiting different stores or looking at different catalogs to compare styles and values before buying.

complementary (kahm-pluh-MENT-uh-ree) **color scheme:** A color group formed from colors opposite each other on the color wheel.

consignment: A system in which a dealer pays only for what he or she sells and returns what does not sell.

cooperative education program: A school program which helps students find part-time jobs while they continue to go to school.

cotton boll: The green pod on a cotton plant which holds the seeds and fibers.

cravat (kruh-VAT)**:** A small scarf tied around the neck.

crosswise grain: The crosswise yarn in fabric.

culture: The customs, beliefs, values, and skills of a group of people.

custom: A long-accepted practice or tradition.

custom-made garment: A garment made especially for an individual by a dressmaker or tailor. Opposite of a mass-produced garment.

cycle: A predictable pattern of events.

Daily Food Guide: A guide developed by scientists to help people make wise food choices. It divides foods into five groups according to the nutrients they contain and lists the number and size of servings needed daily from each group.

darning: The process of mending tears or filling in holes by interlacing stitches.

dart: A tapered fold stitched into a garment so that the garment will fit body curves.

decorative lines: Lines which improve a garment's appearance. They may be formed by trim, special stitching, or by the print of the fabric. They may be functional as well as ornamental. Topstitching on a patch pocket is an example.

dermatologist (dur-muh-TAHL-uh-jist)**:** A doctor who specializes in treating skin problems.

detergent: A laundry product made from petroleum, fats, and oils.

direct printing: *See* **roller printing.**

disposables: Items that are meant to be thrown away after use, such as disposable diapers.

division of labor: A method of producing goods in which the work is divided among many people instead of one person doing all the work.

down: The soft, fluffy growth under birds' feathers.

drape: A characteristic of some fabrics. A fabric with drape lies close to the body when gathered.

draping: Cutting and fitting fabric to a model form according to a garment's design lines. This is one step in the design of a garment.

dressmaker: One who custom-sews dresses and other nontailored garments.

dry cleaning: A method of cleaning garments. It uses chemicals instead of water.

durability: In a garment, toughness of fabric and construction; the ability to withstand repeated wear and cleaning.

dyeing: A method of coloring fabrics by immersing the fibers, yarns, or fabrics in dye or by adding color to chemicals before they are made into manufactured fibers.

ease: (1) Extra room built into a garment for comfort; fitting ease. (2) Extra fullness produced when two edges of slightly different lengths are joined without forming gathers.

economics: The way people produce, distribute, and use goods and services.

elements of design: The "building blocks" of design. They include line, space, form, color, and texture.

embroidery: The art of decorating a fabric with colorful threads in interesting designs.

embroidery floss: A special cotton thread used for embroidery work.

emotions: Feelings.

emphasis: In clothing, the center of interest; one of the principles of design.

employment agency: A public or private agency which tries to match jobs with job seekers.

entrepreneur (ahn-truh-pruh-NUR)**:** Someone who organizes and manages a new business.

entry-level job: A job for people who have not had previous experience in that line of work.

enzyme pre-soak: A laundry product which is added to water. Laundry is then soaked in this water to remove stains.

fabric designer: Someone who designs the construction of a fabric.

fabric finishes: Treatments applied to a fabric to improve its appearance, performance, or safety or to make it easier to care for.

fabric softener: A laundry product used to soften fabrics and reduce static cling.

facing: A piece of fabric used to finish a garment edge if it shows when the garment is worn.

fad: An extreme fashion that lasts for a short time.

fashion: The style that is popular at a given time.

fashion communication: Fashion promotion.

fashion cycle: *See* **cycle.**

fashion designer: Someone who creates a garment based on his or her ideas.

fashion illustrator: A person who draws fashions.

fashion leader: A person who is among the first to wear a new style.

fashion photographer: Someone who helps promote fashions by taking pictures of them.

fashion promotion: Any activity designed to help sell a fashion item.

fashion writer: A person who writes about fashion.

filaments: Long fibers.

filling: The crosswise yarns in a fabric. Also called **weft** or **woof.**

filling knit: *See* **weft knit.**

finisher: A worker in a clothing factory who adds outside stitching, trim, buttonholes, and buttons.

finishes: *See* **fabric finishes.**

fitting ease: Extra room built into a garment for comfort.

flame-retardant: Not catching fire easily or burning quickly.

flax: A slender, annual plant with blue flowers. Its fibers are used to make linen, and its seeds are used for linseed oil.

fleece: The wooly covering of a sheep or other wool-bearing animal.

form: In clothing, the overall shape of a garment. Form is one of the elements of design.

formal balance: A type of balance in which both sides of a design are exactly the same.

fusible patch: A mending patch with heat-sensitive adhesive on one side. It is attached to the garment by pressing with an iron.

fusible tape: A strip of fabric with heat-sensitive adhesive on one side.

fusible web: A weblike material that melts when heated with an iron.

generic (juh-NAIR-ik) **name:** A name given to a whole class of similar items.

grading: Trimming seam allowances so that each layer is a different width.

grain: The direction of yarns in a fabric. Yarns running lengthwise are on the straight grain. Those running crosswise are on the crosswise grain.

greige (GRAY) goods: Newly made fabrics before they have received any finishes.

grooming: The general cleaning and care of the body.

group: People joined together because they share a belief or interest.

guide sheet: A sheet of instructions that is included with a garment pattern.

hand: The way a fabric feels and drapes.

hard water: Water that contains a lot of minerals.

harmony: The principle of design that ties all the elements together for a pleasing appearance.

heat transfer printing: A method of printing in which a paper pattern containing the desired color and design is placed on fabric. Heat is applied to transfer the color and design onto the fabric.

hue (HYOO)**:** The name of a color family, such as red or blue.

impression: An image. It can be physical, such as the impression made by a rubber stamp, or mental, such as the impression made on your mind by someone's appearance.

informal balance: A type of balance in which the two sides of a design are different yet still form a pleasing combination.

information ads: Advertisements that give facts, such as the sizes, fabric, and price of a garment.

insect repellent: A substance that keeps insects away.

intensity (in-TEN-sih-tee)**:** The brightness or dullness of a color.

interfacing: A layer of special fabric placed between layers of the garment fabric to add strength and weight.

inventory (IN-vun-tore-ee)**:** A list of the items on hand.

ironing: Removing wrinkles from fabric by sliding a warm or hot iron back and forth over it.

job application: The official form a company uses to collect and record information about all job applicants.

job interview: A meeting between a job applicant and a potential employer to discuss the applicant's interest in and qualifications for a job.

laminated fabric: A fabric consisting of a layer of foam sandwiched between two layers of fabric.

layaway plan: A form of credit in which the customer pays for an item at regular intervals and the store holds the item until all the payments have been made. No interest is charged, but there may be a handling fee.

layering: *See* **grading.**

leader: Someone who guides, directs, or influences the thoughts, feelings, or behavior of others.

life cycle: All of the stages of a life.

lifestyle: A person's typical way of life.

line of clothing: A collection of garments developed by a designer. There is usually a new line for each season of the year.

lint: Small fibers that have come off a fabric.

loom: A device for interlacing two or more sets of yarns or threads to form cloth. There are hand-operated looms and power-operated looms.

manicure: The special grooming care given to the hands.

manufactured fibers: Fibers made in factories from materials that are not originally in fiber form.

marker: (1) In the apparel industry, the pattern layout. (2) In retailing, a person who puts price tags and labels on merchandise.

market research: Gathering information about consumers' needs and wants, production costs, and competition.

mass production: The manufacture of goods in large amounts.

mercerization (MUR-suh-ruh-ZAY-shun)**:** A chemical and mechanical treatment given to some fabrics to improve their luster, strength, and ability to absorb dyes.

merchandising plan: A selling plan developed by retailers which describes the kind and amount of merchandise to buy and how to promote and advertise it.

mildew: A type of fungus (usually a whitish growth) which can attack fabrics, staining and weakening them.

mold: A type of fungus (usually a furry growth) which can attack fabrics, staining and weakening them.

monochromatic (mahn-uh-kroh-MAT-ik) **color scheme:** A color group formed by using different values of one color.

nap: A soft, fuzzy surface on a fabric.

natural fibers: Fibers that grow as a part of plants or animals.

noncellulosic fibers: Manufactured fibers made from chemicals that are derived from coal, petroleum, or natural gas.

nonwoven fabric: Fabric made by interlocking fibers together without weaving or knitting.

notching: Cutting small triangles out of a seam allowance. Often done on an outside curve.

notions: Items in addition to the pattern and fabric which are needed to sew a garment.

nutrients (NOO-tree-unts)**:** Chemicals the body needs in order to function, grow, repair itself, and provide energy.

off-grain: A condition of fabric in which the lengthwise and crosswise yarns do not run at right angles to each other.

packer: In a store, someone who packs items to be sent to customers by mail or truck.

paralysis (puh-RAL-uh-sus): Inability to move.

patch pockets: Pockets that are sewn on the outside of a garment.

pattern: A sewing pattern; the plan of a garment that shows the shapes of the garment pieces and tells how to stitch them together.

pattern layout: The arrangement of pattern pieces on the fabric.

pedicure: The special grooming care given to the feet.

peer: Someone who has the same standing as another.

personal shoppers: People whose job it is to help others shop or to do the shopping for them.

piece dyeing: A method of coloring in which fabric is dyed after it has been woven or knitted.

pilling: A condition of fabric in which the ends of fibers ball up on the surface.

plain weave: A type of weave in which the filling yarns go under and over alternate warp yarns.

plaque (PLAK): An invisible, sticky film on teeth.

pleats: Straight folds of fabric stitched in place.

plissé (pli-SAY) **print:** A puckered effect achieved by touching portions of a fabric with chemicals which cause these portions to shrink.

posture: The way you carry your body when walking, standing, and sitting.

preshrinking: Washing or dry-cleaning fabric before making it into a garment.

pre-soak: *See* **enzyme pre-soak.**

pressing: Setting down the iron onto fabric and lifting it up again to move it to a different area.

preventive care: Stopping problems before they start.

pre-wash: A laundry product sprayed on soiled or stained areas before washing.

primary colors: The basic colors from which the others are made. They are red, yellow, and blue.

principles of design: The rules which state how the elements of design can be combined to create a pleasing effect. The principles of design are emphasis, balance, proportion, rhythm, and harmony.

printing: In the textile industry, a method of adding color and design to fabrics by applying inks.

production supervisor: In a textile factory, someone who directs the machine tenders and repairers.

promotion: *See* **fashion promotion.**

proportion: The relationship of one part to another and of all the parts to the total look; a principle of design.

psychology (sy-KAHL-uh-jee): (1) The study of the mind and behavior. (2) The mental characteristics or behavior of a person or a group.

quilting: Sewing together two layers of fabric with a layer of padding in between.

ramie (RAY-me): A strong, durable fiber made from the stalks of China grass.

raw edge: On fabric, the side where the lengthwise yarns end.

receiving clerk: In a store, someone who checks goods that have come in to make sure they are the right items and undamaged.

recycled wool: Wool that has been reprocessed from used or unused fabric.

references: The names, addresses, and phone numbers of people who know your character and abilities.

refund: A return of money, as when a customer returns a garment to a store and receives a refund.

reinforced seams: Seams that have been strengthened with additional stitching, seam tape, or other special treatment.

reinforcing button: A small, flat button that is stitched to the underside of the garment at the same time as the outer button is stitched.

remnant: A short length of fabric which is either left over from a bolt or has a flaw.

resilient (rih-ZIL-yunt)**:** Able to regain its original size and shape after being bent, stretched, or twisted.

resource: A source of supply or help.

resumé (REZ-uh-may)**:** An information sheet which lists facts about your education, job experience, and interests.

retail industry: The part of the clothing industry which sells clothing to the consumers.

retailing: The business of selling merchandise to consumers.

reversible: Being the same on both sides; not having a right and a wrong side. Used to describe some fabrics and garments.

revolving charge account: A form of credit in which you are billed each month and charged interest for the amount you owe from the preceding month.

rhythm: The pleasing coordination of all parts of a design; one of the principles of design.

role: A purpose or function.

roller printing: Textile printing which is done by passing the fabric under a series of engraved rollers. Also called direct printing.

salary: A fixed amount paid regularly for work.

sales representative: A person who contacts possible buyers and tells them about a product.

sample stitcher: Someone who follows a designer's pattern or sketches to make sample garments.

satin weave: A type of weave in which the filling yarns go over one warp yarn, then under groups of warp yarns, as in twill weave, but in a random pattern.

screen printing: A type of textile printing in which fabric is placed under a framed screen that contains a design. Color is forced through the screen onto the fabric.

seam: The place where two pieces of fabric have been sewn together.

seam ripper: A small tool with a handle and a curved blade that ends in a rounded tip. Used to cut stitches when opening seams.

seasonal sale: A sale in which all clothing for a certain season is marked down.

secondary color: The color that results when two primary colors are mixed together.

seconds: Garments that have defects and therefore cannot be sold as first-quality merchandise.

self-image: The mental picture that you have of yourself.

self-winding bobbin: A type of sewing machine bobbin which is wound in the bobbin case.

selvage (SELL-vij)**:** On fabric, the side where the crosswise yarns end.

serger: A machine which finishes seams by encasing the raw edges of the fabric with an interlocking thread.

shears: A cutting tool with two long hinged blades, each of which is shaped differently.

shoplifter: A customer who steals merchandise from a store.

shuttle: A tool for moving crosswise threads back and forth through a loom.

singeing: A finishing process in which fabric is passed over a flame or heated copper plate to burn off fiber ends and make the fabric smooth.

sizing: A finish applied to fabric to add body.

soap: A cleaning product usually made with fat, oil, and lye.

solution dyeing: A method of dyeing in which color is added to chemicals before they are made into manufactured fibers.

space: In a garment, the area inside and between lines; one of the elements of design.

spinneret: A device which resembles a shower head and through which a chemical solution is passed. Used in the spinning of manufactured fibers.

spinning: The process of twisting fibers around each other to form long strands.

sportswear: Clothing designed for physical activity.

staple fibers: Short fibers.

status: The rank of a person within a group.

stock clerk: In a store, someone who keeps track of goods that are in stock.

stock dyeing: A method of coloring in which fibers are dyed before being spun into yarn.

straight grain: The lengthwise yarn of fabric.

structural lines: Lines formed by a garment's construction, such as seams, edges, or folds.

style: The design of a garment.

sumptuary (SUMP-chu-wer-ee) **laws:** Laws that control what people are allowed to wear.

tailor: A person who custom-sews suits and other tailored garments.

tape measure: A narrow, flexible strip marked off in inches and parts of an inch (or in centimeters and millimeters).

tartar: A hard deposit that can form on teeth and can cause gum disease.

technology: The way a society uses its resources to produce goods.

tertiary color: The color that results when primary and secondary colors are mixed together.

textile industry: The part of the clothing industry which takes raw materials and makes fibers, yarns, and fabrics.

textile print designer: Someone who develops new patterns and designs to be printed onto fabrics.

texture: An item's surface characteristics; one of the elements of design.

thirty-day charge account: A form of credit in which you are expected to pay the total amount you owe each month. If you don't pay, you will be charged interest or your account may be cancelled.

toddler: A child between the ages of one and three.

toiletries: Grooming products, such as toothpaste or shaving cream.

torso: The body without the head, arms, and legs. Also called the trunk.

trade name: The name given to a fiber by the company that produces it.

triad (TRY-add) **color scheme:** A color group formed by three colors equally distant from one another on the color wheel.

twill weave: A type of weave in which the filling yarns go over one warp yarn, then under two or more warp yarns. Each filling yarn dips under a warp yarn to the right or left of the previous filling yarn.

under collar: The piece that forms the underside of a collar. It finishes the edges of the collar and is not visible when the garment is worn.

union: A group of workers in similar jobs who have joined together to obtain better working conditions, pay, and benefits for themselves.

upper: In footwear, the part of the shoe above the sole.

upper collar: The part of the collar that is seen when the garment is worn.

value: (1) Something, such as a moral principle or quality, which people believe to be right and good. (2) The lightness or darkness of a color.

virgin wool: Wool that has never before been made into yarn or fabric.

wage: An hourly, daily, or piecework rate of pay for work.

wardrobe: A person's collection of clothes.

warp: The lengthwise yarns of fabric.

warp knit: A knitted fabric made by interlocking several yarns.

warranty: A written promise that a product will perform as stated.

water softener: A powder used to soften hard wash water.

weaving: The process of interlacing yarns to form cloth.

weft: The crosswise yarns in a fabric. Also called woof or filling.

weft knit: A knitted fabric made by interlocking loops of a single yarn. Also called filling knit.

woof: *See* **weft.**

wrapper: In a store, a person who wraps gifts that customers have bought.

yarn: A continuous strand of fibers or filaments.

yarn dyeing: A method of coloring in which yarns are dyed before being woven or knitted into cloth.

INDEX

C

D

E

F

G

S

CREDITS

American Sheep Producers Council, Inc., 105 (left)
Lynn Bannon, St. Francis Medical Center, 7 (lower right)
Bausch & Lomb, 75
Bill Blass Ltd. Archives, 266 (left)
British Information Service, Washington, D.C., 6
Browns Sporting Goods, James B. Gaffney, 93, 139, 154, 157
Burlington Coat Factory, Todd Carroll, 28 (right), 38, 40, 46, 50, 51, 96, 99, 114, 137, 145 (left), 196 (right), 198 (middle), 206 (right), 214, 248 (bottom), 258, 269
Burlington Industries, 116, 127 (left), 265
Barbara Caldwell, 77
Cannon Mill Co., 125
Todd Carroll, ix (top) 2, 6, 20, 25, 37 (right), 63, 66, 74 (right), 75, 89, 92, 121, 128, 129 (right), 146, 164, 165, 171, 174, 180, 182 (top), 211 (top left), 212 (lower right), 215 (right), 216, 217 (top left), 218 (bottom), 233 (right), 235, 236 (top), 248 (top), 270, 277, 280
Central Illinois Private Industry Council, N.A. Peterson, 276
Coventry Creative Graphics, 127 (right), 129 (left), 135, 140, 168, 175, 185, 253, 254, 257 (left)
Cranston Print Works Company, 124
Howard Davis, 86, 87, 115, 120 (left), 126, 170, 176, 178, 181, 182 (bottom), 186, 188, 189, 190, 191, 192, 193, 194, 195, 196 (left), 197, 198, 199, 200, 201, 202, 203, 204, 205, 206 (left), 207 (bottom right) 208, 209, 215 (left), 216, 217 (bottom), 240, 241, 242, 246
E.I. du Pont de Nemours & Co., 120 (right), 130
Eric Dusenbery, 61
Eagle Cleaners, Todd Carroll, 230
Figgie International, 7 (top right)
Scott Fishel, 24
Flo & Friends, Todd Carroll, vi (bottom), vii (bottom), ix (bottom), 119, 211, 212, 273
Paul Fusco, Sohio, 84 (right)
James B. Gaffney, 3, 78, 222, 233 (left), 236 (bottom), 245 (top)
The Hirsch Company, 234
Illinois Outdoor, James B. Gaffney, 158
Michael Jenkins, 7 (top left), 281
JMS, 134
Kinney's Shoes, James B. Gaffney, 152
Landmark Recreation Center, Todd Carroll, 83
Library of Congress, 16 (bottom left), 172
Mad-Made Fiber Producers Association, Inc., 107
Manual High School, 3, 184, 271
Manual High School, Todd Carroll, 22 (left), 57
Maytag, 225 (top)
Mohair Council, 106 (left)
Montgomery Wards, James B. Gaffney, 143, 156
NASA, 90
National Cotton Council, 103
National Starch & Chemical Corporation, i, 109
Paul Neakrase, Washington Community High School, 4
North Wind Picture Archives, 8, 19, 254 (top)
Northwoods Mall, Todd Carroll, 142, 144

Gabe Palmer, Burlington Industries, 264, 267

Pennsylvania Bureau of Travel Development, 17

J.C. Penney, James B. Gaffney, 145 (right)

Peoria Area Water Wizards, Todd Carroll, 84 (left)

N.A. Peterson, 54, 68, 69, 72, 76, 94, 106 (right), 147, 227, 229

Liz Purcell, i (right), 10, 11, 12, 13, 14, 15, 16, 20, 23, 27, 31, 33, 34, 35, 36, 37, 45, 47, 52, 59, 62, 64, 65, 81, 85 (right), 95, 98, 138, 149, 150, 151, 166, 167, 179, 207 (bottom left), 243, 244, 247, 284

Richmond Plant, Burlington Industries, 252

Singer Company, 187

Singer Company, Todd Carroll, 274

Social Security Administration, 278 (right)

Sports 'n Spokes/Paralyzed Veterans of America, 80

Stephen's Institute, 30

Techni-Flair, 85 (left)

U.S. Steel, 7 (bottom left)

Cary Wolinsky, Trillium, 105 (right)

Woodruff High School, Todd Carroll, viii (bottom), 22 (top right), 22 (bottom right), 26, 136, 207 (top left), 210, 243 (bottom), 262

Woodruff High School, N.A. Peterson, 74 (left)

Wool & Wick, Todd Carroll, 218 (top)

Ann Wright, 27 (left), 28 (bottom left), 97, 225 (bottom), 232

Duane R. Zehr, 255

Ziptone Cleaners, Todd Carroll, 260